THE
MUSTANG STO

The NA-73X was the start of the Mustang story, an aircraft designed to a British requirement and whose basic design work was completed in a matter of weeks. It was by no means perfect at this stage, but the promise was there. (*FlyPast* Collection)

THE MUSTANG STORY

KEN DELVE

ARMS &
ARMOUR

ARMS & ARMOUR
An imprint of Cassell & Co
Wellington House, 125 Strand, London WC2R 0BB

Copyright © Ken Delve 1999

First published 1999

British Library Cataloguing-in-Publication data:
A catalogue record for this book is available from the British Library.

ISBN 1 85409 259 6

Distributed in the USA by
Sterling Publishing Co. Inc.,
387 Park Avenue South, New York, NY 10016-8810

Edited and designed by Roger Chesneau

Printed and bound in Great Britain by
Hillman Printers, Frome

CONTENTS

FOREWORD

Men stood open mouthed with disbelief. This simply couldn't be true. Mustangs! P-51s! American junk! To exchange our beloved *Spits* for such rubbish! Had the bloody Air Ministry brass gone of their rockers? This was intolerable! How low could they sink? That evening the pilots gave vent to their anger in a drunken brawl, resulting in fairly expensive repairs having to be carried out to the Mess.'[1]

If these fighter pilots of No 65 Squadron RAF had known at the time that they would also have bombs attached to their aircraft and be expected to attack ground targets they would probably have burnt down the Mess! And yet by 1944 this was very much the scenario as Mustangs hunted out the enemy wherever he could be found – in the air and on the ground. Whilst it is in the long-range escort role that the Mustang has basked in the popular memory, the aircraft performed a much wider set of tasks and the ground troops had as much cause to heap praise upon the P-51 pilots as did the bomber crews.

'You fought wide open, full-throttle. With experience, you knew before a kill when you were going to score. Once you zeroed in, began to manoeuvre your opponent while closing in, you became a cat with a mouse. You set him up, and there was no way out . . . you were a confident hunter and your trigger finger never shook. Dogfighting was hard work. You needed strong arms and shoulders. These controls weren't hydraulically operated, and at 400mph they became extremely heavy. Without cabin pressurisation, flying at high altitudes wore you out. And so did pulling Gs in sharp turns and steep dives. After a couple of minutes of dogfighting, your back and arms felt like you had been hauling a piano upstairs.'[2]

'I dropped my wing tanks and turned into the German formation as the lead 109 dropped his nose to start his attack. I gave him a burst with my 0.50 cals, then fanned the rudder left and right to spray the rest of the formation. The lead 109 nosed up, smoke from the engine engulfing the cockpit.'[3]

The North American P-51 Mustang carved for itself an impressive career during the latter part of the Second World War and has gone down in history as one of *the* great fighter aircraft. In the past twenty years it has seen something of a resurgence and is now the most popular – and numerous – fighter type on the international warbird scene. Each year sees a handful more restored to airworthy condition. At certain air shows in the United States it is now possible to see dozens of P-51s lined up, each in authentic markings representing aircraft from, in most cases, the Second World War.

[1] Tony Jonsson, *Dancing in the Skies*, Grub Street, 1994.
[2] Chuck Yeager, *Yeager*, Century Hutchinson, 1985.
[3] Luke Weathers, 332nd FG.

During the Second World War the United States Army Air Forces (USAAF) accepted 14,490 P-51s on to its strength, rather fewer than the total of 15,579 P-47s. During its period of service from 1942 to 1945 the aircraft saw a huge improvement in its operational capability, not least the massive increase in range from 400 miles to 1,800 miles.

Whilst victory and casualty figures are very hard to reduce to absolutes – the statistics published at the time and in the immediate post-war period have been the subject of frequent revisions (some appropriate and some not) – there can be no doubt that the P-51 played a major part in the Allied campaign to achieve and maintain air supremacy in the European Theatre of Operations, without which the strategic bombing campaign would almost certainly have failed. Many critics have suggested that the bombing campaign itself was inappropriate and of lesser import, but this view is certainly not borne out by historical fact – although this is not the place to address this question.

Acknowledgements

As with any work of aviation history, a great debt of thanks is owed to a wide range of individuals and institutions. A great deal of the present work is compiled from primary sources, and to the staff of the Ministry of Defence's Air Historical Branch in London I owe particular thanks for their enormous assistance in accessing official records – and likewise to the staff of the National Air & Space Museum in Washington, DC. A number of individuals have provided material for this book, and special thanks go to Bob Eason and Jack Ilfrey. Thanks are also due to ex-Mustang personnel for their help, to various historian colleagues and to those authors who have kindly allowed me to use extracts from their published works.

Ken Delve

Above: AG345, the first production Mustang I for the Royal Air Force, first flew in April 1941 – by which time the RAF had placed orders for 600 aircraft. (*FlyPast* Collection)

1

THE DESIGN COMES TO LIFE

Below: The XP-51. Two prototypes were built (41-038 and 41-039), with the NA-73 designation, the USAAC putting them under evaluation in late 1941. (Robert F. Dorr)

The story of the great American P-51 fighter has its origins very much with the British. After more than two decades of political neglect, the British military entered an expansion programme in the early 1930s, in large measure prompted by the growing instability in Europe and the militaristic stance of Germany under its Nazi Chancellor, Adolf Hitler. The British aircraft industry was in no position to meet the major orders being placed for all types of aircraft, and so overseas sources of supply were sought, the United States being seen as a prime candidate. The British Purchasing Commission (BPC), under the guidance of Sir Henry Self, had established an office in New York and was busily placing large orders for a variety of types, including hundreds of Curtiss P-40 fighters (despite this type's inherent shortcomings). Curtiss were unable to match the required production rate and so invited North American to undertake licence-production

of the P-40. This idea was not popular with North American's President, 'Dutch' Kindelberger, and in early 1940 he put forward a proposal to the BPC for North American to design and build a new fighter based around the same Allison engine as used in the P-40 but with superior performance through the use of a low-drag airframe and with mass-production techniques to facilitate rapid production. Both aspects were to become important elements in the Mustang programme. On 24 April 1940 a telegram was sent to Raymond Rice, Chief of Engineering at Inglewood, telling him and his team, including Chief Design Engineer Edgar Schmeud, to undertake a preliminary design study, and by the following day a general arrangement drawing and weight study were ready to show Kindelberger.

This rapid progress was to be a feature of the design phase of the new aircraft, as part of the 'deal' with the BPC was that the prototype of the new fighter should be ready within four months.

On 1 May 1940 J. Leland (Lee) Atwood, Vice-President of North American Aviation, wrote to Sir Henry Self outlining the 'agreement' that had been reached:

'In accordance with our outstanding, we are proceeding with the design of a single-seat fighter airplane, our model NA-74, incorporating an Allison engine and fitted with provision for equipment and armament as detailed more completely hereunder.

'We have reached an extremely satisfactory agreement with the Curtiss Aeroplane Company of Buffalo wherein they are furnishing us data covering a compre-

Right, upper: Mustang I AM148 of No 26 Squadron, mid-1942. This aircraft took part in the Dieppe raid of August that year. (Andy Thomas Collection)

Right, lower: AM251 of No 414 Squadron, early 1943. (Andy Thomas Collection)

Left: A fine photograph of an early P-51, showing the distinctive wing shape. The aerodynamics of the P-51, and in particular the laminar flow wing that it later adopted, were key elements in its success. (Ken Delve Collection)

hensive series of wind tunnel, cooling, and performance tests of a similar airplane, which data will assist us in the design and manufacture of these airplanes. We have also received release from the United States Army for the manufacture and export of these airplanes and wish to assure you that all arrangements are entirely satisfactory. We are prepared to construct and deliver to you 320 of these airplanes before 30 September 1941. [The document included a table showing delivery schedules, the first aircraft being delivered in January 1941, rising to over 50 a month by May.] . . . We offer to continue the manufacture of these planes at the rate of 50 airplanes per month until at least the end of the year 1941, should you desire to incorporate and exercise an option for these additional airplanes prior to 30 April 1941.

'We have constructed a mock-up and have completed the initial phase of the detail design and are submitting to you herewith certain data and information regarding the characteristics of the airplane. You will note that we have provided for armor protection for the pilot and a sealing arrangement for the fuel tanks. Provisions are being made for the installation of four .50 caliber machine guns, two of which are in the fuselage and the other two in the wing. As a normal load we are specifying 200 rounds of ammunition per gun, but are making additional provision for more ammunition as a special load. Provisions are being made for four British Type .303 machine guns with ammunition boxes to accommodate 500 rounds of ammunition per gun as a normal load.

'The general provisions for armament have been discussed with Air Commodore Baker and Mr Thomas and it is believed that the arrangement offered is the most practical possible at this time, consistent with the general instructions we have received. It is possible to increase the firepower through the installation of additional guns if absolutely necessary, but the performance will suffer a proportionate loss. We feel there will be no difficulty in making any changes or modifications which you may feel are essential or desirable, and are prepared to co-operate with you technical staff to the fullest extent.

'We have a careful estimate of the price, including sufficient structural tests to guarantee the structural integrity of all parts, wind tunnel testing and flight testing. We have included a price breakdown:

'A) Powerplant, engine accessories	$983.95
'B) Instruments	$1787.35
'C) Electrical Equipment	$890.75
'D) Misc. Equipment	$528.40
'E) Radio Equipment	Customer furnished
'F) Armament	Customer furnished
'Total equipment to be furnished by Contractor	$ 4190.45
'Base Airplane	$33,400.00
'Total per Airplane	$37,590.45
'Total for 320 Airplanes	$12,028.944
'Spare parts (20%)	$2,405,788
'Crating per airplane $675, total	$216,000
'Crating for spare parts (4%)	$96,231
'Total contract amount	$14,746,964

'We are prepared to proceed immediately upon receiving a letter from you accepting this proposal and receipt of down-payment. We desire a down-payment of 10% of the contract amount upon approval of this proposal and a subsequent monthly payment of 2.5% of the contract amount each month until 25% of the contract has been paid. The prices quoted above are intended to include all normal and reasonable modifications and changes which you may require, provided that such changes are agreed upon within three months of the agreement and provided there is no considerable additional expense to us as might be involved in the purchase of additional material or equipment.

'If there are any matters not properly covered in this letter or the enclosed data and it is necessary to withhold the letter until such matters are clarified, we will greatly appreciate it if you will notify us of these matters by telegram or telephone at our expense in order that there will be no delay.'

A great deal of attention was paid to the drag-reducing aspects of the design, with particular care taken in such areas as the cockpit and engine cowling. However, the most unusual airframe element was without doubt the laminar-flow wing shape. This type of aerofoil had been developed by the National Advisory Committee for Aeronautics (NACA) and the basic principle involved was that of smoothing the airflow over the wing and thus delaying the onset of any drag.

The company worked night and day on the NA-73X project and in early August the prototype was wheeled out – minus its engine. In the hands of Vance Breese the new fighter made its first flight on 26 October 1940, an astonishing achievement when one considers that the initial telegram to begin design was only sent on 24 April. The pilot reported no significant problems with this flight other than

Right: The RCAF's No 400 Squadron acquired Mustangs in April 1942 to supplement its Tomahawks. AL971 only served with this squadron – and survived to the end of 1944. (Andy Thomas Collection)

Below: An Allison-engine Mustang I at the A&AEE for weapons evaluation, October 1942. (*FlyPast* Collection)

some degree of engine overheating that would require modification to the cooling system. Sadly, the aircraft force-landed on its fifth flight, due to a fuel-switching error, and was badly damaged. However, it made little difference as both North American and the BPC were confident enough in the design for production to be authorised.

J. Leland Atwood has his own views on the Mustang and the arguments that have raged since the 1940s, and these are expounded in the panel overleaf.

Into Service

The first production Mustang – for that was the name the Air Ministry had chosen for its new fighter in December – for the Royal Air Force, AG345, flew in April 1941, by which time over 600 were on order as the Mustang I. The rationale behind selecting the name 'Mustang' has now been lost, although a number of possible explanations have been put forward, one such being that the name was coined from a popular 1930s song line, 'Saddle your blues to a wild Mustang and gallop your troubles away.' This, however, has the feel of a later 'invention' as it is decidedly 'un-British' – although naming the aircraft after the powerful wild horse would not be unreasonable. It was the second production aircraft, AG346, that first arrived in the UK – the first of many to arrive by ship at Liverpool docks and to be assembled at nearby Speke airport.

Powered by an Allison V-1710-39, the Mustang I was armed with four .50in or four .30in guns and when evaluated by the RAF proved to be 35mph faster than the Spitfire V at 15,000ft (with a speed of 375mph). However, performance fell away rapidly above 15,000ft as the Allison engine was not supercharged; furthermore, the Spitfire was faster to height, taking seven minutes to reach 20,000ft whereas the Mustang, being heavier, took eleven. Factors such as these, and the easing of pressure on Fighter Command in 1941 (the need for fighters was not so frantic in 1941 as it had been in 1940), led to the decision to develop the Spitfire as the primary interceptor within Fighter Command. The Mustangs were, therefore, available for other roles, and another role was just waiting to be filled. It must be appreciated that at this time the role which the P-51 would later dominate – long-range bomber escort – was not perceived as a requirement: the RAF's bombers operated by night and the USAAF daylight bombing offensive was still some months away.

Although many aspects of air power had made rapid advances in the early part of the war, that of army co-operation had seen little change – in large part due to a lack of aircraft and equipment either in the right quantity or with adequate performance. The few Army Co-operation squadrons had performed marvels with such aircraft as the Lysander, but the nature of the low-level role had changed in the face of very heavy anti-aircraft defences and the presence of prowling fighters. What was needed was a high-performance tactical aircraft, the earlier Tomahawks also having proved to be less effective than hoped, and with the arrival of the Mustang the newly formed Army Co-operation Command acquired just what it wanted – and was to put its 'new boy' to good use for the rest of the war. The Command planned for a force of eighteen Mustang-equipped squadrons – although, in the event, the maximum number at any one time was sixteen – and the first of these, No 26 Squadron based at Gatwick, collected its first aircraft from Speke in

A View of the Mustang: J. Leland Atwood, Vice-President, North American Aviation

The Mustang aeroplane, authorised and ordered by the British Purchasing Commission in April 1940, did turn out to be a significant factor in aviation and military history. Its day-to-day service and performance in the latter stages of World War Two and its approach to the speed plateau that faced the reciprocating engine propeller-driven designs of 1903 to 1945 did make it a sort of benchmark and paradigm standard for that class of aircraft.

Not being a qualified pilot, I cannot offer any comment on its military and combat characteristics except for general performance parameters, but I have every reason to believe that its armament, flying characteristics, and general utility were satisfactory and at least average for the time and conditions. Its principal points of merit were more related to basic engineering factors – which were speed and range. These were interrelated, in that range over enemy territory without a speed advantage could be almost sacrificial.

There is a fine article in the June 1995 issue of the *Aeronautical Journal* of the Royal Aeronautical Society by David Lednicer entitled "A CFD Evaluation of Three Prominent World War II Fighter Aircraft." As indicated, he employed modern computational fluid dynamics and finite element analysis to compare the Spitfire, Fw 190, and the Mustang. In summary, he rated the Mustang as 20–30mph (32–48km/h) faster than the others, and defined its drag from the radiator cooling system as only 2 to 3% of the total drag.

'The achievement of this low cooling drag has a legitimate background of research and analysis, primarily from British sources – most prominently presented in Royal Aircraft Establishment Report No 1683 by F. W. Meredith, BA, in August 1935. I had read a modified version of this report, published about 1939, and offered the rear fuselage mounting of the radiator, which I believed would optimise the potential of the Meredith Effect, in my representations to the British Purchasing Commission in 1940. This, along with other considerations, led to the initial order for the original Allison-powered Mustang.

Rather interestingly, a considerable number of competent participants and observers have credited the low drag to other elements such as the wing section profile and the algebraic method of fairing the fuselage lines, etc. Lednicer's analysis supports the cooling drag reduction conclusion, although he does assign a small drag increment to the somewhat steeper slope of the Spitfire pilot's windshield.

In recent years, during retirement, I have spent some time and effort to trace the record of the cooling drag research and have learned quite a lot. David Birch of the Rolls-Royce Heritage Trust and author of *Rolls-Royce and the Mustang* has most generously supplied me with copies of some very pertinent documents involving Royal Aircraft Establishment reports, patents, and wartime research and typed reports from the Rolls Experimental Department then at Hucknall. Among these papers are RAE Report No 1702 by R. S. Capon, OBE, BA, FRAeS, dated 1936, in which he extends and amplifies Meredith's thesis, British Patents No 471, 371 and No 472, 555 in 1937 by Ellor and de Paravicini, and other papers on the same subject.

It is apparent that the principle of cooling drag reduction by restoration of the momentum of the air after it passed through the radiator was well known before the war and had been applied in aircraft configurations of the Spitfire, Bf 109 and others, but it seems that, as is often the case, "the Devil was in the Details." Lednicer's analysis shows aerodynamic losses in the Spitfire's radiator air intake, and a Rolls-Royce report in July 1942 estimates that the Spitfire could have gained 13mph (20km/h) by utilising a more complete air exit closure.

In all candor, I think the Mustang intake would probably have been little better except that flow separation created a serious vibration and irregular buffeting which forced a lot of wind tunnel work and detail improvement. I credit the North American Aviation aerodynamics and powerplant installation engineers with improving the air intake and smoothing the airflow so that most of the potential of the Meredith method could be realised. The difference in speed between the Spitfire Mk IX and the Mustang P-51D with the same engine is generally recorded and agreed as 405 vs. 437mph (652 vs. 703km/h) – most of which can be attributed to the difference in cooling drag at high speed.

January 1942. It was a pilot of this Squadron, Fg Off G. N. Dawson, who flew the first operational Mustang sortie, taking AG418 on an offensive reconnaissance of Berck-sur-Mer on 10 May 1942. By the summer a number of other squadrons had re-equipped with the Mustang and the Tactical Reconnaissance (TacR) force available to ACC was now a potent and effective weapon.

The first two Mustangs for No 414 Squadron arrived on 2 June and the pilots went into a familiarisation phase, soon expressing themselves 'well pleased with the new aircraft'. By the end of the month ten aircraft were on strength and train-

Above: Wearing American insignia and its RAF serial, AM190 was used by the A&AEE for evaluation but subsequently served with No 516 Squadron. (Ken Delve Collection)

ing was intense. Amongst the new units to form in mid-1942 was No 63 Squadron, created out of No 239 Squadron at Gatwick on 15 June and receiving its first three aircraft, courtesy of No 414 Squadron, two days later. With a cadre of experienced pilots, the Squadron was soon heavily involved in the now-standard training routine with its emphasis on exercises with Army units. However, the following month it moved to Catterick.

The first major operation for the RAF's Mustangs came in August when four squadrons were included in the Air Order of Battle for Operation 'Jubilee', the Dieppe expedition. These squadrons flew 72 missions monitoring German troop movements and faced heavy ground fire; losses to flak mounted, and most of the ten aircraft to go down were to this cause. In April 1942 No 400 Squadron at Odiham had re-equipped with Mustang Is to supplement its Tomahawks, and the ORB for August 19 noted:

'Today marked the first occasion when Canadian Army Co-operation squadrons have acted in their orthodox role of co-operating with the Canadian Army in active operations in Operation *Jubilee*. The occasion was the landing and raid in force on the French coast carried out by units of 2 Canadian Division. A detached flight of 17 pilots and 12 aircraft operated out of Gatwick as part of No 35 Wing which included 26, 239, 400 and 414 Squadrons. This Squadron made 24 sorties on 12 tasks out of a Wing total of 72 sorties and 35 tasks. Tasks consisted of deep low level reconnaissance in areas around and behind the ground objectives. The first sortie made by this Squadron was at 0600 hours by F/O Gordon, with F/O Grant as weaver; the last was made at 1315 hours by F/O Grant with P/O Burlingham as weaver. P/O Burlingham was making his first operational sortie and he failed to return. Three aircraft were holed by light flak without injuring the pilots.'

In January 1943 No 400 Squadron heard that Plt Off M. Pepper had been awarded a Mention in Despatches for Dieppe: 'His aircraft was struck by light flak as he began his task on a *Jubilee* operation. Although struck just above the eye by glass splinters so as to affect his sight, he completed his sortie and reported the first enemy movements of the operation. This was his first operational trip.' Fg Off W. Gordon and Fg Off A. Jones also received MiDs for the Dieppe operation.

Left: A Mustang fitted with 20mm cannon, December 1942. An early American report had decided in favour of the .50-calibre gun, but the RAF tested a variety of options. (*FlyPast* Collection)

It was standard operational procedure to fly as a pair, with one aircraft designated to carry out the actual reconnaissance whilst the second, the weaver, provided protective cover.

Another Canadian squadron, No 414, was also active at Dieppe, flying seventeen TacR sorties covering roads in the area. One aircraft was shot down by an Fw 190, although the pilot, Flt Lt Clarke, safely ditched and was picked up by a destroyer. Other pilots suffered from different hazards: 'P/O Stover was jumped by a 190 at low altitude and took violent evasive action, striking a telephone pole, in so doing he tore 3 ft from the starboard wing of his aircraft and half the aileron. He made a successful landing at the aerodrome. F/O Horncastle hit a seagull at high speed – a hole was torn in the leading edge of his starboard wing.' However, it was not all bad news, and the Squadron ORB went on to record : 'F/O Hills was credited with bringing down a Fw 190, this is believed to be the first shot down by a pilot operating in a Mustang. All personnel returned safely, tired but happy to have finally been in action.' Fg Off Hollis

H. Hills (an American flying with the RAF) had taken off in AG470 at 1025 to act as weaver to Flt Lt Clarke.

The tactical employment of the Mustang was such that its pilots were instructed to avoid enemy aircraft whenever possible – their job was TacR, to bring back essential intelligence, rather than to act as fighter pilots – but it was certainly reassuring for the pilots to know that they had an aircraft that *could* fight. The photographic side of the task employed a single F.24 camera in an oblique mounting located behind the cockpit and which produced a 5in ∞ 5in film. The ability to come back with good photographs of heavily defended targets was to prove of vital importance as the Allies looked towards the invasion of Europe. However, photography was only part of the task undertaken by the ACC units. Indeed, the squadrons very much lived up to the 'army co-operation' tag, flying a wide range of missions in support of the ground forces, including artillery spotting. Few of the squadrons were as yet called upon to take part in operations. The majority of the workload involved exercises with army units in

Below: P-51-NA 41-37321 having its Allison engine turned over at NAA's Inglewood factory. This is the second aircraft from the first true P-51 batch.

various parts of the United Kingdom so that both elements could appreciate needs and potentials. Three squadrons (Nos 63, 225 and 241), for example, were in Scotland working with V Corps, part of the land forces allocated to Operation 'Torch', the invasion of North Africa. In July a further order was placed for 150 aircraft, this time for the NA-91 Mustang IA with four 20mm cannon in place of the machine guns.

After 'Jubilee' the main effort for all Mustang units was that of working with UK-based Army units to establish and practise ground-to-air procedures – the use of recognition panels, for example – although a number of squadrons also maintained operational detachments for 'Populars' and 'Rhubarbs'.

'Unobtrusive Cleverness'

Flight magazine for 20 August 1942 carried an article entitled 'Unobtrusive Cleverness – A fighter design which merits close study: North American Mustang embodies many interesting features':

'There was a time when this excellent aircraft came near to being a square peg in a round hole, but fortunately its merits were realised in time and it was allocated to Army co-operation work, for which its 1,150 hp Allison engine with single-stage blower makes it eminently suitable . . . The rather remarkable thing about the Mustang is that one finds it difficult to make up one's mind whether it gets its good looks from the straight lines or in spite of them. Be that as it may, a great deal of care has been taken in the design of the Mustang. In the case of the Mustang, great care has been taken to secure laminar flow by making the surface as smooth as possible, not merely over the leading-edge portion [of the wing] but throughout. Flush riveting and smooth joints between plates are means to this end, but one wonders how much of the effect is spoilt by the camouflage painting. In addition to a smooth surface, the drag of an aircraft wing is also influenced by thickness. Although we have no figures for

the Mustang, in the form of thickness/chord ratio, it is obvious that the wing is very thin, with a fairly sharp nose, both features which are suitable for a high-speed wing.

'The wing/fuselage joint of the Mustang is worth studying. Near the root there is a fairly sudden increase both in thickness and chord, the former being on the under surface and the latter on the leading-edge. In this way it has been possible to avoid large fillets on the upper surface, on which the radius of the fillet is quite small except at the extreme trailing-edge. What probably helps make this possible is the placing of the radiator under the fuselage, the cowling beginning under the wing and ending some way behind it, in a movable cowl which controls the cooling . . . For the work it has to do, the Mustang is fortunately very robust. Army co-operation flying means battlefield airfields with – at the best – only wire mesh runways. If under these conditions a machine is to

Above: A formation of three A-36s over southern California. The first ground attack variant, under the NA-97 designation, was completed in September 1942 and delivery of the aircraft to units commenced in October. (*FlyPast* Collection)

operate and cope on equal terms with enemy fighters, it has to be a very good aircraft indeed.'

These early Mustangs were not to prove 'very good indeed' when it came to air combat, and their legendary status was some time in coming. Nevertheless, for the RAF's immediate needs of a low-level tactical aircraft, the Mustang Is were eminently suitable.

RAF Mustang strength continued to grow. In August No 268 Squadron flew its first offensive patrol with its Mustang Is, having commenced a re-equipment from Tomahawks in March. At the beginning of August Wg Cdr Anderson had chaired a conference for all his pilots at Snailwell to discuss formation flying and the development of fighting tactics with the Mustang. A few days later the Squadron detached to Weston Zoyland for Armament Training Camp (ATC), returning on the 15th for a further bout of training and modifications to the aircraft such as the

fitting of VHF radios. At last, on 30 August, the first operational sorties were flown – patrols off the Dutch coast.

September 16 saw No 268 Squadron on a new type of mission: 'This operation, the first of its type to be undertaken by this squadron, or by any squadron within Army Co-operation Command, proceeded without a hitch. Great dissatisfaction was felt by all concerned when the operation could not be completed because of adverse weather.' Eleven of the Squadron's Mustangs, operating from Attlebridge, were acting as close escort to nine Bostons flying to Den Helder. The RAF had been undertaking offensive fighter sweeps, primarily using Spitfires, over the Continent to draw the Luftwaffe into battle; the Germans were, however, proving reluctant. Thus the concept behind the 'Circus' operation was to add bombers to the package in an attempt to force the Luftwaffe to react. It was a tactic that met with mixed success. As far as our history is concerned, the Mustang played only a small part as the RAF's main fighter type involved with these missions was the Spitfire.

USAAC Interest

At long last the United States Army Air Corps (USAAC) began to take a serious interest in this 'British' aircraft. One of the earliest reports concerning the P-51 is a memo submitted on 26 March 1942 by NACA's Langley Memorial Aeronautical Laboratory concerning 'a profile-drag investigation in flight on an experimental fighter-type airplane – the North American XP-51. Serial No 41-38.' The assessment was carried out at the request of the Army Air Corps and the aircraft was provided by the Material Division. Profile-drag tests were conducted 'on the following surface conditions of the wing section:

'1. Unfinished.
'2. Factory finished.
'3. Factory finished and modified by sanding the insignia.
'4. Smoothened [sic] and faired by filling and sanding.

Left and right: With the RAF serial EW998, this is actually an A-36 under evaluation by the A&AEE in March 1943, although the RAF never adopted the variant. This series of photographs shows the bomb-carrying arrangement to good effect. Note also the air brakes. (*FlyPast* Collection)

'It is estimated that the overall drag reduction resulting from application of the factory finish to this wing would increase the maximum speed of the airplane by roughly 4 miles per hour. However, the best results were obtained with the smoothened and faired wing, giving a lift co-efficient of about 0.10, which corresponds to a shallow dive at an indicated airspeed of about 340 miles per hour.'

It was, however, only when the ACA began a flight trial that the P-51 was first looked at in detail. Two of the original production Mustang Is had been taken on charge for evaluation in the latter part of 1941 (as XP-51s) but little attention was paid to them by the trials unit at Wright Field as a great deal of work was required on other projects and the XP-51 was thus given no special priority.

The Air Corps Technical Report on the 'final inspection performance and acceptance of North American airplane Model XP-51' was dated 15 July 1942 and the following extracts are taken from this report:

'The airfoil is a modified laminar flow and was at the time of construction the closest to a true laminar flow yet built. The armament consists of two synchro-nised caliber .50 machine guns in the fuselage and two caliber .50 and four caliber .30 wing guns. [The .50-calibre guns carried 400 rounds and the .30-calibre guns 1,000 rounds.] In order to expedite delivery of the first airplane for performance testing, no gun charging was provided. The second airplane was equipped with fully automatic gun chargers as developed by the Bendix Corp. Passive armament consists of self-sealing fuel tanks and lines, bullet-proof glass and armor plate in front of the pilot where the engine does not offer adequate protection. Provision only was made for the installation of armor plate behind the pilot.

'On May 4, 1940 the NAA Inc. signed a foreign release document with the AAF for the foreign sale of the Model NA-73 airplane that entitled the AAF to two airplanes of the type contemplated for sale. This release specifically set forth that the AAF would receive the 4th and 10th articles from the production line. The airplanes were built in accordance with the British model specification except that

certain modifications were made to accommodate standard AAF equipment.

'Considerable trouble was incurred with the Allison engine installation in the early stages of the airplane development. At one particular throttle setting the engine was found to be extremely rough and in one instance the engine completely cut out resulting in a forced landing in a plowed field [this refers to the earlier manufacturer's flight trials, as mentioned above]. The first aircraft was delivered to Wright Field on August 24, 1941 and the second on December 16, 1941.

'It was during flight testing of the first AAF airplane that it was discovered that

Left: Two views of P-51B-15NA 42-106767 wearing the 'QP' code of the 4th Fighter Group's 334th Fighter Squadron. (Ken Delve Collection)

engine difficulties previously encountered could be overcome by increasing the length of the ramming air intake scoop.

'Final official performance flight tests at Wright Field took place from October 10 to December 22, 1941 – the reason for the long period of flight testing was due to the higher priority of other airplanes to be tested, bad weather and malfunctioning of the coolant scoop and landing gear mechanism during cold weather.'

The report made no overall judgements on the aircraft but simply listed the performance data achieved:

'Empty weight	6,278lb
'Normal fuel load	105gal
'Max speed	382mph at 3,000rpm (military power 45.9in Hg, 5min time limit)
'Cruise speed	325.5mph at 2,280rpm (29.5in Hg)
'Time to 25,000ft	17min
'Time to 10,000ft	4.41min'

The second aircraft had also been used by the Armament Laboratory for firing tests but these were issued as a separate report.

A follow-on trial by the Tactical Combat Section at Eglin Field used three aircraft (41-37323, 41-37324 and 41-37325) and took place from August to November 1942 to determine the 'Tactical suitability of the P-51 type aircraft'. Report 4-42-7 was dated 30 December 1942, and amongst its conclusion were:

'a. The subject aircraft is the best low altitude American fighter aircraft yet developed, and should be used as the criterion for comparison of subsequent types . . .

'd. Pilots become completely at home in this aircraft immediately after the first take-off due to the remarkable sensitivity of control, simplicity of cockpit, and excellent flying characteristics.

'e. The rate of roll is not as rapid as is desired for combat operations . . .

'h. With the exception of the radiators, the airplane is satisfactory from a maintenance standpoint . . .

'j. Up to 15,000 ft this is faster than all standard American fighters with the exception of the P-47C-1.'

The general handling characteristics of the P-51 were highly praised:

'The flying characteristics of the P-51 are exceptionally good and the aircraft is very pleasant and easy to fly. Its taxiing visibility is limited in view over the nose as are all standard landing gear fighters having engine in front of pilot. There is no objectionable amount of torque on take-off and the ship becomes airborne very nicely. A pilot feels at home when the ship leaves the ground, and he has the feeling that he has flown this ship for a large number of hours. The plane picks up speed very rapidly after leaving the ground and will climb equally well between 165 mph and 205 mph IAS. This ability to climb well at a high indicated airspeed should be a great aid in helping to catch targets having altitude and attempting to escape. In level flight trimmed up, the aircraft will fly practically hands-off. The plane handles nicely in a dive, using a very small amount of trim, and accelerates faster than any other American fighter. At 500 mph indicated the plane still maintains its stability. In normal flight the plane responds quickly to the controls, however, the aileron roll is slower than desired and tightens at very high speeds. It is very easy to put through all normal aerobatics, and it has sufficient speed to perform these aerobatics from level flight without diving to pick up speed. At slow speeds when approaching the field for landing, there is a mushy feeling in the ailerons but the control is still there. The plane lands nicely, has a tendency to skip several times if landed fast, and it rolls in a straight line without attempting to swing or break noticeably in either direction.'

The P-51 was flown in mock combat with a number of other types – a P-39D, P-40F, P-38F, P-47B and even a Mitsubishi '00' – and in general terms was found to be superior in many respects, especially in speed, rate of climb and dive. Its turning capability was roughly on a par with that of the other aircraft, but 'in close "dog fighting" the subject aircraft has the very decided advantage of being able to break off combat at will'. It was not all good news, however. The report was highly critical of the aircraft's altitude performance: 'The absolute ceiling of the subject aircraft was found to be approximately 31,000 ft. It is believed that the fighting ceiling of this aircraft is 20,000 ft as the engine loses power very rapidly above 18,000 ft. This limited ceiling is the most serious handicap to this aircraft, and every effort should be made to increase the power and critical altitude of the engine.'

The report[1] also suggested that the armament should be changed to four .50-calibre machine guns and that additional armour plate should be provided at the rear of the coolant and oil radiators, located in the belly of the aircraft just behind the cockpit, 'for the reason that most hits on an airplane in combat are to the rear of the cockpit and it is believed that this radiator installation may prove quite vulnerable'. Visibility from the cockpit was considered to be acceptable once in the air but very restrictive whilst on the ground. The aircraft was completely serviced – fuel, oil, coolant, oxygen, ammunition and radio check – in five minutes by a team of four armourers, two mechanics and one radioman.

The test results from the three aircraft were averaged to provide performance data as shown in the accompanying table. The average time to 10,000ft was 4min 7sec and to 20,000ft 9min 54sec, at a climb speed of 170mph IAS. A long-range cruise trial showed the aircraft to be capable of a 1,000-mile range when flown at 15,000ft with 1,650 rpm/22.5in Hg, with a reserve of 30 gallons.[2] Other consumption figures included a 'typical' combat range with allowance for a 20-minute combat phase of 3,000 rpm/34in HG; this gave a 1hr 35min sortie covering a distance of 540 miles and with 36 of the original 180 gallons remain-

P-51 Mustang Trials: Performance Data

Altitude	Max. cruise 2,280rpm/ 30.5in Hg	Max. operation 2,600rpm/ 37.5in Hg	Max. power 3,000rpm/ 44.6in Hg
5,000ft	284mph	319mph	343mph
10,000ft	305mph	343mph	369mph
15,000ft	330mph	367mph	385mph
20,000ft		356mph	373mph
25,000ft		334mph	357mph

ing on return to base. The final set of figures was for an escort mission with a 'convoy of medium bombers' at 14,000ft. A 3hr 26min mission covered a combat radius of 305 miles (i.e. a total distance flown of 610 miles) and included a 20-minute combat phase. The aircraft landed with 21 gallons of fuel.

However, in the meantime, and with the British experience of the type as a TacR aircraft and the American entry to the war creating the need for an even more rapid expansion of American air power, 57 of the RAF Mustang IAs on order were diverted to the USAAC for immediate use. Of these, 55 were fitted with cameras to become F-6As, the first aircraft going to the Photo Reconnaissance School at Colorado Springs. It was to be with this variant that the US side of the Mustang story commenced in late 1942. However, North American had also put forward a proposal for a ground-attack version of the aircraft, and the first of these A-36As was completed at Inglewood in September 1942. Deliveries to units began the following month and work-up commenced prior to deployment overseas. The A-36 would be in action by the middle of 1943, but it had to overcome some problems – not the least of which was a number of instances when the wings were lost during a dive. The first batch of reconnaissance Mustangs – 35 aircraft – joined the 68th Observation Group's 111th and 154th Squadrons in the latter part of 1942 at Oujda, operating alongside the unit's P-39s, P-38s and Spit-

[1] See Appendix G for a full copy of this report.
[2] Note that, in the US reports, 'gallons' refer to US gallons, not Imperial.

Below: No 2 Squadron at dispersal. The Squadron operated Mustangs from April 1942 to January 1945. (Ken Delve Collection)

fires. The first operations were flown by the 154th, who promptly lost one aircraft shot down by Allied flak when it was mistaken for a Bf 109.

Increasing Tasks

By October 1942 the RAF's Mustang squadrons were undertaking an increasing range of tasks, including hunting for shipping off the coast of Holland in order to locate suitable targets for the fighter-bombers. With the desire to take the war to the enemy as often and as effectively as possible, the squadrons commenced 'Rhubarbs' in the autumn with offensive sweeps by sections of up to four aircraft against a wide variety of targets. Typical of these was that flown by four aircraft of No 168 Squadron, led by Wg Cdr Anderson, from Duxford on 14 October:

'Landfall was made at a point 6 miles north of Bergen am Zee at 1316 hours. A hutted camp was attacked at this point but no results were seen. The Section then flew east to the canal and followed it to Alkmaar. No barges were seen on the canal, but three locos and about 120 goods trucks were engaged. Two locos were claimed as badly damaged. From Alkmaar the railway line was followed east and a goods train engaged and halted, large clouds of steam were seen rising from the engine. Further along the line another engine was engaged and believed hit in the boiler. Off Ehkhuizen a tug towing two covered barges was seen. Hits were scored on the tug and the leading barge. 15–20 covered barges were seen in the harbour and engaged but without visible results. Course was then set NW, where a tug of about 500 tons was left in flames NW of Workum.'[1]

The TacR role was still dominant, and the standard tactic was for two aircraft to operate together, one to act as the reconnaissance aircraft and the other to provide cover by warning of flak zones and fighters. This was an ideal arrangement as it allowed the reconnaissance pilot to concentrate on his target without any distractions.

Although enemy aircraft were encountered from time to time, the Mustangs were usually able to avoid them and return home with the targets on film. How-

[1] No 268 Squadron ORB.

ever, bad weather and flak were taking a steady toll as the Mustangs operated at ultra low level. Attacking ground targets was always a risky business and relied heavily on the element of surprise – locate a target, take the photographs (or strafe) and run, and don't go back again: the Germans had superb light flak in large quantities and all important targets were well defended.

The squadrons of No 35 Wing were kept busy, and on 22 October Operation 'Petworth I' was launched under the guidance of Gp Capt Andrew Geddes. This was a combined 'Popular' and 'Rhubarb' with the aim of obtaining photographic cover of the enemy-held coast in the neighbourhood of Fécamp. Diversionary attacks were mounted inland to distract the enemy, and typical of these was that by four aircraft of No 400 Squadron against the marshalling yards at Amiens.

A number of Mustang units were now based in Scotland, No 63 Squadron having moved to Macmerry in November to boost the AC strength for a series of major exercises. Late November brought Exercise 'Goliath', a mountain warfare exercise, with the AC units working with the 52nd Division.

Fighter Command Interest

At around the same period, autumn 1942, there was renewed interest from Fighter Command in the Mustang as a fighter. In part this was due to the need to counter the low level 'hit-and-run' raids being carried out by German fighter-bombers such as the Focke-Wulf Fw 190. The AC squadrons were mounting detachments at various bases to provide cover against these raiders, although mostly with no effect. For most of October, for example, No 19 Squadron kept four aircraft at Tangmere and these flew dawn and dusk standing patrols between the Isle of Wight and Beachy Head. Whilst the Mustangs were vectored against a number of targets, sightings were few and opportunities to engage even fewer – although on 27 October Plt Off Hanton managed a three-second burst from 500yds at an Fw 190. In general terms Fighter Command was more than happy with its Spitfires, and the Mustang was seen as a limited acquisition to fulfil one particular role. Little came of this immediately, and indeed Fighter Command was going to have to wait some time to receive its Mustangs: the aircraft was about to take on a new lease of life and become a decisive weapon.

Left: A well-known but nevertheless excellent shot of two Mustang Is, AG550 and AM112, of No 2 Squadron. (Ken Delve Collection)

2

MERLIN MUSTANGS

In April 1942 Wg Cdr Ian Campbell-Orde of the Air Fighting Development Unit (AFDU) invited the Rolls-Royce Chief Test Pilot, Ronald Harker, to Duxford to fly the Mustang I (AG422). Harker flew the aircraft for 30 minutes and in a subsequent memo of May 1 commented:[1]

'This aircraft could prove itself a formidable low- and mid-altitude fighter. It closely resembles an Me 109F, probably due to its being designed by one of the Messerschmitt designers, who is now working with the North American Aviation Co. . . . The point which strikes me is that with a powerful and a good engine, like the Merlin 61, its performance could be outstanding, as it is 35mph faster than a Spitfire V at roughly the same power.'[2]

Harker, with the support of the Hucknall manager, Ray Dorey, took his thoughts to E. W. Hives and convinced him of the potential of such a Merlin-powered Mustang. Putting matters on a more official level, Hives put forward a development proposal to Sir Wilfred Freeman, Air Member for Production and Design. This was followed by a meeting between Rolls-Royce and Air Ministry officials, the outcome of which was summarised in a memo dated May 14:

'At a meeting yesterday on a very high level, it was suggested to the Minister that the LXI should be tried in the above machine . . . I feel myself that it might pay a very good dividend, if it can be done quickly, to install the Merlin XX in this machine. It would be a relatively quick job,

and might fill a very useful interim niche under existing conditions . . . I recall that Mansell and Jones[3] when in the USA did suggest that the Packard should be fitted into the Mustang aircraft, but it did not get any further.'

The Merlin XX option was, in part, put forward as a counter to any possible argument against use of the Merlin 61 as the latter engine was needed for the Spitfire IX (the main Fighter Command type), supplies for which had to be assured. Matters moved fairly swiftly, and Mustang AG518 arrived at Rolls-Royce, on loan, from the Lockheed Aircraft Services assembly site at Speke on 29 May for use by Rolls-Royce as a standard evaluation aircraft; at the same time they were given copies of the A&AEE reports.

A Rolls-Royce memo of June 3 outlined the next stage: 'CRD [Controller for Research and Development] agrees installation of 61 proceed, subject to stress figures being satisfactory . . . [instructions] cabled to General Arnold to arrange for the installation of a Packard Merlin [V1650-1] in the machine immediately and to give

---

[1] Most of the discussion in the following section is summarised from *Rolls-Royce and the Mustang* by D. Birch and published by the Rolls-Royce Heritage Trust. For the full story of the Merlin Mustang development this book is essential reading.

[2] The comment concerning the designer – Edgar Schmeud – is erroneous: although of German descent, he was never a Messerschmitt employee.

[3] Air Cdre R. B. Mansell was Commandant of A&AEE and E. T. Jones was Chief Superintendent at A&AEE.

Priority 1 in the factory.' So, whilst Rolls-Royce were to fit a Merlin 61 to a Mustang in England, North American were also to install a Packard Merlin in an aircraft – although, as will be seen below, this latter was to cause major problems.

Meanwhile Rolls-Royce Performance Engineer Witold Challier had produced a set of theoretical performance curves for a Mustang with a Merlin XX or Merlin 61 and, for comparison, a Spitfire IX with a Merlin 61. His report of 8 June included maximum speed figures of 400mph at 18,600ft for the Merlin XX and 441mph at 25,600ft for the Merlin 61. One of his graphs showed the amount of power required for a particular airspeed in level flight at 20,000ft: '. . . it shows quite conclusively that the Mustang airframe, despite being heavier, produces far less than either the Spitfire V or IX, to such an extent that when all three are compared at the Mustang's top speed of around 375 mph, the latter's engine was producing around 200bhp less at 20,000ft.'

Hives was convinced of both the potential of, and the need for, the Merlin Mustang, and on 17 June he wrote to Freeman expressing his concern over the future position regarding fighters, and particularly that of Griffon-powered Spitfires:

'The best bet at the moment is the Mustang. We have now got it agreed that we shall convert three machines instead of one . . . somebody has got to make sure that there is a good supply of Mustang airframes. Another variation we are looking at is that for a super low-altitude fighter Mustang with the Griffon 11-B engine; we have not got the final figures for this, but I mention it as an indication that you cannot get too many of these machines. The risk of course is that we make the Mustang into a first class machine [and] the USAAC will want to collar them, because the information we have had from the USA is that the fighter position is by no means clear.'

This latter was a very perceptive comment from Hives and is, in effect, what was soon to take place. Ten days later, on 28 June, Hives wrote to Freeman again on the same subject:

"We feel very depressed about the fighter position, both in this country and the USA . . . We are sold completely on the Mustang. The Merlin 61 goes into it with no alteration to the engine cowling or to the radiator cowling. We are pressing for-

Right: No 268 Squadron's AM104 looking the worse for wear, 13 July 1942. The aircraft was repaired and went on to serve with Nos 414 and 430 Squadrons, eventually being lost to flak on 21 October 1944. (Ken Delve Collection)

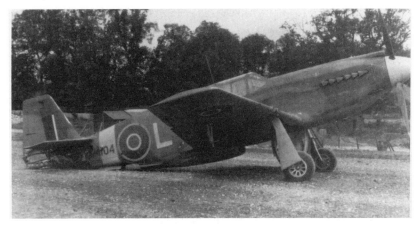

three? I should like to send no less than two to the USA.'

A memorandum of 10 July confirmed that five aircraft were to be converted, the intention being to send two to the United States; AM121 arrived in early June as the first aircraft, the decision having been taken not to convert AG518 as it was not to the latest production standard and therefore would be inappropriate. The next to arrive were AL963 and AL975, joined in August by AM203 and AM208.

In August Challier, following an examination of the test results from AG518 and the proposal to use a Rotol wood laminate Hydulignum propeller of 11ft 4in diameter rather than 10ft 9in (and to change the reduction gear ratio to 0.42:1), revised his performance estimates:

ward with the conversion of these machines, but as hundreds of small detail drawings have to be produced, special radiators, etc., it will be towards the end of August before it is flying. We have asked that 250 sets of conversion parts shall be put in hand . . .'

Freeman replied on 30 June: '. . . it has proved over and over again that technical superiority confers an almost overwhelming advantage on its possessor . . . I agree with you that 250 conversion sets should be put in hand, but why only 250? In the old days we should have chanced our arms. Anyway, I will do what I can to get an order for 500 sets put through today. Can you convert six Mustangs instead of

	Merlin XX	Merlin 61
All-up weight	8,600lb	9,100lb
Max. speed	393mph @	432mph @
	18,600ft	25,500ft
Operational ceiling	32,700ft	37,200ft

Although progress was being made at the British end, there were problems in the United States as licence-production of the Merlin 61 was not yet under way and

Left: It was the marriage of the Merlin engine, in its Packard Merlin form, with the Mustang airframe that was to produce the exceptional P-51 fighter. This is P-51B-1NA 43-12166 (*FlyPast* Collection)

Right: The TacR team. Squadrons often worked with the artillery, as here with a British 25pdr gun. (Ken Delve Collection)

a proposal to use the Merlin 28 was rejected; a memo issued by the Army Air Forces Material Command on August 28 stated: 'Dutch Kindelberger says that the Merlin 28 is out for installation in the P-51, but they are going full blast on the Merlin 61. About all the redesign necessary is to move the wing forward three inches and down one inch, also the nose will be dropped a little to give better visibility. If the aerodynamics isn't ruined, looks like they might have a pretty good airplane.'

On 9 September Lappin wrote to Jimmy Ellor of the Packard Motor Car Co.: ' I brought Mr Legara to Hucknall yesterday to discuss the further development of the Mustang, and the situation in the USA does not seem to be a happy one. Here we have an aircraft, which from the point of view of aircraft [aerodynamics?] is outstanding, and even with a Packard 28 it would perform probably about 400mph ... However, we are taking energetic action as far as possible in order to impress upon the Air Ministry here and the Army Air Corps, that this machine should enjoy a very high priority, which at the moment it has not got.'

On 27 August a meeting was held between the Air Ministry and MAP to discuss Mustang requirements and Hives commented: '... a telegram had been sent to the British Air Commission asking that the possibility of extending Mustang production in the US to provide, say, 120 a month without engines for the UK be explored. If Mustang with Merlin 61 proved satisfactory the Americans might be asked to supply 200 a month for use in the Middle East, India and Australia in return for the equivalent number of Spitfires for US Pursuit Groups in the UK. VCAS [Vice Chied of Air Staff] expressed doubt as to whether the Spitfire IX would have good enough performance for 1943 and recommended increasing order for 1,200 Merlin Mustangs to 3,000 of which we should insist on a 50% share.'

A few days earlier, on 4 September, Brig-Gen A. J. Lyon, Air Technical Section of HQ ETO, had written to Hives: 'The Mustang, now known in America as the P-51, will be known as the XP78 when fitted with the Merlin 61. North American estimate that the first airplane will be ready for flight by October 1, and the second two–four weeks later ... North American estimate the following performance figures for the XP78 airplane:

'Gross weight   8,350lb
'High speed   445mph @ 28,000
'Service ceiling   42,400ft

'Colonel Chidlaw reports that no action has been taken relative to the Griffon en-

Right: A Mustang fitted with two 'S' guns, May 1943. (*FlyPast* Collection)

Left: A Mustang IA (FD843) of No 170 Squadron, September 1943.

gine, as there is little doubt that the Mustang would have to be largely redesigned to install this engine.'

Authority for the XP-51B project had been granted on 12 June 1942 (under CTI-710) for 'Immediate negotiations with North American Aviation for the procurement of one airplane fitted with a Packard Merlin 61 engine. Addendum 1 to this CTI, dated 15 June 1942, directed that action be taken to procure mock-up engine, flight engines, and header tanks in order that initial flight date would not be delayed.'[1] The XP-78 designation was superseded in a Technical Instruction of 2 September stating that the P-51 designation was be retained – as the XP-51B.

Maj Thomas Hitchcock, Assistant Military Attaché in London, had followed progress with all aspects of the project and was without doubt one of its greatest supporters. On 8 October he issued a memo summarising the history of the project to date – a memo that included a number of very perceptive comments that demonstrated that 'national self-interest and commercial bias still held sway in the midst of war':

'The Mustang is one of the best, if not the best, fighter airframes that has been developed in the war up to date. It has no compressibility or flutter troubles, it is manoeuvrable at high speeds, has the most rapid rate of roll of any plane except the Fw 190, is easy to fly and has no nasty tricks . . . The development of the Mustang as a high-altitude fighter will be brought about by cross-breeding it with the Merlin 61 engine. While the prospects of an English engine in an American airframe may appeal to the sentimental qualities of those individuals who are interested in furthering Anglo-American relationships by joining hands across the water, it does not fully satisfy important people on both sides of the Atlantic who seem more interested in pointing with pride to the development of a 100% national product than they are concerned with the very difficult problem of rapidly developing a fighter plane that will be superior to anything the Germans have.' Sadly, he does not elucidate on who the 'important people' were or the details of their arguments.

An official American study of the AAF in the Second World War puts this interpretation on the development of the Mer-

Right: An Allison-engined Mustang II under evaluation, July 1943. (*FlyPast* Collection)

---

[1] Air Corps Technical Report 5134.

Left: Merlin Mustang X AM308, with its 'prototype' markings, under evaluation at the A&AEE in April 1943. (FlyPast Collection)

lin Mustang and Hitchcock's role: 'In the autumn of 1942 Major Thomas Hitchcock . . . reported on the P-51 as "one of the best, if not the best, fighter airframe that has been developed in the war up to date" *and suggested* the development of the Mustang as a high altitude fighter by "cross-breeding it with the Merlin 61 engine".[1] The parochial attitudes to the aircraft would still seem to be present as this implies that the uprated Mustang was Hitchcock's idea!

The comment regarding the Fw 190's rate of roll is of interest: attempts were made to emulate this with the Mustang, as Eric Brown recalls in his book *Wings of the Weird and Wonderful*: '. . . in an attempt to find the correct lateral control formula the RAE Mustang I AG393 was fitted with linearly geared aileron tabs. I flew this aircraft at five different gearing ratios, and on the fourth attempt the magic formula was found and we had a set of ailerons even lighter and more effective than those of the Fw 190. By the time these experiments were made the Mustang III was already in service, and it had a rate of roll only slightly inferior to that of the Fw 190.'

First Flight

The first flight of a Merlin-equipped Mustang took place on 13 October 1942 when Captain R. T. Shepherd flew AL975, powered by a Merlin 65. The aircraft performed well, other than the fact that the cowling came loose; a series of high-speed tests was carried out to determine whether a redesign of the cowling was needed. The flight test programme continued, although the aircraft was performance-limited on the first eight sorties as it was still fitted with the standard fuel tanks and pumps. Few problems were discovered during these flight trials, although one that did cause trouble was a tendency for the undercarriage doors to open in flight, usually in a high-speed dive. Various modifications were tried but the problem was not cured (and indeed was still present on P-51Bs in operational service). On sortie No 9 the port wing was fitted with one of the new tinned-steel fuel tanks and an immersed fuel pump and in the early part of November a number of performance evaluations were flown, the aircraft reaching 422mph on the 13th.

The second aircraft to be converted, AM208 (first flight 13 November) was sent to the A&AEE at Boscombe Down. They were not altogether impressed, criticising the lateral stability of the Mustang X: '. . . it appeared that there was a large change in the directional trim with power and speed applied and the aircraft side-

[1] W. F. Craven and J. L. Cato (eds), *The Army Air Forces in World War Two*, Vol. VI, Washington, 1983.

slipped easily during manoeuvres. This, it was thought, was due to a lack of fin area, coupled with the effects from the four-bladed airscrew. However, the tests concluded that there was no real deficiency in the fin area but the fitment of a dorsal fillet to the base of the fin would improve matters to some extent.'

Directional stability 'problems' were highlighted by others over the next few weeks, and a meeting was held at Hucknall on 2 February 1943 to discuss matters, the minutes of which included the following: 'AFDU cannot accept the aircraft as a 100% success as a fighter machine at present and their criticisms are, in general, confirmed by Mr Greenwood and Capt Shepherd. It became apparent that there are two problems. The first is to provide sufficient directional stability and the second is to overcome the large change of directional trim with power which is objectionable owing to the heavy rudder forces involved.'

Meanwhile, the first of the US 'Merlin Mustangs' had flown. In July the contract had been issued for two aircraft (41-37352 and 41-37421) to be fitted with Packard-Merlins; the first flight took place at Inglewood on 30 November 1942: 'The delay in making this flight was caused by repeated failures of the Packard V-1650-3 engine during tests at Wright Field. Although the engine was installed for several weeks prior to the first flight, the failures at Wright Field prevented the engine from being released for flight. The second airplane, 41-37421, was first flown on 2 Feb 1943.'[1]

Although the USAAC already had substantial numbers of P-51As on order, a further 2,000 of the new variant were ordered – even before the prototype had flown. New construction facilities had to be built to cope with the orders being placed by the USAAC and RAF. The Mus-

[1] Air Corps Technical Report 5234.

tang had truly arrived, although it was to be some months before the Merlin Mustangs reached operational units.

The AAF history has this comment to make regarding part of the P-51 story: 'The story of the P-51 came close to representing the costliest mistake made by the Army Air Forces in World War Two. By 1943 it was becoming all too clear that the big bombers would require the protection of full fighter escort if an effective campaign of strategic bombardment of Germany was to be maintained . . . but an opinion that had first been stated in 1940 still prevailed that "no fighter plane can be designed to escort Heavy and Medium bombardment to their extreme tactical radius of action and there engage in offensive combat with enemy interceptor fighter types on equal terms. The escort plane in order to have the range and speed of the aircraft it accompanies may be as large and at least as expensive as such aircraft." In August 1942 a special Board, under Brig-Gen Alfred J. Lyon, recommended the use of modified B-17s and B-24s to act as destroyer escort planes; this in due course led to experiments by the 8th Air Force in early 1943 with the YB-40.'[1]

The cost of a P-51 in 1942 was $58,698 (this eventually fell to a low of $50,985 in 1945) whereas its two main 'sister' fighters were appreciably more expensive, the P-47 being $105,594 and the P-38 $120,407. Oddly enough, this price variation still applies in the warbird market for these types – although in this case the much higher cost of a P-47 and P-38 (over $1 million) is due to the rarity of these aircraft.

Sliding Hood

In December a Mustang IA was with the AFDU for trials on a new canopy arrangement: 'In accordance with instructions from Air Ministry (DAT) reference CS/11800, trials have been carried out on a Mustang IA aircraft, AG618, fitted with a sliding hood. This hood has been designed by North American representatives in this Country and fitted to the aircraft by RAF Henlow, and is merely an interim measure in order to ascertain the tactical advantages of having a sliding hood on Mustang aircraft . . .

'2. The aircraft has been flown at Duxford for 5 hours and the following comments are forwarded:

'Advantages

'(i) The view for take-off and landing is considerably improved with the hood in the open position. Previously pilots have felt a trifle cramped when landing the Mustang fitted with the standard hood as the long nose restricts forward view and the view to the side panels is poor when compared with most British fighters.

'(ii) The aircraft has been flown at cruising and fast speeds with the hood open and the view for search was found to be greatly improved. Night flying was not actually possible on this aircraft as flame damping exhausts were not fitted, but it is certain that the improved view would make this aircraft most suitable for night flying.

'(iii) The view forwards and sidewards is now completely unrestricted and this gives much confidence to pilots when flying in bad weather.

'(iv) It was found possible to fly with the hood open without using goggles, as apart from a slight eddy at the back of the cockpit, there is no draught.

'(v) With the sliding hood entry and exit from the cockpit is much easier. It was found with the standard hood that it was advisable for a Rigger to make quite certain that the hood was securely locked before taxying out and with the sliding hood this procedure is now unnecessary.

'(vi) The aircraft fitted with the sliding hood was limited from diving, but maximum level speed runs have

Below: An atmospheric photograph of Mustang III FX893; note the modified canopy. The aircraft was sent to the Middle East after it had completed its trials work. (Ken Delve Collection)

---

[1] Craven and Cato, *op. cit.*

been carried out without any problems developing. The hood, although only a lash-up model, showed no signs of blowing away and stayed in the open or shut position at all speeds. It is necessary to use both hands to open or close the hood even at slow speeds and although at first this was found a little difficult, it became reasonably easy after practice. The hood has been opened at an indicated speed of 250 mph and closed again at 300 mph, though at these speeds the opening movement was found rather difficult.

'(vii) Level speed runs have been made with this aircraft fitted with the standard hood and with the sliding hood. With the sliding hood there appeared to be a slight increase in speed which is probably due to the removal of the aerial mast and rear ventilators. It was also compared with a standard Mustang from an Army Co-operation squadron and again showed a slight superiority in speed.

'Disadvantages

'(i) The radio mast has to be removed from its present position behind the cockpit to allow the hood to open. This will necessitate re-positioning the mast.

'(ii) There is a very slight up-draught through the cockpit when the inboard wheel fairings are open when operating the undercarriage, but this is not considered sufficient to worry about. [The next section concerned criticisms that only affected the 'lash-up hood' and so has been omitted.]

'Conclusions

'3. The tactical advantages of being able to open the hood of the Mustang in the air are very great and pilots have been most enthusiastic about the improved view, particularly during bad weather flying. This should be a great asset when carrying out "Rhubarb" operations.

'4. The sliding hood will make the Mustang most suitable for night flying due to the view for search and night vision being greatly improved.

'Recommendations

'5. It is strongly recommended that as tactical advantages of having a sliding hood on Mustang aircraft have proved so great, a hood should be carefully designed and fitted to all Mustang aircraft as soon as practicable.

'AFDU/3/20/33
'7th December 1942'

Pilot visibility from fighter aircraft was a subject of constant discussion and evaluation but it was only with the advent of 'blown' or 'bubble' canopies that a practical solution was achieved. (The Bf 109 had perhaps the worst canopy arrangement of any fighter and, unlike most of its opponents, saw very little improvement.)

As 1942 came to a close, a year in which Allied fortunes at last brightened and the previously 'invincible' Axis forces suffered a number of reverses, the Mustang was still primarily a low-level tactical aircraft. The superlative fighter was, however, soon to enter the fray.

New Year – New Roles

The invasion of France by the Allies was the major planning element of Allied strategy from mid-1942. It would happen; all that was uncertain was when. The Russians continued to press for this 'second front' to be launched as soon as possible to relieve pressure on the Eastern Front, but Allied planners knew that a great deal of background work and military build-up had yet to take place before any such operation could be attempted. One of the first essentials of such planning was intelligence, and the reconnaissance units, including those equipped with the TacR Mustang, had a vital role to play. The other prime concern was that of air superiority. The P-51 was to be a key element in both. As 1943 opened, the acquisition of this intelligence began to play an increasing role.

Right: Mustang AM106/G (the 'G' code meaning that this aircraft required additional security protection), March 1943. (*FlyPast* Collection)

No 63 Squadron, although still based at Macmerry and devoting most of its attention to AC exercises, maintained an operational detachment at Odiham tasked with oblique photography of the French coast. Typical of the missions detailed in their ORB was that for January 18:

'S/L Walford and F/O Alston briefed for low level oblique photography of digging at Airon Notre Dame . . . with two aircraft of 168 Squadron and two aircraft of 613 Squadron. 168 Sqn were Blue Section, 63 Red and 613 Black. Weather was 9/10 cloud at 600–1,000 ft with haze below and this made the trip to the coast lengthy and hazardous. Blue 2 lost the remainder of the formation and returned to base. At Beachy Head, Blue set course for Dieppe and Red and Black, led by S/L Walford, set course for Berck. Berck was sighted on ETA with cloud approx 10/10 at 3,000 ft. Speed was increased to 300 mph and aircraft flew up the Bay of D'Authie, thence Black 2 broke off to photograph Berck aerodrome while Red 1 and 2, with cameras switched on, flew a pre-deter-

mined course at about 30 ft. The objective was sighted and no enemy activity seen, but a number of gun positions were noted. On way out to coast Red 1 saw dummy aircraft under camouflage netting and Red 2 fired a 2 second burst at about 20 German soldiers on sand dunes. The aircraft landed at Odiham at 1200 hours. Red 1 had a camera failure due to a blown fuse after about 20 exposures so that the objective was not covered; Red 2's cameras worked throughout and some useful photos were obtained.'

Later in the month the Squadron was using a camera with a 14in lens: '. . . some useful photos were obtained which will be of great value in future coastal reconnaissance.'

It was still fairly early days for the PR aspect of the Mustang and new equipment and tactics were frequently under evaluation. In March No 268 Squadron tested a new 14in lens vertical camera: 'Photographs taken from 8,000 ft were very satisfactory. The test also included a fast climb to 20,000 ft and this too was satisfactory.'[1] Two months later the ORB reported: '. . . work was started today to fit a vertical camera in a Mustang. This Squadron had already fitted a vertical camera in a Mustang but our latest installation has been approved by HQ ACC and it will be fitted by all units.'

Over a period of months thousands of photographs would be taken, and the analysis of this material has all too often been ignored in histories of the air war. The value of air reconnaissance cannot be overemphasised, and if the Mustang had played no other role in the war this alone would have been a significant contribution.

The Mustangs also attacked opportunity targets during many of these missions, such low-level escapades proving quite hazardous: 'Whilst flying through the steam of a damaged locomotive, F/O Watson collected some telegraph wires from the side of the line. He landed with 10 yards of this wire hanging from his starboard wing-tip.'[2] Mustang AM154 was soon repaired and back in action. Such low-level hazards were something that pilots had to accept as the risks from enemy ground defences and aircraft were, in general terms, far higher: the lower you flew the less likely you were to fall victim to flak or fighter, notwithstanding the fact that at very low level there was an increased risk from small-arms fire.

The RAF units generally continued in much the same range of roles as before but underwent organisational changes with the creation of Composite Groups as part of the preparation for the invasion of Europe. Exercises with ground forces were stepped up and tactics and techniques of air support were revised and rehearsed, in many instances putting into practice the lessons learned in the Western Desert, where the Desert Air Force had developed such work to a fine degree. The largest peace-time exercise ever held by the RAF, 'Spartan', took place in March. 'One of the primary purposes of the exercise was a full-scale try-out of the use of a Composite Group working through a common operations room in direct contact with the Army commander. This Squadron worked in conjunction with 414 Squadron out of Dunsfold.' Between 1 and 12 March thousands of sorties were flown by RAF and Allied units and valuable lessons were assimilated by the planners – all of which would prove useful when the Allies returned to the Continent.

Tragedy was never far away, much of it nothing to do with the enemy. On 13 May one of No 63 Squadron's armourers, AC2 Dorrington, decided to fly one of the Mustangs (AP184). He started up, taxied and took off into wind but stalled at 40ft and crashed – with fatal consequences.

By mid-1943 the RAF Mustang strength stood at sixteen squadrons, and despite the heavy training commitment there was still plenty of operational work being carried out, offensive missions over the Continent being the major task. A number of the units now had Mustang IAs on strength. However, the introduction of the new variant was not without problems, as reported by No 268 Squadron: '. . . almost 100% unserviceability of the IA owing to failure of the auto boost control in conjunction with the fitting of the low altitude supercharger'.[3]

There had also been a great deal of moving from airfield to airfield, frustration being expressed in the No 414 Squadron ORB, the unit having moved from Harrowbear to Portreath after little more than a week: '. . . seven days doesn't give one time to become bored at a station'. Two weeks later they were on the move again, to Dunsfold: 'Definitely a mobile squadron with a capital M. Not too bad under ordinary circumstances but as an indication of what we mean, we quote the words of an American who watched our trucks labour into Portreath – "are you guys fighting this war or the last one?"'

In June Army Co-operation Command disbanded, to be replaced by the 2nd Tactical Air Force (TAF). However, as early

Right: Mustang AG357 undergoing trials with rocket projectiles (RP), July 1943. Although the trials were a success, these weapons were not used to any great extent by RAF Mustangs, although some Italy-based units did use them. (*FlyPast* Collection)

[1] No 268 Squadron ORB.
[2] No 63 Squadron ORB for 12 February 1943.
[3] No 268 Squadron ORB, August 1943.

as January the Mustangs had been called upon to fly fighter escort for day bombing missions. For example, on 22 January No 268 Squadron escorted Mitchells of No 98 Squadron to targets in Holland. The Mustangs engaged Fw 190s and shot one down, but two Mustangs failed to return, one of which was lost to flak. Most of the anti-air work undertaken by Mustangs during 1943 was not air-to-air but attacks on enemy airfields. The anti-airfield work was also continued at night, albeit on a small scale by the Mustangs, as part of the Allied strategy of destroying the Luftwaffe in order to achieve air superiority by day and night. Daylight attacks on, and reconnaissance of, airfields became increasingly important as Allied bomber losses mounted during 1943.

Drop Tanks

July brought the introduction of 62°-gallon drop tanks in an effort to increase the radius of action of the RAF Mustangs, partly in response to Operation 'Haunch' to counter German minesweeping aircraft. Drop tanks of various capacities were to become a standard fit for most P-51s, and it was the use of such tanks that was to give the escort fighters the incredible range for which the Mustang became famous. Indeed, trials on new weapons and tactical employment were a continuing routine, and this history can only touch on a limited number of examples. Amongst the weapons being evaluated for the Mustang was the rocket projectile (RP), and two aircraft (AM130 and AG357) were used for such trials by the A&AEE. The RP was not widely used operationally by Mustangs – the Typhoon adopted it as a standard weapon – but a number of units in the Desert Air Force, operating in Italy in 1944, did employ RPs.

A great deal of effort was also expended on armed shipping reconnaissance (later to be termed 'Jim Crow' operations) throughout the summer of 1943 and various Mustang units played a part in this. Typical of the work undertaken was that of No 309 Squadron under Sqn Ldr Piotrowski and based at Snailwell. The Squadron recorded the following operations for August 1943:

'Aug 1 – 8 ac shipping recce
    '4 – 4 ac shipping recce
    '8–10 – Ex *Snaffle* in support of

1st Polish Armoured against 5th Canadian Armoured; 24 sorties over 3 day period.

'13 – 8 ac shipping recce, 4 "M" Class minesweepers plus convoy

'16 – 10 ac shipping recce, strafe convoy

'19 – 8 ac shipping recce, MTBs plus tugs

'22 – 6 ac shipping recce

'23 – 4 ac shipping recce, minesweepers plus cargo vessels with two Me 109s as escort

'25 – 8 ac close escort for ASR Hudson

'26 – 2 ac shipping recce, convoy in entrance to Den Helder

'28 – 8 ac on standby for Op *Disti* to act against mine clearing aircraft

'29 – 2 ac shipping recce

'31 – 4 ac shipping recce'

The training routine continued throughout the month as well, with pilots going to Hutton Cranswick for four-day air firing detachments and regular small-scale exercises taking place with Army units.

By midsummer the Mustang units were also flying night intruder missions over enemy airfields in France and Holland. No 400 Squadron took a leading role in this and for 14 August the ORB records: '. . . four pilots placed at immediate readiness from 0300 hours. F/L Stephens and F/Os Morton, Seath and Henton flew to targets in France. No activity was seen by the first three pilots but F/O Henton attacked an enemy aircraft at Rennes and claimed one Me 110 destroyed and one Ju 88 damaged; he also damaged a train south of Vire.' Although there is no comment to the effect in the Squadron's engineering report, one assumes that the Mustangs must have been fitted with appropriate exhaust flame dampers. These operations were being flown from Ford, as were daytime sorties to attack any suitable targets. Typical were a pair flown by No 414 Squadron

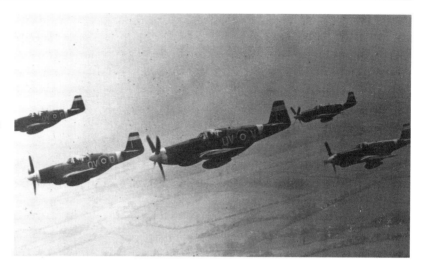

on 21 August: '. . . F/L Stover and F/O Theriault left base at 1600 hours to carry out a *Ranger* in the Paris area. Smoky Stover attacked a tug towing 10–15 barges, strikes were seen and the tug was enveloped in steam. Lou Theriault attacked a goods train and tug, steam was seen coming from both. Two other engines were attacked and probably damaged approximately 10 miles east of Houdon and at Rambouillet. F/L Stover pursued and destroyed a Ju 88 that was flying above an aerodrome, believed to be Enghien/Moiselles.' Lou Theriault failed to return from this sortie, the Mustangs having becoming separated after the attacks on the trains.

No 268 Squadron was also chasing trains and other enemy land targets. Typical of their operational records is that for 25 September: '. . . an excellent day of train busting . . . claim 12 trains, eight barges, two tugs, two lorries, two staff cars – and one hangar'. Over the coming months the prowling Allied fighters and fighter-bombers wreaked havoc in the areas of Occupied Europe that fell within their radius of action.

AEAF

By summer 1943 planning for the invasion of north-west France had assumed immense proportions, not least with the creation of the Allied Expeditionary Air Force (AEAF) under Trafford Leigh-Mallory. One of the major problems was

Right: P-51B-1NA 43-12201 was one of the first production batch of 400 P-51Bs.

Left: No 19 Squadron Mustang IIIs on escort duty. The Luftwaffe was reluctant to engage Fighter Command's sweeps, and so 'Circus' operations involving escorted bombers became a standard tactic. (Ken Delve Collection)

that of persuading air commanders to allocate resources to the AEAF, especially if such resources had to come from the American strategic forces. In a memo to the USAAF's Commanding General in the United Kingdom dated 23 September, Leigh-Mallory expounded his case for the tactical employment of fighters:

'Due to the relatively short range of fighter aircraft, the disposition of fighter squadrons requires careful consideration. The principal functions of fighter aircraft for this operation are:

'a. To provide fighter cover for the beaches.

'b. To provide fighter cover for the shipping lanes leading to the beaches.

'c. To make fighter-bomber attacks against enemy ground forces and installations.

'd. To provide fighter escort for medium and light bombers.

'e. To provide reconnaissance.

'The other three functions, c–d–e, are essentially offensive in character. The P-51 appears to be an ideal type for fighter-bomber operations, and is equally good for escort. In order to achieve the maximum

benefit from aircraft which have such flexibility, they should be grouped under a single command agency.'

There is no word here about the needs of the 'heavies' for escort during their strategic bombing campaign, but it was intended by Leigh-Mallory and others that the bulk of such bombing effort would be switched to targets in support of the landings, and even to what could be termed tactical targets. Many arguments were about to brew on this very subject, with both Bomber Command and Eighth Air Force commanders being distinctly unhappy about what they saw as misuse of strategic bombing resources. The bottom line was that Leigh-Mallory, with the support of the Allied Supreme Commander, General Eisenhower, was determined to employ the maximum amount of air power in order to ensure the success of the Allied invasion. If that meant that fighters had to carry bombs, then so be it.

In a memorandum dated 27 September 1943, Leigh-Mallory outlined aspects of the 'target force for single-engine squadrons within TAF/ADGB'. In part this said that 'the eight FR squadrons will be

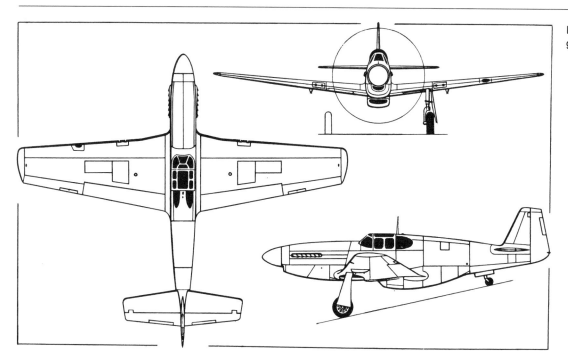

Left: P-51B Mustang
general arrangement.

equipped with Allison Mustangs until the supply of these gives out, and these will be replaced with Merlin Mustangs . . . with regard to the 46 Spitfire squadrons, if Mustangs with Merlin 68 engines become available I would be prepared to regard this type as a replacement for the Merlin 66 Spitfires in some of the squadrons.'[1] This was further highlighted at the C-in-C's conference held on 11 November to discuss the force adjustments of TAF/ADGB:

'The eight FR squadrons are to be equipped a follows:

'(a) the 5 squadrons in TAF to remain equipped with Allison Mustangs. It was estimated that if action referred to at 5 below is taken, they can be maintained on this type until mid July 1944.

'(b) the 3 reserve squadrons to be re-equipped forthwith with Hurricane IV aircraft.

'5. In order to maintain the 5 FR squadrons on Allison Mustangs, the following action is required:

'(a) close down FR OTU to half size. There is already a large surplus of FR pilots.

'(b) all *Rhubarb* ops by Allison Mustangs to cease.

'(c) Inquiry to be made as to whether No 516 Squadron at Dundonald which holds one Flight of 8+2 Mustangs can give up Mustangs and adopt another type.'

The suggestion that the ten Allison Mustangs held by No 516 Squadron could make such a critical difference says much about the detailed nature of the planning and also the acute shortage of suitable aircraft. The Squadron did indeed give up its Mustangs – in February 1944.

Developments aimed at producing an effective tactical air element for the invasion also involved the creation of a number of specialist units, one such being 3 Tactical Exercise Unit (TEU) at Hawarden to convert pilots to the 'invasion support' role. Mustangs were included within the Unit Establishment.

On 8 November No 63 Squadron moved from Turnhouse to Thruxton, where 'most of the pilots were given a flight in a IA aircraft to familiarise them with the performance of the aircraft and to do a Sector Recce'. Four days later the unit had moved to Sawbridgeworth with a complement of twenty Mustang IAs. However, this airfield was in such poor condition

---

[1] *Planning and Preparation of the AEAF for the invasion of NW France*, AHB history series.

that within a week it had moved to North Weald, from where it continued the training routine as well as flying operational sorties such as 'Lagoons'.

The Mustang was, however, not without its problems. The No 309 Squadron ORB for 19 November noted that 'Inspection of AM211 showed badly marked plugs; there have been other similar instances and so [there will be] no further operations until the engine problem has been rectified. It is thought that the problem is caused by lead forming on plug points due to the engine running at too low a temperature and we are trying to secure blanking shields for the radiators.' Within days the Squadron had fitted locally made blanking shields to fourteen of the Mustangs, but these proved unsatisfactory when tested on 28 November. The following day six of the aircraft were given shields at the back of the radiator which gave a satisfactory temperature but too low an oil pressure. With a few more minor adjustments the rear shields seemed to provide the solution to the problem. However, this proved to be a premature assessment, and the following January the Group Engineering Officer was visiting the Squadron to discuss the continuing engine problems.

The Merlin Mustang development continued through the first half of 1943 and was certainly not without its problems. On 25 February Hives held a meeting with Sir Wilfred Freeman, and one of the problems under discussion was who would put the aircraft together. In a memorandum the following day Hives wrote: '. . . [their] capacity would be inadequate, even if the whole of it was given up to the Merlin-Mustang . . . the aircraft pieces were going to be delivered in balanced sets complete less engines and airscrew . . . Sir Wilfred Freeman informed the meeting that the essential jigs and tools for building the aircraft could not be expected to arrive from America in this country before November. It appears therefore that even if an early decision is reached as to who is to build the aircraft, the engines will not be required for about 12 months from now, and no production of complete aircraft can be looked for much before the middle of 1944.'[1]

Final Report

In June the Tactical Combat Section at Eglin Field issued its final report on the 'Operational Suitability of the P-51A-1 airplane'. The trials had been carried out on three aircraft (43-6012, 43-6013, 43-6014) between 1 April and 10 May 1943 and included basic flight and armament trials as well as comparative tests against a P-38, a P-39 and a P-47. The general conclusions were that:

'a. The P-51A-1 is the best medium altitude fighter aircraft tested to date at this station . . .

'e. The P-51A-1 has the longest combat range of any current type American fighter.

'f. The P-51A-1 has a potential operational ceiling of 30,000 ft. However, due to the progressive ignition trouble of the Allison engine encountered on consecutive flights to an altitude of 30,000 ft, its practical operational ceiling is limited to approx 25,000 ft. . . .

'h. The cockpit heater is unsatisfactory in design.

'i. The four .50 caliber machine guns are insufficient armament for most theaters of operation.'

The major part of the report looked at manoeuvrability and combat performance, much of this being related to the performance of the comparative types. Typical of the comments made here was that relating to aileron roll: 'Aileron roll is satisfactory up to a speed of 400 mph, at which speed the ailerons tighten and become very stiff. Experiments should be carried out to improve aileron roll, but not at the expense of loss of feel as in the P-39NO.' This characteristic of the P-51 was one that continued to be highlighted for much of the aircraft's wartime career. In a push-

---

[1] *Rolls Royce and the Mustang.*

over and dive the P-51A was better than any of the other types, and in a zoom climb it was at least equal to or better than its competitors up to 25,000ft; indeed, the report stated that 'The P-51A-1 has the greatest zoom of all types tested from high speed (400 mph), continuing to climb after others had lost speed and leveled off.' In level turning combat the aircraft was superior to all three of the other fighters, except that when using manoeuvring flaps the P-38 could out-turn the P-51. The scenario was different, however, from 25,000ft upwards, when the P-51's engine problems made it inferior in almost all respects.

The comments regarding pilot comfort and visibility are interesting: 'Pilot Comfort is considered satisfactory for the average fighter mission. It is believed that the P-51A-1, with the longest combat range of any current American fighter, has neared the limit of range in which a fighter pilot can undertake operational missions without excessive pilot fatigue followed by long rest periods.' Aircraft 43-6013 was used for a 'range check' as part of the evaluation and, fitted with two external 75-gallon tanks in addition to its normal 180 gallons of internal fuel, flew a 1,520 mile cross-country sortie at an average of 15,000ft. The aircraft burnt an average of 43 gallons per hour and total flight time was 6hr 40min – not including a mid-point refuelling stop. Pilot visibility was criticised:

'Visibility could be improved. The wide formers on the hood seriously interfere with the search view. The clear vision panel, the lights, vents and numerous metal formers, and brackets greatly reduce available visibility and add to the difficulty of formation flying, especially at night. If practicable, a solid Perspex canopy of similar shape would offer fewer blind spots. The air intake scoop limits the average downward deflection through the gunsight to approx 65 mils.'

A team of seven ground crewmen (four armourers and three mechanics) could carry out an operational service – 1,260 rounds of .50 ammunition, two 100lb bombs, fuel, oil and oxygen – on the aircraft in 7min 30sec.

The major recommendations were:

'a. Corrective action to be taken immediately to provide an ignition system that will be dependable under all operating conditions and at all altitudes up to the service ceiling of the airplane.

'b. Six normal rate of fire .50 caliber guns to be installed.

'c. The clear vision panel to be eliminated . . .

'e. A sliding, solid perspex canopy of similar shape and size to the present type with a minimum of formers be provided.'

At about the same time the AFDU issued a comparison between the Mustang I and the P-51A-10, based flight evaluations carried out by the AFDU and the USAAF's School of Applied Tactics. In this the AFDU summarised the major differences between the two aircraft and the overall performance of the P-51A-10. Of note are the following comments:

'The combat range at 12,000 ft is about 420 miles, allowing a reserve of approx 20 gallons after landing. This range is calculated on the following basis [see accompanying table]:

'The maximum level speed is approx 410 mph true at 18,000 ft; with the coolant shutters open or bomb shackles fitted the top speed is reduced by approx 15 mph. The P-51A-10, with several improvements incorporated which are not incorporated in the Mustang I, has a better rate of climb and an increase of max speed of 30 mph. The flying characteristics of the P-51A-10 are in every way similar to those of the Mustang I, and the turning circle is ap-

P-51A-10 Range Calculations (see text)

	miles	Time	MP	RPM	IAS
Out	210	45 min	38.3"	2600	293 (Buster)
Combat		15	44.0"	3000	305 (max 15 min)
Back	210	60	28.9"	2280	255 (Liner)

Right: P-51C-10NT 42-103506.

preciably reduced when the trailing edge flaps are used as maneuver flaps (30 degrees max). When the maneuvering flaps are lowered in a turn the aircraft becomes nose heavy and trimming is desirable. The time taken to climb to 22,000 ft is 10 minutes.'

Combat experience and comprehensive trials were maturing the P-51 – and not before time, as the daylight bomber offensive was approaching a crisis.

Escort Fighter

In the period from July 1943 the USAAF's Eighth Air Force extended both the scale and penetration depth of its bomber operations; however, the German defences had undergone a period of expansion and improvement and were in a position to provide an effective defence – as the Americans soon discovered. The 17 August raids on Regensburg and Schweinfurt were little short of disastrous:

'Owing to limitations on fighter range, escorted raids could only reach fringe targets in Germany, and limitations of operational activity to such attacks meant therefore the abandoning of the planned programme of a systematic onslaught on the German war industry deep in Reich territory.'[1]

The Eighth Air Force renewed its unescorted deep-penetration raids on 8 October, but in four raids between 10 and 14 October the loss rate was 11 per cent, a completely unsustainable rate that would have bled the bomber groups dry in a matter of months. The net result was little short of a crisis of confidence at the Eighth Air Force – the great hopes of the Combined Bombing Offensive, and the much-vaunted ability of the American bombers to look after themselves, were shattered. Without an escort fighter it looked as though the daylight offensive over Germany were dead. Various options were examined. The P-47 Thunderbolt did not have adequate range even with drop tanks fitted, although it had proved itself a capable fighter; great hopes had also been placed in the P-38 Lightning, but deliveries were slow and the type suffered a number of technical problems.

---

[1] *Rise and Fall of the German Air Force*, Arms & Armour Press, 1987.

The first Merlin-powered Mustangs entered service at the end of 1943, the RAF receiving Mustang IIIs and the USAAF receiving P-51Bs. The first RAF unit, No 65 Squadron at Gravesend, received its first aircraft in December to replace its Spitfire IXs. The RAF's Mustang IIIs flew their first operations the following February, the month in which two further squadrons (Nos 19 and 122) also re-equipped with this variant. The first operational American Mustang unit to arrive in the European Theatre of Operations (ETO), the 67th Tactical Reconnaissance Group (TRG), moved into Membury with P-51As and F-6As in October.

The first American Merlin Mustang unit, the 354th FG (later known as the 'Pioneers' because it was the first such unit) had arrived in the United Kingdom (at Greenham Common) in October 1943 and had had to wait until the following month to receive its P-51Bs. The unit, under Lt-Col K Martin, was allocated to the Ninth Air Force, but following pressure from the hard-pressed Eighth Air Force was attached to VIII Fighter Command of that organisation and moved to Boxted. The first mission was flown on 1 December 1943, 24 aircraft taking part in a 'familiarisation' flight down the Belgian coast and the Pas de Calais, led by the experienced 4th FG's Don Blakeslee. Four days later the Mustangs undertook their first escort mission, accompanying B-17s to Amiens. However, it was with the third mission that the USAAF began to make full use of the capabilities of its new fighter in respect of its range and performance. Fitted with two 75-gallon drop tanks, the fighters escorted their B-17 charges to Emden on 11 December and two days later undertook the longest mission to date, a 1,000-mile round trip to Kiel.

It was on this sortie that the first combats took place, Lt Glenn Eagleston damaging a Bf 110. The first victory was scored on 16 December, Lt Charles Gumm shooting down a Bf 110 over Bremen. Despite this, December was a frustrating month, with a number of technical problems that had to be overcome – problems caused mainly by the new environment in which the aircraft were operating, long flight times in sub-zero temperatures. The freezing of oil and lubricants put a strain on

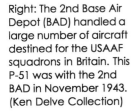

the engines, ammunition belts froze or jammed under G loading, and engines had a habit of overheating and the plugs of fouling. Most of these were readily overcome, but the majority of aircraft losses during December were put down to one or other technical problems.

Nevertheless, the ability to escort the bombers to the heart of Germany had a great effect on the morale of both the bomber crews and the enemy fighter pilots; the unwieldy twin-engine Bf 110s were surprised to find single-engine fighters over the middle of Germany. The Mustangs of the 354th 'Pioneer' Group had also done enough to convince the air commanders that here was an aircraft that was needed in large numbers – and as soon as possible: Maj-Gen William Kepner, VIII Fighter Command's commander, stated that the P-51B was 'distinctly the best fighter that we can get over here', and the race was now on to get more units equipped and operational.

The reference to guns freezing is recurrent in a wide range of reports relating to bomber and fighter types and it was certainly a significant problem. The Mustang was provided with an electric heating system for the guns, the switch being next to the gun master switch; once selected 'on', the heaters were meant to function automatically when the temperature dropped. The RAF Pilot's Notes for the Mustang III (AP2025G) contain a reference to gun heating of another sort: '*Warning*. If a continuous burst of between 50 and 75 rounds is fired, very high barrel temperatures are reached and the guns may fire whether the master switch is on or off.' The gun and camera master switch was located on the left-hand switch panel.

The Packard Merlins were causing some problems and a number of aircraft were sent to Rolls-Royce for investigation. The major difficulty was that of excessive oil loss from the engine breather system, which could in extreme cases lead to engine failure over a period of time. Hucknall used up to five Mustangs on tests to evaluate and cure this problem, the first of which, 43-12425 (with a Packard Mer-

lin V1650-3) arrived in October from Bovingdon. It was subsequently joined on the trials by AL975, FX852, FX858 and FX901, the last three of which, all with 1650-3 engines, were delivered via the Lockheed facility at Speke in October/November 1943. It turned out to be a complex problem with more than one contributing factor and thus was hard to resolve. A different oil tank and breather system were devised, but in the meantime the Mustangs were restricted to using a limit of 2,700rpm for the first two hours of any flight. Another significant problem arose with the fuel system: the aircraft had been designed with a four-position manual mixture control – fully rich (for use on take-off), auto-rich (for use above 30in Hg or +4lb boost), auto-lean (for economic cruise) and idle cut-off (used when starting and stopping the engine). In practice it was found that when auto-rich was used at around 21,000ft and in FS (maximum supercharger), then the engine had a tendency to cut out, accompanied by a cloud of black smoke and an engine failure. This indicated that the mixture was too rich, and if auto-lean was selected then all was

well. The solution was to delete the full-rich and auto-rich positions and also to add a 'gate' so that idle cut-off could not be selected by accident.

'Operational Suitability'

On 23 October 1943 a report was issued by Eglin Field on the 'Operational Suitability of the P-51B Airplane'. The unit had received three P-51Bs and had begun the evaluation on 6 July. Unlike earlier instances where the Mustang had been put forward for evaluation, this was a Priority One test. Many of the conclusions were similar to those issued in June with respect to the P-51A-1, for example the inadequacy of four .50 guns and the engine trouble suffered at altitude which 'seriously affects the aircraft performance'. Amongst the other comments made were:

'c. Oil leaks from the propeller and engine restrict vision through the windshield and gunsight.

'd. The use of maximum allowable power is limited in high blower operation because of insufficient mixture aftercooling due to corrosion products blocking the intercooler and

Right: 311th FBG line-up at an unknown location. (Roger Freeman Collection)

Left: P-51B *Peggy* of the 354th FG poses for the camera as ground personnel attach one of the underwing tanks.

radiators. A high percentage of engine failures will occur if full power is used in high blower after 50 hours of engine operation . . .

'g. The bomb racks are unsatisfactory from an operational standpoint and cause excessive drag at high speed.

'h. Excessive oil is thrown by the engine through the oil breathers. Gas siphons out of tanks of aircraft in flight (this condition might prove serious on long missions) . . .

'p. Oxygen supply is barely adequate for long range high altitude missions . . .

'r. The overall visibility from the cockpit of a P-51 is unsatisfactory . . .

't. The angle of the pilot's seat is uncomfortable causing excessive pilot fatigue on long flights.'

However, despite the long list of problem areas, the report also stated that, 'Considering over-all performance, handling characteristics, and general maintenance, the P-51B is the best fighter type aircraft tested at this station to date' and that 'the present P-51B [should] be produced in the largest quantity possible'.

One of the greatest requirements with escort fighters was that of range, and North American had devised an additional 85 gallon fuselage fuel tank (giving a total of 269 gallons). Tests were conducted using two standard aircraft with this fit, and Eglin Field issued its report on 22 December, the conclusions stating that:

'a. The 85 gallon fuselage tank is desirable as a production item because of the additional range it affords.

'b. With the internal fuselage tank fitted with 85 gallons of fuel, the airplane is so unstable longitudinally that violent pull-outs or tight turns must be executed with caution as the stick loads rapidly reverse, with the fuel tank half empty these maneuvers may be executed in practically the normal manner.'

The report's recommendations included:

'2. Missions be planned that the greatest possible is offered to enter combat with the fuselage tank not more than half full.

'3. Fuel be used for long-range combat missions in the following order:

'a. fuselage tank – approx 20 gallons for warm-up, take-off and climb, leaving 65 gallons in fuselage tank.

'b. droppable tank – expended in cruise towards destination.

'c. fuselage tank – continue cruise and use approx 30 more gallons, at this point the fuselage tank will contain about 35 gallons and the airplane is ready to participate in combat.

'd. main wing tanks.

'4. Pilots given extra time to become accustomed to handling qualities of airplanes with full fuselage tanks before engaging in tight turns.'

Left: A 1943 photograph of 27th FBG A-36A aircraft in Italy. Note the white mission marks. (Roger Freeman Collection)

Warnings of the instability were re-issued throughout 1944 (see later).

F-6 Units

The USAAF's TacR force had been expanded with the creation of more F-6-equipped units, such as the 7th and 10th Photo Reconnaissance Groups (PRG). The F-6 was eventually to appear in four main variants, each being the equivalent of a 'standard' fighter version:

F-6B   (P-51A)
F-6C   (P-51B/C)
F-6D   (P-51D)
F-6K   (P-51K)

The main cameras were the K-17, K-22 and K-24 with various lenses:

'The K-22 with a 12" lens gave excellent, finely detailed photographs from an altitude of 6,000 ft, whilst the K-17 with a 6" lens was used for altitudes up to 3,500 ft (this was later replaced by a 6" lens on the K-22 that provided a 2 second rewind cycle for overlap coverage at low altitude). For missions that required oblique photography, the F-6 carried either the K-24 camera, which had a 7" or 14" lens, or a K-22 with a 12" lens. The K-24 was used for low altitude oblique cover of railways bridges, cuts and tunnels. The K-22 camera was used for taking Merton Gridded Oblique Photographs; these were generally taken at altitudes of 2,500–4,000 feet and at an angle of 12–17 degrees. These gridded photos were quite valuable to both artillery and field commanders in planning barrages and assaults.'[1]

It was inevitable that later versions of the P-51 would be converted for photoreconnaissance as the type had already proved to be effective in this role. The arrival of the P-51C led to the creation of the F-6C reconnaissance version. An AAF Material Command memorandum dated 14 August 1944 detailed the '. . . photographic installation in P-51C 42-103639, an aircraft modified for use as an F-6C with provision for the following alternate single camera installations:

'vertical 7" K-24
'vertical 6" K-17 or K-22
'vertical 12" K-17 or K-22
'vertical 24" K-17 or K-22
'oblique 12" K-22
'oblique 7" K-24

'A B-3B intervalometer, electrical controls and sighting device are installed in the cockpit. The camera compartment is just forward of the tail wheel, with a magazine access panel near the top of the fuselage. There is a bottom window for the vertical cameras, an upper window for the oblique K-22 and a lower window for the oblique K-24. The sighting aid is composed of three crosses on the left side of the canopy and corresponding crosses on the

[1] Tom Ivie, *Aerial Reconnaissance – 10th PRG,* Aero Publishers, 1981

wing, lining up two pairs of crosses and directing them at the target will aid aiming of oblique cameras. Due to the increase in weight with cameras, a maximum of 25 gallons is carried in the fuselage tank in order to maintain proper flight characteristics. Considerable structural re-work was necessary in the vicinity of the magazine access panel and window for the oblique K-22.

'The intervalometer is located on the floor beneath the left corner of the seat. The camera switch box has two switches – Master ON/OFF and selector for continuous/intervalometer, plus green 'blinker'

light which flashes when an exposure is being made. Operating the throttle button when the selector switch is in manual will operate the camera continuously. The three black crosses on the canopy and wing, along with three marks on the leading edge, correspond to the three positions of the K-24 oblique – the middle one being 15 degrees below the horizon. They can also be used to aim the K-22.'

North Africa

Mustangs first appeared in North Africa with the RAF's No 225 Squadron in October 1942, the Squadron arriving at Maison

Right: Two photographs showing 'bazooka' rocket mountings under the wings of a Mustang. The unit is not noted, but it is possibly the 311th FBG in India. (Ken Delve Collection)

Blanche on 13 November, although it moved to Bône a week later, in support of the First Army (Operation 'Torch', the Allied landings in French North Africa, took place on 8 November). Within a year No 225 Squadron had given back its Mustangs and acquired Spitfires, and the Kittyhawk remained the backbone of the RAF's Desert Air Force (DAF) tactical operations throughout 1943.

It was in the final stages of operations in North Africa that the Mustang in American service had its operational début. In March 1943 the 86th BG moved to North Africa with its A-36s. By May there were 300 aircraft of this type in the theatre, some of which were also allocated to the 27th BG. The first missions were flown in June against the fortified island of Pantelleria as part of the Allied preparation for the invasion of Sicily. The basic attack profile was for a section of four aircraft to arrive over the target at 8,000ft, extend the dive brakes, half-roll over the target and set up a 90-degree dive angle (!) at around 300 mph. Bomb release (the aircraft usually carried two 500lb bombs) was at about 4,000ft, and the idea was to recover from the dive as low as possible in order to escape 'on the deck' and avoid the defences.

By July the squadrons had moved to Sicily following the Allied landings in order to stay as close as possible to the troops they were supporting. It was a dangerous role, and losses mounted at such a rate that the Groups had to be reduced from four to three squadrons each, there being insufficient numbers of replacement aircraft available. Indeed, in January 1944 the 27th re-equipped with the P-40 whilst in July the 86th BG re-equipped with P-47s, bringing to an end the short career of the A-36 in this theatre of operations.

China–Burma–India

July 1943 also saw Mustangs en route to the China–Burma–India (CBI) theatre of operations with the arrival of the 311th Group. Two of the Group's squadrons were equipped with the A-36A whilst the third, the 530th, was equipped with P-51As. By the autumn the Group, as part of the Fourteenth Air Force, was performing the complete range of tactical tasks as well as providing escort for bombers and transports flying 'over the Hump', the supply route between India and China. The 8th Photo Reconnaissance Group (PRG) was also undertaking vital missions, some of which were flown by F-6 Mustangs. With a move to Kurmitola in order to escort Liberators and Mitchells to targets in the Rangoon area, the 530th undertook what were the first long-range fighter escorts of the war. Their P-51As were equipped with two 75-gallon drop tanks in order to fly the 900-mile round trip. Unfortunately, six Mustangs were shot down by Japanese fighters during the first two such missions, the American pilots claiming two of the 64th Sentai's fighters in reply. After only four missions the 530th was down to half strength and operations had to be restricted.

The 311th, led by Col Henry R. Melton, had its first brush with the 'Oscars' of the 64th Sentai on 25 November whilst escorting B-25s of the 490th BS. They were intercepted over Mingaladon by twelve 'Oscars' of the 64th plus five 'Nicks' of the 21st Sentai. The first victory went to 2nd Lt Clifton Bray, who at point-blank range blew a 'Nick' out of the sky; however, it was at that point that the 'Oscars' joined in and the combat soon became somewhat more heated. Lt Hinoki shot down Henry Melton: 'Colonel Melton made the mistake of flipping his Mustang over. If he had dived away to the left or right without exposing his belly I'm sure he could have escaped. I got a clear shot at him from close range and gave him a burst from my guns . . . I made just one firing pass on his fighter before breaking off to help my comrades.'[1] Two days later Hinoki fell victim to 2nd Lt Robert F. Hulhollen of the 311th.

---

[1] Lt Hinoki in Henry Sakaida, *Pacific Air Combat World War Two*, Phalanx, 1993.

3

INTO EUROPE

Below: A classic
airborne study of a P-
51D, in this case P-51D-
3NA 44-13366. Note that
the aircraft does not
have the modified
empennage. (*FlyPast*
Collection)

The year 1944 was that in which the Mustang really began to make a name for itself and in which these sleek fighters, the 'Little Friends' of the bombers, would become the scourge of the Luftwaffe. As the year opened the Luftwaffe had almost 2,500 fighters on strength – 1,535 single-engine and 905 twin-engine – in large part due to the measures taken by Milch to improve production:

'The impact of the long-range fighters was only felt slowly but with growing power. Surprisingly, it had only a limited effect upon monthly bomber losses, which averaged 4.5% from January to April and showed a sharp fall to 3.11% only in May, when Mustangs began to fly the majority of escort missions. The real success of the American long-range fighters was in forcing the *Jagdgruppen* into a battle of attrition they could not win, with loss rates

rising alarmingly from February to undermine the *Luftwaffe*'s plan for expansion.'[1]

The same general point was mentioned by the Air Historical Branch's post-war study of the German Air Force:

'The long-range fighter escort at a stroke capsized German defensive air strategy. The *Luftwaffe* planning staff had been lulled into a false sense of security during the winter of 1943–44 on the assurance of the Research and Development Branch that such an aircraft was an impossibility. Its appearance at the shortest notice in large numbers meant that the German defensive commitment had overnight been magnified beyond all expectations.'[2]

Between December 1943 and March 1944 the Jagdkorps lost 529 pilots killed or missing. As we shall see below, it was this loss of pilots – and in particular experienced pilots and leaders – along with shortages of aviation fuel, that became the critical factors in the ultimate collapse of the Luftwaffe.

Even the well-established TacR units with their Allison-powered aircraft still suffered problems as the aircraft was not without its technical 'snags'. The No 26 Squadron ORB records two such instances in January 1944: 'Aircraft of A Flight are grounded pending mods to their radiator scoops, several of which have come adrift in flight.' The aircraft were flying again

[1] E. R. Hooton, *Eagle in Flames*, Arms & Armour Press, 1997.
[2] *Rise and Fall of the German Air Force, op. cit.*

Left: An anonymous P-51D. From this angle the six .50-calibre guns are distinct. One of the great improvements with the D model was the increase in fire power from four to six guns. (Ken Delve Collection)

Right: Boxted, January 1944: 1st Lt Frank Hendrickson, 1st Lt William Pitcher and 2nd Lt Edward Phillips. (US National Archives)

within a week, but the following day 'AM966 flown by F/O Stokes had to return to base with the front radiator scoop half off – all aircraft are grounded again.' It took another week for the problem to be sorted out and by that time the Squadron was trying out an engineering fix for a continuing engine problem: 'Aircraft "A" was air tested on 21 January 21 and this aircraft has to be watched for 10 hours as it has a set of single-point plugs in it to see if they lead-up any less easily.' Likewise, the RAF's introduction of the Mustang III was by no means as smooth as most had hoped it would be. The minutes of the C-in-C's conference at AEAF HQ for 23 February '. . . expressed dissatisfaction with the present state of the Mustang III. In particular:

'a) The four bottles of oxygen provided were insufficient.

'b) Oil was thrown out on the windshield in considerable quantities at high altitude, obscuring the pilot's vision and greatly increasing his difficulties in combat.

'c) Carburettor trouble develops when changing over from drop to wing tanks.

'd) The range of the Mustang III in 2nd TAF appeared less than that of the 9th Air Force P-51s.

'e) D/SASO reported that 9th Air Force had experienced trouble with the guns, only one of the four guns would fire on a tight turn. This difficulty had been remedied by the incorporation of a gadget to adjust pressure. He recommended the adoption of a similar modification in Mustangs of the 2nd TAF.

'STechSO said that the inclusion of two additional bottles of oxygen was already under consideration. He said that tests were in progress to improve the oil trouble. He confirmed that air lock was likely to develop if drop tanks were completely emptied before switching to wing tanks. The remedy was to switch over before the drop tanks were emptied. With regard to range, some of the 9th Air Force P-51s were fitted with 85 gallon tanks. To fit similar tanks to aircraft of 2nd TAF would require 450 man-hours per aircraft, which was out of the question at the present stage of the war.

'STechSO added that the present policy with regard to modifications was an equal division as between British and US Mustangs. Strenuous efforts were being made to overcome the troubles referred to by AMC, 2nd TAF, but it must be remembered that Mustangs were required urgently for operations and if modifications were to be effected aircraft would have to be withdrawn from operations. STechSO further added that one of his engineers had recently visited Boxstead [sic] to compare notes with his American counterpart.

'AMC 2nd TAF stated that his third squadron should receive its aircraft within a week, and that seven squadrons should be formed up by the end of March.

'AOA AEAF confirmed that 93 aircraft were at present in 41 Gp in process of modification.

'USE OF CAMOUFLAGE PAINT
'AOA AEAF stated that Mustangs now arriving from the US were without camouflage paint, consequently in addition to other modifications such aircraft had to be painted. Commanding General 9th Air Force said that his policy was to remove paint from US Mustangs and to fly these aircraft polished to facilitate identification. STechSO remarked that the object of painting was not only for camouflage purposes, but also to produce a smoother finish and thereby increase the speed.

'The Air C-in-C considered that uniformity between US and British was important, and either all aircraft should be polished or all should be painted. It was necessary to determine which was most advantageous. STechSO deplored the suggestion that paint should be removed from 2nd TAF aircraft. This was a lengthy process and shortage of manpower was an urgent consideration. The Air C-in-C directed:
    '(i) that RAF and US technicians should discuss and report their recommendations with regard to the use of paint.

'(ii) that AOA AEAF should investigate the possibility of finding additional technicians from other sources, such as Servicing Commandos from 2nd TAF, to assist with Mustang modifications.'

USAAF policy on camouflage had officially changed with a Technical Order (07-1-1, dated 26 December 1943) which stated that '. . . painting of the exterior metal surfaces of AAF aircraft is hereby discontinued. This does not, however, eliminate the required identification date, insignia, anti-glare coating and corrosion prevention. Man-hours expended on maintaining existing camouflage finishes, now considered unnecessary, will be held to a minimum.'

Gun Feed Problems

January 1944 opened with a particularly successful mission, the Mustangs of the 354th claiming eighteen Bf 110s and Fw 190s for no loss on 5 January during an escort mission to Kiel. It was during this mission that 1st Lt Bob Welden of the 356th FS scored his first success, claiming one Bf 110 and sharing in the destruction of another. Like most of his colleagues within the Pioneer Group, he had little experience on type and was, of course, new to combat:

'As a result of the rush to get the Mustang into combat as a long-range escort fighter, operational testing was never completed. This caused some problems when the 354th FG started flying the Mustang in combat. For instance, the P-51B's four .5 cal machine guns had to be canted about 45 degrees in order to fit into the very, very thin laminar aerofoil . . . the ammo belts and the trays in which the ammo belts lay were positioned outboard along the wing; the belts had to feed over the tops of the gun breeches. Before feeding into the guns, however, each belt had to make a sharp inboard turn. The feeding path of the ammo belts resulted in a whole bunch of problems when engagements occurred and deflection shooting was required — when you had to pull 3g or 4g to get the

Right: Mustang III FB104 served with four RAF squadrons – Nos 19, 65, 309 and 316 – and survived the war, being struck off charge in February 1946. (FlyPast Collection)

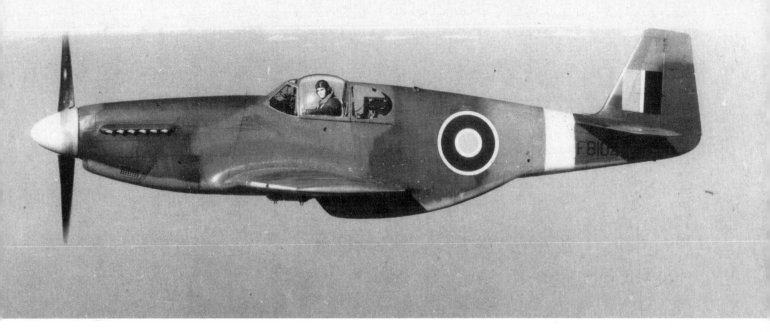

gunsight on an enemy airplane the ammo belts crimped where they crossed the gun breech. This pulled the bullet linkages apart so that, many times, the guns would not fire. This problem became so enervating that, on two separate occasions, pilots in my squadron, whose guns had jammed, flew right up the tails of enemy fighters and ticked the enemy's rudder and fins with their propellers. Each of the Mustang pilots was credited with a kill, but there was no longevity in their solution!'[1]

The frustration level of such problems was immense and an urgent solution was sought. North American Aviation technical personnel looked at the gun feeds of other aircraft to see if any useful lessons could be learned. From the B-26 they adopted the idea of boost motors, and the Fighter Group's ground crew spent two days carrying out modifications to the aircraft (and see below for the P-51C armament trial in May 1944, when the problem was still evident.)

Although the P-51B had undergone extensive operational trials in mid-1943 it was only in February 1944 that a major report was issued for circulation to the squadrons. This extensive document (dated 12 February 1944) summarised the 'Tactical Employment Trials of the P-51B-

1' and gave advice on such aspects as manoeuvring, using the flaps and power settings. Most of the comments made were similar to those mentioned above in relation to the original evaluation reports, although, for obvious reasons, this report is not so critical of the aircraft and does not include recommendations. Extracts of the report are included in the trials appendix, but the report's general conclusion regarding the escort role was that 'with its long range, high cruising speeds, and excellent fighting qualities, the P-51B airplane is very good for escort work. Pilot fatigue caused by poor cockpit ventilation and the not too comfortable seat are disadvantages for long-range flights.' Concerns were expressed that pilots would be unable to cope with very long sorties in such single-seat fighters and that their combat effectiveness would be decreased; experience was to show that this concern, whilst not misplaced, was overstated.

The success of the 5 January mission was repeated a week later, with the Group claiming fifteen kills, plus eight probables and sixteen damaged, again for no loss – and with Maj James Howard, CO of the 356th Squadron, being awarded the

[1] Bob Welden in *Aces Against Germany*, Praesidio, 1993.

57

highest decoration, the Medal of Honor. It was not all one-way trade and the Mustangs did suffer a number of losses during this period, including Col Martin who collided with a Bf 109 (he survived and was made a PoW). More Mustangs were arriving in theatre and in February the next two Groups, the 357th FG and the 363rd FG, commenced operations. VIII Fighter Command was still involved in something of a political wrangle with the Ninth Air Force over the allocation of Mustang-equipped Groups, perhaps having its origins in the tactical role of the type, and had to argue very forcefully to get these two Groups under its command; indeed, the 357th was acquired only when a P-47 Group was 'swapped' for it. The 363rd became the first operational Mustang Group with the Ninth Air Force, flying its first mission on 24 February, an offensive sweep by 42 aircraft over the Low Countries and Northern France.

The Eighth Air Force P-51 Groups were now being employed on escort duties, either as close escort or with more freedom to act as a sweep. The bombers obviously liked the former but, as the Luftwaffe fighters had found over Britain in 1940, this tended to reduce the effectiveness of the fighter. This was an argument that was never resolved throughout the war and some Groups developed their own tactics. What was certainly true was that any bomber stragglers were easy targets for enemy fighters unless they were able to pick up a fighter escort – and in most cases the Mustang pilots performed this task without a second thought.

To Berlin

The latter part of February saw a series of missions to Berlin. February 20–24 became known as 'Big Week': some 4,231 bomber sorties were flown (for a loss of 158 aircraft), along with 3,839 fighter escort sorties (425 by P-51s, of which eleven were lost). The fighters took particular care to look after any straggling bombers as these were easy targets for prowling enemy fighters. Bob Welden recalled one such instance when he was part of 'Starstud Green' Flight led by Lt Goodnight and they spotted a B-17 under attack by a Bf 109 and an Fw 190; the 109 was soon despatched by another member of the Flight, Lt Miller, '. . . then we went after the Fw 190. We went straight in at the fighter and we both fired from maximum range, about 300 yards, [and] I observed strikes from both sets of guns on the 190's wing, fuselage and tail. The German fighter broke to the right very quickly, and Miller and I were sucked into a rat race – a steeply banked circle to the right. The 190 was turning much more sharply than Miller and me, but I finally got my sight on him from above by applying 30

degrees of flaps and full RPM. This was a perfect use of one of the P-51's best features. Dropping the flaps increased the lift of the wing and allowed me to come around more tightly so I could get the desired lead on the 190. But I had to leave on full RPM and suck the flaps right back up as soon as I could see strikes on the enemy airplane.'[1]

During his tour with the 356th FS/354th FG Bob Welden was credited with 6.25 enemy aircraft destroyed (in the period January–June 1944), plus one damaged.

Don Blakeslee's 4th Fighter Group was the next to take up the Mustang and converted from its P-47 mounts in only one day as Blakeslee was determined not to be out of the fight for any longer than was absolutely necessary. The Group was ready therefore to take part in an escort trip to Berlin on 4 March. The weather was poor and the mission was doomed to failure. Only 29 bombers made it through to the target area – but Blakeslee's P-51s were there. One of the other Mustang Groups, the 363rd, was bounced by a large formation of enemy fighters near Hamburg and lost eleven aircraft.

Two days later the Eighth Air Force raided Berlin again, and this involved major air battles. The fighter force was led by the 4th FG, which claimed fifteen of the 81 enemy aircraft shot down that day. However, the major honours fell to the 357th FG, which, although losing almost one-third of its number to technical aborts, intervened on behalf of the 3rd Division when the bombers were under attack by over 100 enemy fighters. The Mustangs broke up the attacks and shepherded the B-24s away. On the way home Col Hayes took a flight of aircraft down to strafe the airfield at Ulzen, damaging a number of machines. All of the Group's P-51s returned safely to Leiston, claiming twenty destroyed and eight others probable or damaged.

The 4th FG was rapidly becoming aggressively expert in the use of its Mustangs and was amongst the Groups to score well on the deep-penetration raid to Augsburg and Friedrichshafen on 16 March. Once again the Luftwaffe rose in some strength, and once again it was hammered by the American fighters. Of the

---

[1] Bob Welden in *Aces against Germany, op. cit.*

59

Left: *Ferocious Frankie*, P-51D 44-13704 of the 374th FS/361st FG. (US National Archives)

75 German fighters claimed that day, thirteen fell to 4th FG pilots. Indeed, by the end of the month the Group's total for March had risen to 156 destroyed.

The air battle was by no means won – the Mustangs had plenty of hard fighting left to do – but the mission to Berlin was certainly a milestone in the air war, since at long last effective fighter cover could go with the bombers all the way to the Reich capital. For the Luftwaffe, the writing was very much on the wall. Likewise, the strafing of German airfields, though not, as yet, an official policy, was soon to pay dividends as part of the overall reduction of Luftwaffe strength. Indeed, at around this time the USAAF decreed that

ground victories would carry the same weight (for scoring purposes) as air victories. Airfield attacks were later code-named 'Jackpots'.

During Exercise 'Thunderbolt', the RAF's post-war analysis of the bomber campaign, ACM Sir Norman Bottomley stated that '. . . it was evident from the outset of these daylight operations over Europe that even their heavy armament was not sufficient protection against German fighters and they therefore began to build up as rapidly as they could a force of long-range escort fighters . . . this necessitated a battle for air superiority which fell principally to the Americans. It was to be achieved mainly by the destruction

Left: Don Blakeslee's P-51D 42-106726 at Debden in mid-1944. (Andy Thomas Collection)

of enemy airframe assembly factories, and by attrition in the air by fighters and bombers . . . but gradually they were able to equip their force with ample long-range escort fighters and in December 1943 the P-51s appeared. With this aircraft came a change of tactics; the fighters sought out German fighters instead of clinging to their bombers. It was then a matter of providing fighter cover rather than escort.'[1] In 1944 the Allies claimed 16,000 enemy single-engine fighters destroyed (excluding those on the Eastern Front), a figure that included a tally of almost 1,700 a month by the latter months of 1944.

In the same report Maj-Gen Kepner commented:

'The tactics of the escort fighters developed through the following stages. At first they remained close to the bombers. As their strength, experience and knowledge of German tactics increased Fighter Groups were detached to attack enemy fighters forming up to attack the bombers. By early 1944 escort fighters were leaving the bombers freely to hunt out the German Air Force. The climax and turning point of the air war was the series of successful fighter engagements over Berlin. The next stage was the despatch of fighters ahead of the bombers deliberately to provoke a German fighter reaction, and the final stage, reached after D-Day, the complete freeing of the fighters to attack any suitable opportunity targets.'

German fighter ace Adolf Galland, as Inspector of Fighters, commented in April 1944:

'The problems which the Americans have set for the fighter arm – I am speaking solely of daytime – is quite simply the problem of superiority in the air. As things are now, it is almost the same thing as command of the air. The ratio between the two sides in day fighting at the present time is between 1:6 and 1:8. The enemy's proficiency in action is extraordinarily high and the technical accomplishment of his aircraft is so outstanding that all we can say is – something has got to be done! In the last four months well over 1,200 day fighter pilots have been lost, including of course many of the best unit commanders. We are having great difficulty in closing this gap, not in a numerical sense, but with experienced leaders. I have often spoken of the last chance and the danger of the air arm collapsing. The enemy's numerical superiority has reached such proportions that we must realise that operations are beginning to become extremely unproductive for us. Secondly, there is the fact that owing to the enemy's superior technical and tactical training we are still lagging behind.'[2]

Air Superiority

Whilst P-47s and P-38s continued to be important elements of the fighter force, it was increasingly the P-51 Groups (whose numbers continued to increase) that created the conditions for air superiority over Northern Europe.

April saw the first mass strafing mission by the USAAF Fighter Groups. Bad weather on 5 April grounded the bombers, but over 450 fighters (from eleven Groups) were let loose against German airfields, although the weather was so poor that only three Groups were able to find suitable targets. The 4th FG hit five airfields near Berlin and although they lost four aircraft to ground fire, including leading ace Maj Duanne Beeson (CO of the 334th FS and with a total of 17.33 air victories and 4.75 ground victories – mostly with P-47 – when shot down by flak at Brandenburg and taken prisoner), they claimed a large number of kills, Don Gentile putting in a claim for five Ju 88s.

Gentile had been with the 336th FS in its P-47 days and had already become an ace when the squadron converted to P-51s; with the new type, however, he was soon registering an impressive tally of victories. His first score with a P-51 came on 3 March when he downed a Do 217 near Wittenberg. A further eleven, plus one

---

[1] From 'Thunderbolt' report, August 1947.
[2] Galland at the Fighter Staff Conference, 27 April 1944, from *Translations of German Documents*, AHB.

shared, fell to his guns in air combat during March, to which he added four further aerial victories in the first week of April – including three Fw 190s on 8 April – before being grounded and sent to the United States on leave. His score at this point was 21 plus a share in two others.

Returning to the 5 April mission, Mustang 'new boys' the 355th FG also did well, claiming six aerial victories plus 43 destroyed and eight damaged on the six airfields they attacked near Munich, for the loss of three aircraft.

Major aerial battles were still being fought, and on 8 April the 4th FG set a new record with a 31-to-four tally against the Bf 109s they encountered.

A fifth P-51 Group, the 339th based at Fowlmere, became operational within VIII Fighter Command at the end of April, with at least two other P-47 Groups scheduled to re-equip during May. During April the four P-51 Groups scored nearly three-quarters of the Command's victories for the month – but also lost 70 aircraft.

Lt Ed Heller was with the 486th FS/352nd FG operating out of Bodney. Typical of the missions he was flying was that of 7 May 1944:

'We crossed into Holland at Haarlem and flew on to the RV point without incident, located the bomber stream, and identified our bomber group by the symbol on the bombers' tails. They were at about 25,000 ft, heading towards the target – we spread the Flights out over the bombers, doing S-turns to match speed with them. At the distance we were from Bodney and at the rate we were consuming fuel S-turning over the bombers, we expected to stay on escort station for only 35 or 40 minutes.'

Combat was soon joined and Ed Heller engaged a Bf 109, ending up on the deck in a turning fight:

'The Jerry got so tight that we both had to slow down to about 130 kts. I had to put about 10 degrees of flap down just to stay even with him. We started out eyeball to eyeball across the circle, but I was able to slowly increase my advantage. That was only because his engine was bad.

When I finally dumped flaps to decrease my turning radius, he broke out. Maybe he had to break out because he knew his engine was going to go.

'He didn't have any choice about where he was going. He just headed right for a little river and set up over it to make a belly landing. There was a little bridge in his way, and he was just lifting up to go over the bridge when I got in a last-second burst from 500 feet. I saw some strikes and then he pancaked into the river. As I flew over him, I saw some people jumping off the bank of the river, going to rescue him. I zoomed up, shut my guns off, and did a wingover so I could take a picture of him. Unfortunately, I was still flying right on the deck while maintaining a manifold pressure of 62 inches of mercury. Just as I took my pictures, my coolant popped – blew up in front of my face, all over the windshield. The loss of coolant was the death knell for a P-51's liquid-cooled in-line engine. I instinctively jammed the manual switch to open up the coolant door, which would cool the engine off a little.'[1]

With judicious management – and a little luck – Ed Heller made it back to Bodney.

On 8 May Ed Heller shot down two Bf 109s during a morning sortie mounted by the 352nd FG; indeed, during the day the Group claimed 22 enemy aircraft shot down plus four probables and one damaged, earning them a Distinguished Unit Citation. Heller's usual aircraft was P-51B 43-6704 PZ-H *Hell-er Bust*. He remained with the 486th to the end of the war, taking his tally of victories to 5.5 plus one damaged; post-war he joined the USAF and subsequently flew the F-86 in combat in Korea, adding 3.5 MiG-15s to his score.

May 8 had involved bomber attacks on Berlin and Brunswick and saw one of the biggest air battles in what was otherwise a fairly quiet month. Highest honours went to Heller's 352nd FG with 27–2–7[2]

Right: Re-arming a P-51 at Boxted, 20 January 1944. (Ken Delve Collection)

Right: Boxted January 1944: fitting a drop tank. (Ken Delve Collection)

Right: Part of the same Boxted series of shots: an aircraft being refuelled. (Ken Delve Collection)

---

[1] *Aces Against Germany, op cit.*
[2] Scores were usually expressed as Confirmed–Probable–Damaged and recorded simply as numbers.

for the loss of just one Mustang, with Lt Carl Luksic (487th FS) claiming two Bf 109s and three Fw 190s – the first 'five in a mission' for an VIII Fighter Command pilot.

The Mustang was greeted with near universal acclaim by its pilots; almost to a man they found the aircraft a delight to fly. The acclaimed British test pilot Eric 'Winkle' Brown flew a wide variety of aircraft types during (and after) the war at the RAE; he recorded his overall impressions of the Mustang in his book *Wings of the Weird and Wonderful*:

'The Mustang III was an effective fighter over Europe and a pleasant aeroplane to fly. The cockpit was neatly laid out and not the usual over-large American style. View ahead on the ground was poor, so for taxying the nose had to be swung from side to side, but this was made easy by virtue of the tail-wheel being capable of being locked to the rudder controls and steered over a range of 6 degrees either side. This steerable position was achieved by holding the control column past the neutral position. For take-off the elevator was trimmed 5 degrees back, the rudder 5 degrees right and the ailerons neutral. The fuel cock was set to Main Tanks and the master booster pump to Emergency. The supercharger was set to Auto, the carburettor air intake to Ram Air and the radiator and oil cooler shutter to Automatic.

'The stick was held back as the engine was opened up to 61 inches Hg boost, 3,000 rpm, and this helped eliminate swing. The aircraft was very blind forward during the early part of the take-off run, but got off very smartly in the tail-down position. Actually a normal take-off could be comfortably made using only 46 inches of boost. The master booster pump was switched to Normal before commencing the climb at 160 mph. The stalling characteristics of the Mk III were mild without fuel in the fuselage tank, with slight tail buffeting at some 3–4 mph before the actual all-up stall at 90 mph when the right wing dropped gently. The all-down (dirty) stall occurred at 75 mph. With full fuselage tank there was no buffet stall warning, but a series of stick reversals just before the wing fell sharply.'

Mustang III

It was not only the USAAF fighter squadrons who were taking the war to the enemy: at the very end of 1943 the RAF had begun to receive its own version of the P-51B, the Mustang III. No 122 Wing (Nos 19, 65 and 122 Squadrons) at Gravesend was the first to re-equip, operations commencing in early 1944. These aircraft did not have the radius of action of their American counterparts as they were not equipped with the extra 85gal fuel tank, the RAF having no perceived requirement for long-range escort fighters. The No 19 Squadron Operational Record Book recorded the unit's first mission with the new type: 'We now have sufficient aircraft operational to put a squadron in the air, and everyone was very keen to test out our new machines against the wily Hun. Unfortunately the weather intervened and the show did not come off.' However, on the following day, 15 February, it was different:

'Offensive fighter sweep of Holland/ Northern France by three flights of four (White, Dick, Green) led by S/L N. J. Durrant. Take-off 0950 and climb to 26,500 ft and cross the coast near Flushing. To avoid smoke trails angels were reduced to 25 and the Squadron swept the area Antwerp–Brussels–Cambrai without any enemy reaction and crossed out just south of Boulogne. Although uneventful, everybody felt very happy with their new kites and our cruising speed at altitude was very high (approx 250 IAS).' The Squadron flew another uneventful sweep in the afternoon.

In March Flt Lt St John from the Handling Flight at Hullavington was leading a tour of a Mustang II and P-51C around various units. On 8 March he arrived with No 63 Squadron: '. . . received information that this squadron was to be re-equipped with Mustang IIs and that he

Rolls-Royce Developments

Rolls-Royce was convinced that the Mustang could be developed even further and a number of aircraft were tested with other engines. FX858 was fitted with a Merlin RM.14.SM (Merlin 100) and achieved 453mph at 18,000ft, whilst FX901 was given an RM.16.SM (Merlin 113) and reached 454mph at 26,800ft. In November 1944 MAP had approved the construction of three flying test-beds with Griffon 65s, based upon a fighter aircraft proposal put forward by Hucknall in January. This 'Hucknall Private Venture' was based around the Mustang airframe using a two-stage Griffon 61 in a buried installation driving contra-rotating propellers. The first mock-up was constructed using a Merlin as no Griffons were available, but no priority was given to this work, even after the MAP agreement, and so progress was slow. A 1/10 scale model was wind-tested by the RAE but in the end it all came to naught as in February 1945 the project was cancelled, its potential having been overtaken by that of the jet-powered fighter.

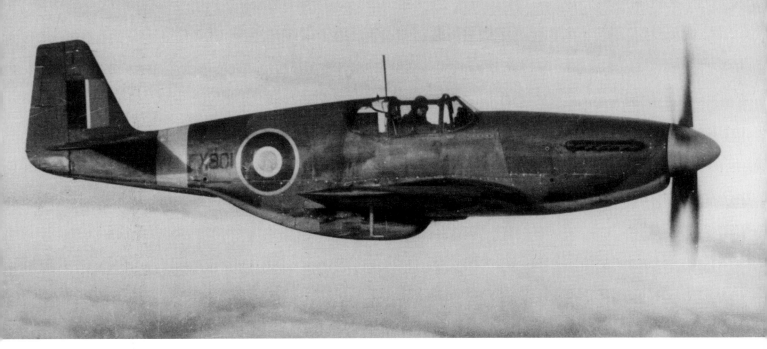

had come to demonstrate one.' The Squadron was re-equipped that same month – but with Hurricane IIs!

It was also increasingly evident that 1944 would, at last, see the Allied invasion of France. A major reorganisation and training programmes were established in the first few months of the year, and these, inevitably, affected the RAF's Mustang units. Work with ground units intensified, much emphasis being placed on co-operation with amphibious forces. A number of squadrons also took part in naval exercises, the primary role being that of spotting 'fall of shot' for naval bombardments. In March No 414 Squadron was at Dundonald on one such exercise, lectures on naval bombardment being followed by shoots with Royal Artillery 25pdr guns and, finally, live shoots with HMS *Diadem*, *Enterprise* and *Sheffield* using the Kintyre ranges.

At Dundonald No 516 Squadron was formed on 28 April from the nucleus of No 1141 (Combined Operations) Flight under the command of Sqn Ldr B. G. F. Drinkwater with a mixed establishment of Mustangs, Blenheims, Lysanders and Ansons – although it was intended that it should become exclusively a Mustang unit as soon as possible (its establishment of 15 Mustangs was in place by the end of

May). Straightaway the unit was taking part in exercises with amphibious forces as Army units throughout the United Kingdom intensified their training for the coming invasion. Increasing use was made of Forward Air Control as a way of improving the speed and accuracy of tactical air support to the ground troops.

Build-Up to D-Day

The RAF involvement in the escort role all but ended by April as more USAAF units were available and there was a pressing need to increase capability for TAF operations over Europe. Much of the Allied air effort, strategic and tactical, was now being devoted to the preparation for a 'second front', the return of the Allies to the European mainland.

A great deal of effort was expended against the enemy's lines of communication and in particular the rail network. Whilst these types of target had been attacked since the earliest offensive sweeps over the Continent, they now became key targets to be actively hunted, the instruction being to destroy the locomotives as these were in limited supply. The Germans had demonstrated their ability rapidly to repair rail lines that had been cut, and whilst bridges remained hard targets to destroy, the planners decided that locomotives were the most vulnerable part of the system. The effectiveness of the so-called Transportation Plan have been debated at great length since 1945 – and, indeed, were during the implementation of the plan itself. The USAAF fighters flew their first 'Chattanooga' (anti-transportation) mission on 21 May with 550 or more fighters hunting suitable targets and claiming 91 locomotives and other targets. Road targets were equally likely to come under attack: Don Blakeslee's 4th FG had a flair for finding 'juicy' targets and on 22 May came across a German road convoy. The fighters raced back to Debden to bomb up with 500lb bombs, a feat that was achieved in record time. When they returned to the area, however, they found that the weather had closed in. Nevertheless their luck held: they found a hole to sneak through and were able to identify the target. 'We didn't wipe it out completely, but we sure did shake the hell out of 'em,' Blakeslee is reported to have said.

Typical of such rail attacks was that by the three squadrons of Gravesend's No 122 Wing against the marshalling yards at Tours on 19 April:

'On arrival at Tours we formed up and delivered the attack in such a deliberate way that it resembled nothing more than a Wing training exercise. The only difference was that we became acutely aware of the flak. Black smoke-puffs appeared in the sky around us as we neared the target, and one shell exploded so close to my aircraft that it was jolted. I heard a loud bang over the engine noise and felt the thud of shrapnel hitting metal, but I was not aware of any changes in the handling of the plane. As the large workshops were disappearing under the nose of my aircraft, I rolled over and pulled back the stick to go into a vertical dive and followed this up with the usual procedures practised during training – keep the centre of the gunsight on one side of the sheds and watch the altimeter unwind rapidly . . . through 5,000 ft . . . pull slightly on the stick and count to three . . . press the but-

ton . . . the bombs are away . . . pull hard on the stick to come out of the dive . . . try to turn a little to avoid the flak . . . climb steeply . . . re-form on the leader.'[1]

There was an enormous requirement for photographic coverage of thousands of targets, and the Allied tactical units had to carry out much of this work. Added to this was a major increase in the fighter-bomber work being conducted, both as part of the overall counter-air campaign and as part of what was to become known as the Transportation Plan, the latter involving attacks on all enemy lines of communication – road, rail and river/sea. A number of the RAF's fighter squadrons found themselves changing roles:

'Our role in the early stages was to escort the bombers but because of the Mustang's range and carrying capacity a decision was taken to form us into an inde-

Above: Lt Graham's 339th FG *Miss Max*, 1 September 1944. (Ken Delve Collection)

[1] Tony Jonsson, *op. cit.*

Right: A red-nose P-51 about to receive six .50-calibre machine guns plus ammunition – an effective, if posed, photograph. (US National Archives)

pendent offensive unit as 122 Wing within 2 TAF. In place of drop tanks, two 500lb bombs were hung under the wings and we were despatched to attack either planned targets or to search for targets of opportunity.'[1]

Allied tactical aircraft of all types ranged over the near part of the Continent attacking almost anything that moved – but it was dangerous work. The No 268 Squadron Operational Record Book recorded the unit's first operational Mustang sortie from its new base at North Weald on 22 January:

'F/L Brees and F/O Jenkins covered Cambrai/Epinoy airfield and were engaged by three Fw 190s south of Hesdin, in the course of violent evasive action, F/L Brees flew through trees and the enemy aircraft followed him. It is thought to have crashed as it disappeared and F/L Brees saw smoke. Both aircraft were damaged.'

Although enemy fighters were encountered on a number of occasions, the greater danger at low level remained that of flak and natural hazards such as trees and

[1] Tony Jonsson, op. cit.

Right: A 4th FS/52nd FG P-51D (Ken Delve Collection)

wires. The sturdy nature of the Mustang meant that many a pilot managed to return safely despite contact with these 'enemies'. (As will be seen in the section dealing with Israeli Mustang operations, the aircraft could even be used intentionally to cut wires.)

A great deal of effort was also expended in acquiring photographic coverage of the beaches to be used for the assault. No 268 Squadron again (3 March):

'F/L Lissner and F/O Moyle completed a *Popular* of the beach defences in Boulogne area. Diving from 3,000 ft the run was made from south to north at a height of 750 ft according to plan. No 1 only took photos, from a range of about one mile. Some flak from the harbour area.'

This type of task intensified as the date for the invasion approached. Four sorties flown over two days in late May by No 268 Squadron illustrate the nature of the tasks, and the risks involved. On 19 May Flt Lt M. Lissner (FD561) and Fg Off B. F. Rachinger (FD535) carried out 'an unusual task involving finding of stake and wire anti-glider obstacles in set areas near Le Havre. The obstacles were found and photographed successfully.' The same day Flt Lt R. G. Brown (FD498) and Flt Lt V. E. Lewis (FD526) conducted 'PR in Estrees St Denis area. Both pilots took successful photos and both took photos of a rail halt at sheet 4 N2916. Visual recce reported 20+ MT on rail tracks. Sidings full of tarpaulin-covered trucks. No locomotives seen. Medium flak from Roye Amy airfield and intense flak from Carmaches.'

On 24 May Flt Lt T. B. Winslow (FD497) and Fg Off A. D. Fraser (FD552) carried out '. . . PR in Neufchatel area. Photos required of the RDF installation from zero feet and as close as possible. The Section crossed in south of Boulogne and made a sweeping, diving turn on to the target. Both pilots made a perfect approach despite heavy flak. Photos were taken but F/L Winslow had been hit by flak. The aircraft was badly damaged and on reaching Brenzett F/L Winslow made a successful

belly landing. F/L Winslow received emergency treatment for facial and wrist burns and was then flown to base and taken to hospital. It transpired that a sheet of flame had filled the cockpit and forced the pilot to jettison the hood. His helmet had gone with it. The targets were claimed. F/O Fraser flew on to base.'

Also on 24 May Sqn Ldr A. S. Mann (FD532) and Fg Off D. M Ashford (FD505) carried out '. . . zero feet oblique photography of a radar chimney on the NE outskirts of Boulogne, adjacent to the Napoleon monument. The Section crossed in and was at once met by intense and heavy accurate flak. The Section made a diving turn on to the target

Below: Honington, 28 July 1944: a P-51 of the 383rd FS/364th FG is worked on. (Ken Delve Collection)

amidst heavy flak. F/O Ashford received a 20mm-type shell in the wing root and a very large number of shrapnel splinters penetrated the port side of the aircraft.' Neither of the two damaged aircraft were repaired.

The Eighth Air Force summary for May 1944 records that in that month the bombers suffered their lowest loss rates to date – 2.2 per cent (although that still equated to 361 aircraft). The average daily strength during the month was 1,304 bombers and 856 fighters, and together they flew over 36,000 sorties; fighters claimed 622–31–252 for the loss of 171 (a 1.2 per cent loss rate) aircraft, whilst the bombers claimed 377–115–170 for their loss of 361, the majority of the claims being made by the B-17s of the 3rd Division. Seven more Bomb and one Fighter Group had become operational during the month, and targets had ranged from oil refineries in Czechoslovakia to various communications and airfield targets in France and the Low Countries – and, of course, Berlin.

The statistics for the three Fighter Wings were:

Unit	Sorties	Results
65th FW	4,523	153–13–43 for 51 aircraft lost, plus 32–0–29 ground
66th FW	5,667	172.5–6–46 for 58 aircraft lost, plus 56–0–54 ground
67th FW	4,811	168.5–12–32 for 62 aircraft lost, plus 80–0–58 ground

Using the British-made 108gal drop tank, the P-51 escort fighters were now regularly flying round trips of over 1,400 miles – a figure that the previous year few planners would have thought possible. By late May, VIII Fighter Command's strength of fifteen Groups included seven equipped with P-51s, a figure that continued to rise in 1944 until by the end of the year most Groups had Mustangs. In addition the Ninth Air Force/XIX TAC was able to field three Mustang Groups.

Continued Testing

Aircraft trials and testing continued throughout the war, as often alluded to in this history, and in many instances trials of a particular variant appear to coincide with its entry to service – or in some cases take place after it had entered service and problems had arisen. This was inevitable under wartime conditions where the degree of testing that could take place before a type entered service was often very limited, and it was only when units began to operate an aircraft in realistic conditions that difficulties and limitations became evident.

The P-51C-1-NT underwent cold-weather tests in May 1944 ,and in a report dated 20 May it was concluded that '. . . the P-51C type aircraft is satisfactory for operations in temperatures as low as –44 deg F, except for the limitation placed on operations by the failure of the engine to operate correctly with highly diluted oil. The P-51C test airplanes [42-102979 and 42-102980] were not completely winterised upon arrival at Ladd Field, and several of the winterisation items were unsatisfactory.'

The same report was, however, somewhat more scathing about the armament fit on the aircraft: '. . . armament trials have proved unsatisfactory – recommend that guns be installed in erect position or inclined in opposite direction to eliminate the 180 deg turn in ammunition feed chutes; ammunition boxes need to be more securely installed. The armament of the subject aircraft failed to function properly throughout the test. New guns were installed from time to time after having been tested on the range and found to be in perfect condition; nevertheless, when installed in the airplane they failed to function properly.'

There had been 46 gun stoppages during the tests, 21 of them caused by the failure of the gun to extract a round from the belt. Problems with the guns were to be a feature of the Mustang during much of its operational career, as mentioned above, and many combat reports include reference to stoppages – often caused by high-g manoeuvres.

Right: Clear blue sky – perfect conditions for a fighter: a P-51D of the 353rd FS/55th FG. (Ken Delve Collection)

Left: Fowlmere, 10 May 1944: the 339th FG Mustang of Lt Everitt. (US National Archives)

Right: A No 122 Squadron Mustang on a forward airfield. The Squadron operated Mustang IIIs from May 1944 as part of the 2nd Tactical Air Force. (Ken Delve Collection)

Also as part of the training routine for the invasion, a number of squadrons underwent naval bombardment courses as 'fall of shot' for naval gunnery would be an important role during the invasion period. Indeed, the tactical squadrons were kept incredibly busy both operationally and with training during the first half of 1944 as air, land and sea forces were working themselves up to the highest possible level of operational efficiency for D-Day. On 6 June the massive naval armada was in place and the landings began. The role of air power was critical and the Mustangs, of all varieties, played a full part with sorties being flown throughout the daylight hours.

Invasion Sorties

The major RAF strength comprised a large number of Spitfire squadrons, and for the USAAF's Ninth Air Force/XIX TAC there were twelve Groups equipped with P-47s and three with P-38s; the P-51s were, therefore, only a small part of this total effort. However, the Eighth Air Force was able to put up seven P-51 Groups. As an aside, the Ninth Air Force statistics showed 125 P-51s available for the 67th RG against a Group UE (Unit Establishment) of 72 – a salutary lesson in interpreting the statistics provided in Order of Battle records as these invariably give only the UE and not the actual strength. On 4 June pots of paint had been issued and the fighters duly appeared with their white and black identification stripes.

As part of the Air Spotting Pool (ASP), No 414 Squadron, led by Sqn Ldr Stover, flew its first naval spotting task at 0500, landing back at Lee-on-Solent and then flying a second sortie. The afternoon brought no calls on the Squadron and the

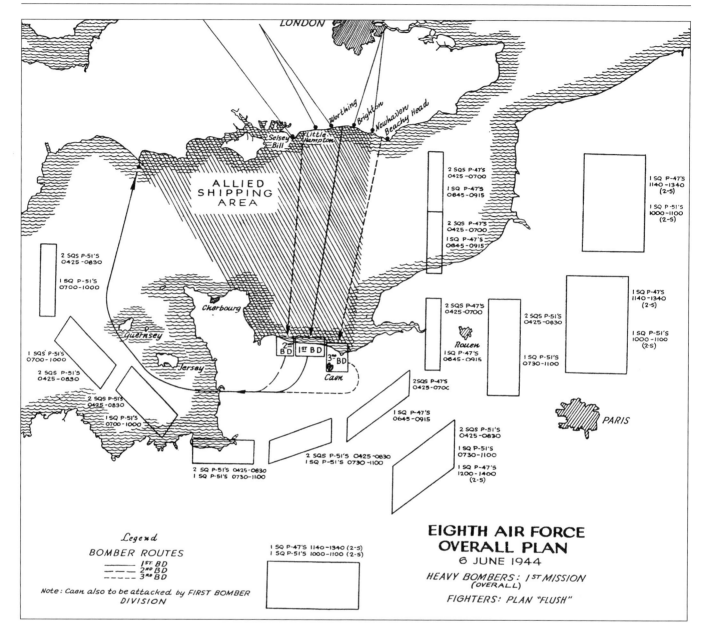

ALLIED
SHIPPING
AREA

2 SQS P-51'S
0425-0830

1 SQ P-51'S
0700-1000

Cherbourg

Guernsey

1 SQS P-51'S
0700-1000

2 SQS P-51'S
0425-0830

Jersey

2 SQS P-51'S
0425-0830

1 SQ P-51'S
0700-1000

2 SQ P-51'S 0425-0830
1 SQ P-51'S 0730-1100

Selsey
Bill

Little
Hampton

Worthing

Brighton

Newhaven

Beachy Head

LONDON

2 SQS P-47'S
0425-0700

1 SQ P-47'S
0645-0915

2 SQS P-47'S
0425-0700

1 SQ P-47'S
0645-0915

2 SQS P-47'S
0425-0700

1 SQ P-47'S
0645-0915

2 SQS P-47'S
0425-0700

1 SQ P-47'S
0645-0915

2 SQS P-51'S 0425-0830
1 SQ P-51'S 0730-1100

Rouen

1 SQ P-47'S
1140-1340
(2-5)

1 SQ P-51'S
1000-1100
(2-5)

1 SQ P-47'S
1140-1340
(2-5)

1 SQ P-51'S
1000-1100
(2-5)

2 SQS P-51'S
0425-0830

1 SQ P-51'S
0730-1100

2 SQS P-51'S
0425-0830

1 SQ P-51'S
0730-1100

1 SQ P-47'S
1200-1400
(2-5)

PARIS

2ⁿᵈ
BD   1ˢᵗ BD   3ᵗʰ BD

Caen

Legend

BOMBER ROUTES
——— 1ˢᵗ BD
— — — 2ᴺᴰ BD
- - - - 3ᴿᴰ BD

Note: Caen also to be attacked by FIRST BOMBER
DIVISION

1 SQ P-47'S 1140-1340 (2-5)
1 SQ P-51'S 1000-1100 (2-5)

EIGHTH AIR FORCE
OVERALL PLAN
6 JUNE 1944

HEAVY BOMBERS: 1ˢᵗ MISSION
(OVERALL)

FIGHTERS: PLAN "FLUSH"

final sortie of the day was a pairs TacR flown at 1800. The Squadron had flown a total of 34 sorties during the day. No 268 Squadron was also involved in the naval gunfire task, their first pair being airborne at 0455: '. . . first target successful, second failed owing to R/T weakening. Intense and accurate heavy flak.' The second pair, airborne five minutes later, had to carry out an impromptu shoot as the designated target had already been neutralised. This was true of a number of targets during the day and a few of the sorties were re-tasked by the HQ ship with TacR. Most sorties recorded heavy flak,

one commenting: '. . . intense inaccurate light flak from target area AND unit of the Royal Navy'. The Squadron flew 26 sorties between 0455 and 1135, one aircraft, Flt Lt E D Woodward's FD477, failing to return. Two further TacR sorties were flown in the evening.

The pace of operations continued into the late evening of 6 June. No 19 Squadron did not fly its first operation until 2030, when its aircraft acted as close escort for the airborne operation by the 5th Landing Brigade and with armed reconnaissance over the beach-head, eventually landing at 2215. Armed reconnaissance

Above: Plan showing the fighter patrol areas for 6 June 1944. The P-51s were stationed in the outer and middle screens. (USAF)

Right: A 361st FG aircraft coming in to land at Bottisham. (Ken Delve Collection)

D-Day Order of Battle: P-51 Units

No 12 Group
No 316 Squadron	Coltishall	

2nd TAF
No 122 Wing	Funtingdon	Nos 19, 65, 122 Squadrons
No 133 Wing	Coolham	Nos 129, 306, 315 Squadrons
No 35 (R) Wing	Gatwick	Nos 2, 268 Squadrons
No 39 (R) Wing	Odiham	Nos 168, 414, 430 Squadrons

Eighth Air Force
4th FG	Debden	334, 335, 336 FS
339th FG	Fowlmere	503, 504, 505 FS
352nd FG	Bodney	328, 486, 487 FS
355th FG	Steeple Morden	354, 357, 358 FS
357th FG	Leiston	362, 363, 364 FS
359th FG	East Wretham	368, 369, 370 FS
361st FG	Bottisham	374, 375, 376 FS
496th FTG	Goxhill	Training unit

Ninth Air Force
67th RG	Middle Wallop	12th, 15th, 107th, 109th Sqns

XIX TAC
100th FW:
354th FG	Lashenden	353rd, 355th, 356th Sqns
363rd FG	Staplehurst	380th, 381st, 382nd Sqns

remained the order of the day for most units over the next few days, with Mustangs attacking a variety of ground targets – and suffering losses. On 14 June the 19 Squadron ORB recorded: '. . . whilst bombing and strafing an enemy road convoy F/Sgt Kairton's aircraft blew up and went straight in. It is believed that he flew too low and was caught in the blast of his own bombs.'

In response to the massive Allied air effort the Luftwaffe flew only 70 single-engine fighter sorties in the invasion area and few combats took place. Indeed, the Fighter Command Intelligence Summary recorded that '. . . no major encounters took place throughout the first day of the invasion of Normandy. Enemy air activity was negligible. It is estimated that both escorting and protective fighters over the assault area and defensive fighters over France did not exceed 50 to 70 [enemy] sorties.' The Allied expectation had been somewhat different, and of the 10,344 Allied aircraft declared available for D-Day, 1,977 were fighters. The defensive air plan was impressive in its scope, with screens of fighters being provided around the invasion area (see map). The directive issued to the fighter forces stated that '. . . the intention of the British and American fighter forces is to attain and maintain an air situation which will assure freedom of action for our forces without effective interference by the German Air Force, and to render maximum air protection to the land and naval forces in the common object of assaulting, securing and developing the bridgehead'. The fighter pilots were prepared for a hard fight. Don Blakeslee, for example, briefed his pilots at 0300 hours on 6 June and left them in no doubt as to what he expected: 'I am prepared to lose the whole Group.' The first of the fighter screen squadrons was to be in place by 0425 and the entire screen was to be in effect for the 'peak operational period' of 0500 to 1000 hours, and at two further periods during the day. Fixed patrol lines were given to VIII Fighter Command's P-51 and P-47 units, and at the end of each patrol, once relieved by the next group of pilots, the fighters were clear to attack ground targets. The P-51s provided a vital part of the outer screen, the inner defence lines being made up of P-38s and Spitfires.

The Mustangs of the 355th FG, led by Lt Col Dix, had a quiet first 'Full House' mission:

'For the first mission of D-Day, the 355th FG was divided into two parts, A Group composed of the 354th FS 357th FS and B Group consisting of the 348th Squadron. Actually, this first mission of the Big Day turned out to be a Milk Run, for neither division of the Group saw any enemy planes. The A Group patrolled an area, labelled M, in the forefront of a giant U-shaped shield behind which the mammoth ground and heavy bomber operations were taking place. This area was to the SW of Paris. Handicapped by weather and the darkness, the Group was soon split up into sections and flights. It was impossible to orientate the outfit definitely over its assigned area. They flew through it, around it, and around Paris. However, since the Group was flying under Type 16 control and were rather freelancing it, they could still have taken care of any bandits reported in their vicinity. All told, it seems that not one member of the Luftwaffe was on hand to offer resistance to the first phase of the invasion.'

Most combats that did occur took place late in the day, the most successful coming when the 355th FG jumped a formation of Ju 87s. Two squadrons of the Group had taken off on a 'Royal Flush' mission at 1810 and went first to the Châteaudun area, 'then dropping through the clouds onto the deck, the Squadron sighted three trains in the Chartres area. All flights fired with the results that four oil cars were set afire and the other two trains were damaged. Four trucks were also claimed. At 2115, in the Chartres-Dreux area, approx 15 Ju87s were encountered. In this encounter some of the enemy aircraft tried to crash-land in the open fields.

This attempt accounts for the Squadron claims:

'Capt Marshal   1 Ju 87
'Lt Fortier   1 Ju 87
'Lt Perry   1 Ju 87
'Lt Ray   1 Ju 87 (+ 1 shared)
'Lt Col Dix   2 Ju 87 (1 on ground)

'The second squadron fared even better, spotting a similar formation near Janville. Flying in vic formation of three plane vics and going westward towards the beachhead and flying on the deck. The formation was bounced with claims as listed below. Lt Douglas was hit by flak near Calais and is missing in action:

```
            S E C R E T                      X-R-5
                                               SECRET
            H E A D Q U A R T E R S        AUTH: CG ASUPC
        363rd Fighter Bomber Group, Army Air Force    INITIALS: erc
                                              DATE: 7 June 1944

                                              APO 141, US Army,
                                                  7 June 1944.

TO:  CG, Ninth Air Force, (Att: 26th SCU) APO 696, US Army
     CG, XIX Tactical Air Command (Att: Stat Control) APO 141, US Army
     CO, 100th Fighter Wing (Att: Stat Officer) APO 141, US Army

FROM: 363rd Fighter Bomber Group, APO 141, US Army

REF:  Oprep A No. 68 for 24 hours ending Sunset 7 June 1944. Mission No. 74.

     A.  Transport and glider escort mission to Cherbourg Peninsula, France.
Up 0556, down 0830. L/F out at 1,000 feet over Bill of Portland at 0625. Did
not R/V with transports but followed course as briefed to area north of Cherbourg
and picked up 150 to 200 transports returning to England from France at 0730 hours
10 miles north of Pte. De Barfleur. Fighters at 1,000 feet, transports on deck.
Escorted transports to Bill of Portland and left them at 0807, 1500 feet. Several
stragglers were escorted in. Saw cruiser which appeared to be on fire at approx-
imately 4936N, 0146W. Two stacks of another vessel protruding from water at
approximately 4935N, 0110W. A C-47 protruding from water at approximately 4950N,
0250W. Saw sunken 4 stacker vessel between St. Marcons Isles and mainland. No
E/A encountered. No flak.
     Weather: 9/10 strata cumulus, ceiling 1,000 feet, visibility 15 miles.

     B.  (i) 37 P-51B's, 6 P-51C's, 2 P-51D's. (ii) 37 P-51B's, 6 P-51C's,
2 P-51D's completed mission. (iii) Nil. (iv) Nil. (v) Nil. (vi) Nil. (vii) Nil.
(viii) 45.

     C.  (i) 90 American Universal - 75 American gallons. (ii) Nil.

     D.  (i) P-51B's 106:30, P-51C's 17:30, P-51D's 5:45. (ii) Nil.

     E.  (i) 62,800 rds. 50 cal. (ii) 320 (iii) Nil.

     F.  Nil.

     G.  Nil.

     H.  Nil.

                    For the Commanding Officer:

                                        Raymond B. Raub
                                        RAYMOND B. RAUB,
                                        1st Lieut., Air Corps,
                                        Statistical Officer.

                    S E C R E T
                        -1-
```

Opposite and above: Opreps issued by the 363rd FBG to the Ninth Air Force, 7 June 1944. (USAF)

'Capt Kelly	2 Ju 87
'Lt Bernoske	1 Ju 87
'Lt James	3 Ju 87
'Lt Fuller	1 Ju 87 (+ 1 prob and 1 damaged)
'Lt Cotter	1 Ju 87
'Capt Wilson	1 Ju 87 damaged
'Lt Minchow	1 Ju 87 damaged
'Sqn shared	1 Ju 87'

The P-51s of VIII Fighter Command flew 505 sorties during the day at a cost of 22 aircraft. Comparative figures for the Ninth Air Force/XIX TAC are not available, although the total fighter sorties mounted by the Ninth/XIX were 2,576.

With the troops ashore, TacR once more increased in importance as Allied ground forces came to rely on the presence of air power. June 1944 was one of the most intense operational periods of the war, with many units involved in tactical low-level operations. Losses were appreciable (the RAF lost over 60 Mustangs between 6 June and the end of the month), the majority being to flak. Although the Luftwaffe put in few appearances, there was a significant air threat from friendly aircraft, with numerous instances of attacks or attempted attacks. The P-47 units seemed most prone to making this error, although many RAF squadrons also record 'unwarranted attention' from P-38s.

The fighter-bomber role was to become increasingly important to support the precarious ground position. Lt Jim Starnes was with the 505th FS/339th FG operating out of Fowlmere on such missions:

'On the morning of June 8 we took off one hour before daylight on another dive-bombing mission to France. Each airplane carried two 500lb bombs instead of the 250lb bombs we had carried on all our previous dive-bombing missions. I do not know why the field order for this mission called for these bombs as the P-51 flew a bit more sluggishly with the larger bombs. Our airfield at Fowlmere had no lighting, so we had to use the lights of several jeeps to help us line up with the runway. After assembly into flights of four, we climbed out on course 150 degrees – to our target area, which was in the vicinity of Dreux. At about 1500 feet we entered the overcast, and I soon lost sight of my element leader. Since I was on his left wing, I went onto instruments and took up a heading of 140 degrees to avoid a possible mid-air collision with other members of the flight. When I broke out on top of the clouds at 5,000 feet it was still totally dark.'

Failing to locate any other members of his flight, Jim Starnes set course for the target area:

'When I arrived in the Group's area of responsibility I descended to about 5,000 feet and began to search for a suitable target. Just as dawn was breaking, I spotted a steam locomotive moving through a rail yard near a small French town and I decided to attack it. I circled once to look the area over. Using the cockpit arming switches I armed the nose and tail fuses of my bombs. I also turned on my gunsight. Our bombing technique consisted of flying to the right of the target so that it appeared halfway along the left wing. My bomb run was made parallel with the tracks in order to minimise the chance of hitting French civilians. As the locomotive started to disappear underneath the left wing, I rolled left and down at an angle of 60–70 degrees. I had to fly smoothly to keep the gunsight pipper [a dot in the centre of a 100-mil reticule] on the target. As my speed was increasing I adjusted the rudder trim to avoid slipping or skidding. I let the aircraft's nose rise slowly. As the target disappeared underneath the nose, I pressed the pickle button on the control stick and immediately began a hard pull-out to avoid going below 1,000 feet. I felt the concussion from the bombs as I pulled up, and I circled left to see what they had hit. I had missed the locomotive but apparently had cut the tracks ahead of it.

'I turned on my gun switch and made two broadside strafing passes at the steam engine. I estimate that I expended 30 to 40 rounds from each of my four guns on each strafing pass. The strikes caused steam to billow up.'

Jim Starnes could hear other pilots from his Group on the radio but saw no one – until he spotted a Bf 109 at tree-top height and gave chase. He caught up with his quarry, who was still unaware of his presence, and promptly shot it down, taking his score to three. He became an ace on 4 August when he shot down another Bf 109, and a final victory on 2 March 1945 took his total to six. Almost 25 years later he was in combat again, flying a tour out of Udorn, Thailand, in 1968–69, during the Vietnam War.

By 10 June the Germans had moved 300 fighters into the area, but a tactical change meant that many sorties were being devoted to ground attack work. However, this misuse of the fighter force was cancelled on 12 June under orders from Berlin. The increased Luftwaffe presence was soon being felt, as in a sortie flown by No 19 Squadron:

'Squadron airborne 1530 to dive bomb M/T at Rambouillet. Whilst approaching Dreux aerodrome, 16 Fw 190s were sighted slightly above. Bombs were jettisoned and the Squadron climbed hard

Right: 44-13341, an anonymous P-51D. (Ken Delve Collection)

Below: 44-13254 was one of a batch of 800 P-51D-5NA aircraft. (Ken Delve Collection)

until above the E/A [enemy aircraft]. Green section were the first to attack, closely followed by Tonic and White, and a first class dog fight developed, which cost the Hun two destroyed, one probable and five damaged for the loss of P/O Schofield, who was last seen going down on fire and must be presumed killed.'[1]

German fighter-bombers were equally vulnerable, as demonstrated on 10 June when the 328th FS (352nd FG) ran into 40 bomb-carrying Bf 109s heading for the beaches. The enemy 'jettisoned their bombs and dispersed', Capt John Thornell claiming two to bring his P-51 score to ten and his total to 14 (he finished his tour on the 328th with a score of 17.25 confirmed). More and more dogfights were taking

[1] No 19 Squadron ORB.

Below: Mustang IV TK589 still bearing traces of its USAF serial 44-13332, August 1944. This was one of two such aircraft received from the USAAF in July 1944 (*FlyPast* Collection)

place at low level, one side bouncing the other, and the P-51s were proving quite capable of outmanoeuvring most of their opponents in these conditions. It was just as well, however, that the P-51D began to enter service in June: its improved visibility (it had a full-view teardrop canopy) and eight rather than six guns made it an even more effective fighter.

With air superiority assured and aggressively maintained, a high proportion of tactical air effort was applied to the land battle. The Allies were ashore, but it was by no means certain that they could stay there; indeed, without the massive levels of both tactical and strategic air power the invasion would have proved impossible. The key to success lay in preventing German reinforcements reaching the battle area, and so road and rail sweeps were the order of the day. Lt-Col Tom Hayes of the 357th FG decided to drop half-empty fuel tanks amongst the rail cars at the St Pierre marshalling yards. When the P-51s ran in a second time they strafed the area, and the tanks – along with a selection of

rail cars – vanished in a series of spectacular explosions. This somewhat *ad hoc* 'tactic' does not appear to have been widely used and it was some months before a special weapon along these lines, napalm, was used in combat.

June had seen a major reorganisation of the Ninth Air Force in order to provide the right type and level of tactical air support for the Third Army once it was established in France, and as part of this reorganisation the 10th PRG acquired the P-51-equipped 12th and 15th TRSs. The 15th TRS had been operational since 26 March under the command of Lt-Col George Walker and was already establishing a fine reputation – including an aggressive attitude to enemy fighters, with at least seven shot down to date. For the 15th TRS the transfer to the 10th PRG (from the 67th Observation Group) took place with effect from 13 June, by which time one of the unit's pilots, Capt John Hoefker, had already scored his first victory, shooting down a Bf 109 near Le Mans airfield. By the end of June this pilot had added two more Bf 109s to his score, one

Right: Lt Murphy's Jersey Bouncer, *364th FG, 20 December 1944. (US National Archives)*

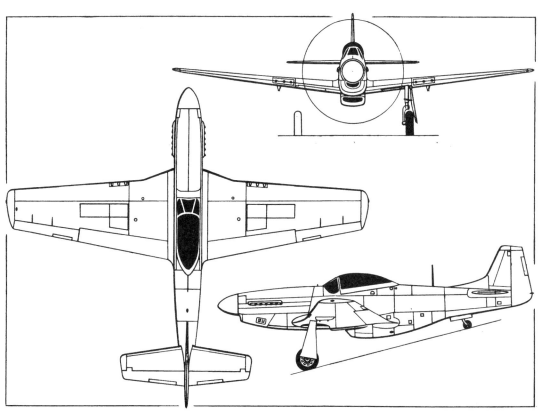

Left: P-51D Mustang general arrangement.

on the 20th and one on the 29th. Hoefker went on to become one of the few aces in the reconnaissance role, ending the war with 8.5 confirmed kills, all scored whilst flying F-6Cs and F-6Ds.

Into France

With the Allied armies safely ashore, further reorganisation of the air elements took place as units began to move to airfields on the Continent. The first RAF Mustang unit to move to France was No 122 Wing, which took up residence at B-7/Martigny on 25 June. Three days later No 39 Wing began the move to B-8, No 430 Squadron's Mustangs being the first to take up residence.

The 10th PRG began to move to France in early July to assist the 67th PRG, undertaking a similar range of missions to those of the RAF TacR units; the primary task was to locate targets suitable for attack by the growing number of Allied fighter-bombers. The

12th TRS was acting in support of Omar Bradley's First Army and was particularly heavily engaged during Operation 'Cobra', the ground offensive in the Coutances area.

The various Allied squadrons quickly settled into this nomadic life with few amenities, but one thing that was missing was beer, and for aircrew this was not acceptable! The solution adopted by one RAF Wing was to modify a 75gal underwing tank for use as a beer container: '. . . four tanks were sent to a factory for their insides to be coated with a substance to prevent the taste of metal contaminating the beer and taps were fitted. A contract was agreed with a brewery in London and on an appointed day every week a Mustang flew with two empty "beer" tanks to Croydon aerodrome and brought back two full – one containing Mild and the other Bitter. These tanks were placed on trestles in our mess tent – which quickly became known as the best pub in

Normandy.'[1] The squadrons were often moved to landing grounds within range of enemy artillery: '. . . we were shelled by German artillery the next day, three groundcrew were killed and only four aircraft were serviceable. The decision was taken to move the aircraft to B.6 and to find a new campsite.'[2]

The PR Spitfire-equipped No 541 Squadron had acquired a Mustang detachment in June: '. . . towards the end of the month three Mustang IIIs and three pilots trained in low level photography were attached to the Squadron but are still working up to operational standard'. By early July the ORB was recording that 'the three SAAF pilots with Mustang IIIs started operations in July on essential targets where high-level cover has been impossible owing to cloud. In such circumstances the Mustangs go in at 3–5,000 ft with a short focal length camera to obtain their pictures from below cloud.' The first mission was flown by Capt Williams in FB182 on 8 July, the target being the V-weapon site at Wizernes. The air effort expended both in finding and attacking these targets expanded daily.

V-Weapons

Only a few days after the Allies had landed, the Germans brought a new weapon into play, the first of the V-1 flying bombs landing on London on the night of 12/13 June. The existence of the weapon had long been known and Allied air power had been attacking launch sites – and, in the case of the Mustangs, photographing sites – for some months. The problem now was how to counter this new threat. The tactical operations to locate and attack these 'Noball' sites were stepped up, as was the use of strategic bombing against elements of the target system (such as production and storage sites), in addition to which extra fighter units were stationed in southern England to intercept the V-1s before they reached their target. Part

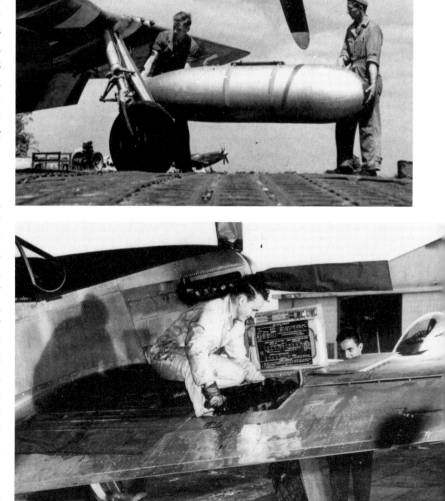

[1] Tony Jonsson, op. cit.
[2] No 19 Squadron ORB, the Squadron having moved to B-12 on 15 July 15.

Left: An auxiliary tank being fitted by S/Sgt D. Ratcliffe and S/Sgt E. Rowe. (US National Archives)

of this reinforcement included four RAF Mustang squadrons. The P-51 was a stable gun platform and had a high diving speed; it therefore had a reasonable chance of catching a V-1 as long as the initial approach was satisfactory. The three squadrons of No 133 Wing (Nos 129, 306 and 315) based at Brenzett were soon giving a good account of themselves and in two months claimed 179 V-1s destroyed, a further 75 falling to No 316 Squadron which had joined two Spitfire squadrons. The 54th FG also flew anti-'Diver' patrols out of Lashenden prior to its move to the Continent at the end of June.

In order to escort bombers to more distant targets 'shuttle' missions were planned from the United Kingdom as well as Italy (see below), with aircraft landing in Russia afterwards. Base facilities had to be provided in Russia, and three airfields in the Kiev area were allocated to the Americans and developed by US engineers. The first such mission from the UK took place on 21 June when Don Blakeslee led 61 P-51s as escort to a B-17 force attacking oil targets in Germany. (The 486th FS, from the 352nd FG, joined the 4th for this mission.) The B-17s were bounced by Fw 190s near Siedlice but the P-51s intervened, claiming six at the cost of one

Mustang and one Fortress. The P-51s landed at Piryatin and eventually returned via Italy on 5 July, having chalked up a number of other missions.

The reconnaissance effort continued unabated with TacR Mustangs ranging far and wide. The three Mustangs attached to No 541 Squadron were still active with their singleton operations against targets that the high-flying PR Spitfires could not cover, although the concept of operations with lone aircraft rather than a pair on TacR was somewhat unusual.

The weather in early July was poor, hampering Allied air operations and thus making the task of the ground forces even harder. With the ground forces continuing to advance but meeting stubborn resistance, tactical aircraft were called upon to play an increasing part in smashing German defences. Armed reconnaissance became the order of the day for the majority of Mustang units: operating within the battle area and the surrounding area, the aircraft, along with other Allied types, attacked German ground forces and made road and rail movement by day all but impossible. There was a great determination amongst pilots to 'press on' and get the job done. This was especially true of the reconnaissance units, where vital in-

Left: Mounting guns in the wing of a P-51, November 1944. (US National Archives)

Right: A No 19 Squadron Mustang III undergoing maintenance near a damaged church in Normandy. (Ken Delve Collection)

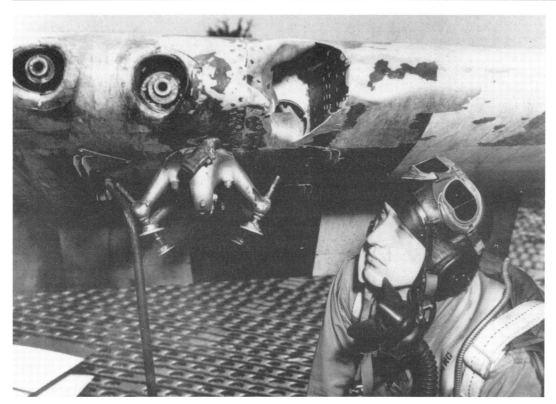

Left: Lt Howard Spalding 'admires' the damage caused to his aircraft when he struck a tree whilst strafing a train near Chartres. (Ken Delve Collection)

Right, top: Artillery being directed by a Ninth Air Force P-51 against a German-held château. (US National Archives)

Right, centre: A direct hit on a train. The artillery was 12 miles away and its fire was directed by a P-51. (US National Archives)

telligence information just had to be obtained to enable the ground commanders to fight an effective battle.

One critical question was the status of the bridges over the Loire, and on 10 July Lt Sal Mecca and Lt John Miefert of the 10th PRG were amongst those trying to help clarify the ground situation:

'Our squadron was assigned to do some behind the German lines reconnaissance to determine troop and tank strength. Sal Mecca drew the mission and I had been assigned as his wingman. The weather was bad so it was over the clouds we went with a let down near the Loire river so Sal could orientate himself and then fly north to the battle lines observing all he could see. The ceiling over the Loire was under 5,000 ft. As we worked our way north, the ceiling got lower and lower and eventually we had to abort – having observed nothing. Army was not satisfied and we were sent out the next morning with orders to go as low as necessary. Weather conditions were the same, but Sal kept on flying and looking. We came on some encampments and picked up some flak, which I reported to Sal. He kept on going and the flak increased till I thought that the whole German Army was shooting at us. It was the worst flak I ever received. Sal finally gave the order to climb into the cloud cover. We returned to base with my gas very, very low. It was decided the information Sal had gathered was not enough and he must go back again to try and complete this mission.'

Four aircraft were sent out by 15th TRS that afternoon – all singly as the weather had deteriorated to such an extent that a wingman was thought unnecessary. Sal Mecca failed to return. The ground commanders had come to rely on their 'air picture' of the battlefield, and such missions were often flown 'at any cost'.

Even the squadrons on fighter escort would, having left their bombers under the care of the return escort, use their fuel and ammunition to good effect by attacking targets on the ground; many VIII Fighter Command pilots ran up appreciable scores of German aircraft destroyed in this way. This offensive spirit was noted by the USAAF's Commanding General, 'Hap' Arnold, in his 'Third Report to the Secretary of War' (dated 27 February 1945):

Right: Lt Taylor plus groundcrew, 20th FG. (Ken Delve Collection)

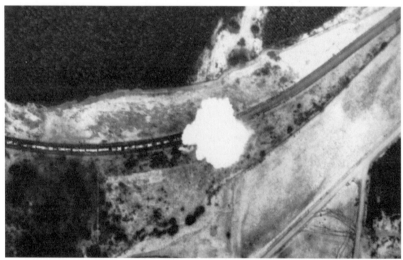

'The reluctance of the Luftwaffe to give battle except under favourable circumstances meant that our fighters often finished their leg of the bomber escort mission with surplus fuel. So they began attacking ground targets on the return trip. Their spirit was typified by Lt Thomas Biel who returned to his base one afternoon after 4 hours of combat. He had destroyed one airplane and damaged two others, but on the return trip he spotted a small airdrome with a dozen planes on it. He hadn't the gasoline or ammunition to attack. On landing at his base he approached another pilot – "I spotted an airdrome. Nobody else knows where it is. Let's gas up and give it a bounce. It won't be dark until 8 o'clock."'

Scouting Force

On 16 July an Experimental Scouting Force had flown its first mission (to Munich), and in the period up to 12 September it flew a total of 35 missions. The concept had grown out of an earlier proposal by Col Bud Peaslee of the 348th BG that weather reconnaissance by a fighter force scouting ahead of the bomber force would prove invaluable. The concept was supported by General Kepner, and Peaslee was posted to implement the idea:

'The Experimental Squadron has been selected from the 355th FG at Steeple Morden. There will be no administration or command changes involved, but the mission of the squadron will be, for the next two weeks, the training of eight bomber and eight fighter pilots for scouting employment, and thereafter the employment of this force with the 1st Division.'[1]

The selected bomber pilots were initially sent to the FTG at Goxhill, the Eighth Air Force's 'European Theater fighter orientation base', for initial checkout on the P-51. Typically this would involve a T-6 check ride followed by three or four solo P-51 sorties and then a series of pairs sorties covering aerobatics and gun-

[1] Note by Col Walter E. Todd, Chief of Staff for Operations.

nery. Lt Merill Dumont recalled this conversion:

'Check out in a P-51 was a couple of rides in an AT-6. You got a P-51 manual to read and off you went. Honington had steel mats for a runway and after much bouncing up and down over the soft spots I became airborne. Flew an average sloppy departure, all the time wondering why I was wallowing around the sky instead of being a hot-shot P-51 jock. After I woke up I discovered that, unlike a B-17, you had to pull the gear up yourself! The result was utterly amazing and I am in "Hog Heaven".'[1]

Ed Beaty commented: 'How effective were we? On en-route weather we helped a lot to alert bomber streams to climb instead of wallowing into the stuff. In target areas, when it was socked in below, as it often was with air mass conditions over Europe, it was easy to report these conditions early on to help set up PFF runs. In such conditions we were strictly Deduced Reckoning so could not be sure of our own position. Fighter navigation was crude. In addition to a flight plan of times, headings and altitudes, Kodak leaders carried a one foot square plexiglass-covered map of the route and target. Luckily we got to know the area pretty good, flying over it so much, that, with some ground reference here and there, we probably got where we were supposed to most of the time.'[2]

Maj-Gen Kepner provided an overview of the Force's contribution: 'During the bad weather of winter operations, many missions were saved from failure by the excellent scouting of this force. The weather Scouting Force as part of heavy bomber operations is well proven and tested. The excellent plan developed by the SF has made it possible to exploit changing weather conditions in target areas distant from home bases and under conditions that weather forecasting is unable to cope with.'

By 17 August it was being stated that 'the establishment of a Scouting Force within each Division has been determined

Above: Col Bud Peasley, who was responsible for the creation of the 1st Scouting Force. (US National Archives)

to be a requirement which is highly desirable . . . Recommend that one Group in each fighter Wing be designated a fourth squadron as a means of providing a Scouting Force for each Division.'[3] On 2 September Lt-Gen James R. Doolittle, Eighth Air Forces commander, circulated a memorandum authorising a Scouting Force for each Division and the following day Kepner instructed the following changes to be made:

364th FG (Honington)	1st SF (first mission 1 Aug.)
355th FG (Steeple Morden)	2nd SF (first mission 26 Sep.)
55th FG (Wormingford)	3rd SF (first mission 15 Sep.)

[1] E. R. Atkins, *Fighting Scouts of the 8th Air Force*, Scouting Force Association, 1996.
[2] *Ibid.*
[3] Col Robert Landry.

Above: The 379th FG's Col Niven Cranfill, with Sgt Tony Chardella at left. (Anthony Chardella)

Right: A 25 February 1944 line-up of aircraft at the 2nd BAD. (Ken Delve Collection)

Meanwhile the 363rd FG was one of the units taking part in offensive sweeps over northern France, and on 18 July Lt Dick Asbury was leading one of the two 382nd FS four-ships that left Maupertus. They engaged a group of twelve Bf 109s and Asbury recalled:

'I started a tight circle to the left that soon went from level to half vertical. The 109 pilot on my tail was very good; he stayed with me through several circles, perhaps as many as four. As I went around, every time I crossed another 109 in range in front of me, I fired. I saw definite strikes on two of them, but I was unable to see the results. Finally I decided

to pull the circle as tight as I could; I was willing to spin if I had to. I pushed the throttle and prop pitch full forward, pulled the nose up quickly to bleed off a little speed and thus allowed greater manoeuverability at lower speeds. By increasing the lift over the wings in this manner, I was able to complete a much tighter turn where otherwise I might have spun out. Flaps could be used this way only momentarily, but I had become fairly proficient at this maneuver. I had a lot of confidence in the P-51. As long as I kept the air flowing over the wings, it would fly for me. *Queenie II* was a great airplane, and she didn't let me down. By applying stick and rudder, I pulled the airplane around so quickly that the 109 on my tail could not stay with me. In fact, I immediately wound up on its tail. As soon as the enemy pilot saw what was happening he reversed his turn and Split-essed – turned upside down and headed for the deck as fast as he could. As the 109 dived away, I followed. I finally closed to within firing range on him at low altitude and pulled the trigger. Lo and behold, only one of my four .50-caliber guns would fire – the outboard gun in my right wing. All the others must have jammed tight when I was firing them in my tight turns above. It was a common problem on the P-51B.

'I moved my gunsight to the 109's left wingtip and fired again. The recoil of the one gun kicked my airplane to the right slightly, but the motion allowed my bul-

lets to go from wingtip to wingtip. After the first burst, the German pilot did nothing more to evade me. This leads me to conclude that I wounded him. I fired twice more, dragging the bullets from my one gun from the left wingtip to the right wingtip both times. During the last burst, the 109's engine erupted with black smoke and appeared to stop. By this time we were at low altitude, so the German pilot headed to a little field and then crash-landed into it. He plowed a furrow and stopped, then the whole airplane erupted in flames.'[1]

Dick Asbury headed back to where he had left the main dogfight and found that more 109s had joined in, some of which he engaged without result. It had been a good day for the eight aircraft of the 382nd FS: they had claimed at least ten Bf 109s destroyed. Asbury's first combat tour was with the 382nd FS from August 1943 to August 1944, his first aerial success being scored on 25 June near Lisieux. The 18 July sortie was, however, his most successful with the unit – the confirmed Bf 109 plus two others damaged. Having completed his 200 operational hours, he was sent back to the United Kingdom, returning to the war in Europe in November with the 356th FS. April 1945 brought further success, and on three missions between 7 and 15 April he claimed three more German fighters and a half share in an He 111 bomber. Dick Asbury was one of those to be reunited with the Mustang for another war, flying F-51s (as the P-51 was designated by then) in the Korean War, whilst acting as an adviser with the Korean Air Force.

July also saw the 20th FG and 55th FG become operational with P-51Ds, flying their first combat missions on 19 and 20 July. At the end of the month the 364th FG at Honington was also in the process of converting to Mustangs, all part of the plan to re-equip the P-38 Groups in summer 1944.

The Mustang was proving to be an effective fighter in most combat scenarios. True, there were problems: the low

firepower provided by the machine guns, especially when these had a habit of jamming in high-G manoeuvres, caused a great deal of frustration. However, the young American pilots soon learned how to get the best performance out of their aircraft, particularly in the all-important turning fight. Lt Bob Goebel flew Mustangs with the 308th FS/31st FG:

'We concluded that our best chance to meet enemy fighters was to loiter in the target area after most of the attacking force had left for home. The logical thing

Top: Capt Binkley plus groundcrew, 20th FG. (Ken Delve Collection)

Above: Capt R. Phipps of the 20th FG explains his mission to the groundcrew. (Ken Delve Collection)

[1] *Aces Against Germany, op. cit.*

Top: Capt Hurst, 20th FG. (Ken Delve Collection)

Above: Maj Jack Ilfrey with *Happy Jack's Go Buggy*, 20th FG. (Ken Delve Collection)

nant sow. The standard procedure was to burn the fuselage tank down to 50 gallons immediately after take-off, even before going on external tanks, so that if the tanks had to be jettisoned unexpectedly you were already in a condition from which you could fight. Leaving 50 gallons in the fuselage tank involved some risk, but I didn't give it a second thought; I was getting pretty cocky, assuming that attitude of invincibility so common in fighter pilots. I had gained tremendous confidence in the Mustang and in my ability to fight with it.'[1]

During an escort sortie on 28 July the 359th FG's pilots reported a new threat – Me 163 rocket fighters, which they estimated were flying at over 500mph. Allied fighter pilots were aware of the existence of the German jets, but the initial combat experience against these aircraft (the Me 163 and, a short while later, the Me 262) was to prove unpromising. The 359th FG claimed one Me 163 shot down, by Col Murphy, and one damaged, by Lt Cyril Jones, on 16 August. Both pilots had seen the Me 163s of 1/JG 400 some way off and had predicted that they would head for a straggling bomber, thus allowing the Mustangs to get into a favourable position. The usual high-speed slash attack tactic by jets gave the escort fighters very little chance; indeed, the most successful counter-tactic was to be that of hitting the jets at their bases.

'Operational Suitability of the P-51D'

On 5 August 1944 Eglin Field issued its report on the 'Operational Suitability of the P-51D', having had P-51D-5-NA 44-13254 under evaluation from May. Once again, this latest Mustang variant acquired the accolade of 'the best long-range escort fighter tested at this station to date'. Throughout the report comparison and cross-reference was made to various version of the P-51B, the P-51D being in essence 'basically similar to the P-51B-5,

for us to do was to pull back the power as much as possible, thereby saving fuel and increasing our time in the target vicinity. Another way to extend the time aloft was to cheat a little on the fuselage tank. During the design of the early prototype P-51, an internal 85-gallon fuel tank was installed aft of the cockpit to supplement the 92 gallons in each wing. With a full fuselage tank the aircraft flew all right in normal attitudes, but, in a high-G turn, the aft center of gravity caused a stick reversal – the plane tended to wrap the turn tighter without any back pressure on the stick and to generally behave like a preg-

[1] *Aces Against Germany, op. cit.*

differing from it in four main respects: the power plant, the armament, the bomb racks and the canopy'. In fact it was nearer to the P-51B-15 as they both had the V-1650-7 engine and carried the same fuel – 185 gallons in the wings and 85 gallons in the fuselage tank. Amongst the general conclusions were that:

'f. The operational ceiling is approx 36,000 ft.

'g. The combat radius is approx 780 miles.

'h. With the fuselage tank full, the airplane is too unstable to perform combat maneuvers with safety . . .

'j. The six machine guns represent a very desirable increase in fire-power over the P-51B, and constitute adequate armament for this airplane. However, the installation as furnished requires some modification to attain functional reliability . . .

'l. Both the bubble and semi-bubble canopies provide a very marked improvement in search view and general visibility. The bubble canopy is preferable to the semi-bubble canopy in that it affords much better vision forward and downward . . .

'n. The green tinted canopy is very desirable in that it reduces the glare when flying in bright sunlight . . .

'p. The canopy leaks when flying through heavy rain.'

The main recommendation related to the question of fuel in the fuselage tank: 'Whenever possible, missions be so planned that the fuselage tank will contain no more than 35 gallons at the point where the pilot has a reasonable expectation of engaging in combat.' The Stability and Handling section expanded on this comment:

'When the fuselage tank is full, the airplane shows very marked static instability about the pitching axis. The airplane cannot be trimmed hands-off level flight, and stick forces reverse very rapidly in turns. Under this load condition, the airplane is not considered satisfactory for combat maneuvers. This instability is characteristic of all P-51 airplanes equipped with the fuselage tank, but it appeared to be a little more pronounced in the P-51D. The expenditure of ammunition or of fuel from any of the tanks moves the center of gravity forward and hence tends to improve the stability. Trials by five experienced pilots showed

Right: Capt Kolb, 350th FS. (US National Archives)

Below: A P-51D of the 351st FS/353rd FG. (US National Archives)

fine scratches. These scratches, though often too small to be noticed in a casual inspection, show up as bright concentric circles when the pilot looks at the sun. It is therefore desirable to keep the canopy covered with a hood when the airplane is not in use, and to exercise extreme care in cleaning and polishing the canopy.'

Despite the overwhelming nature of Allied air power, German ground forces were still able to put up strong resistance and on many instances the tactical aircraft were called upon to clear a 'blockage'. TacR aircraft hunted for suitable targets, often in liaison with ground-based tactical controllers (the concept of Forward Air Controllers operating with the ground forces was now well established), and then either attacking those targets themselves or, more usually, calling on the nearest squadron of fighter-bombers to come and deal with the problem. The P-51s of the 10th PRG were particularly adept at this and frequently led P-47 attack forces to targets – although this was in itself hazardous as on occasion the P-47s were inclined to have a go at the Mustangs that were trying to attract their attention! The Luftwaffe was also to be found from time to time, as Tony Jonsson noted in his Log Book for 29 July:

'Armed recce Dreux-Evreux. An exciting trip. We met a formation of aircraft in the Evreux area going in the opposite direction. At first they were reported as Spits, but turned out to be 109s. This left us at a disadvantage, but we jettisoned our bombs in a hurry and engaged them. We were outnumbered 3 to 1. The CO shot down a 109 and Sgt Holland was seen to be hit and blew up in the air. After a while the Huns withdrew, but a few moments later we met another large formation of 109s and 190s, and again we had a dogfight. We (only five of us) were badly outnumbered and therefore no-one had a chance to keep his sights on a Hun for any length of time. I had snapshots at about four different Huns, but each time I had to break away because I was being attacked myself. During this time I got hit

that with full ammunition load, and with the wing tanks full, the airplane becomes satisfactory for combat when 50 to 55 gallons have been expended from the fuselage tank, i.e. when 30–35 gallons remain.'

The new bubble canopy was greeted with great enthusiasm by all the test pilots, although a note of caution was sounded: 'As in any plexi-glass canopy, exposure to dust and careless polishing will mar the surface of the canopy with

Below: Lt Stapp and Lt Monaham re-live an encounter; 350th FS/ 353rd FG. (US National Archives)

in the tailplane, fuselage and port wing. At last I managed to get three bursts into a 190 and he went vertically into the ground.'[1]

As Allied forces spread out over France the air effort against German lines of communication, and especially rail communications, increased and all Allied tactical air power was called upon to attack trains, the aim being to destroy the locomotives as these remained the most critical aspect of the rail system (hence the medium bombers were targeted against locomotive repair facilities). River transport was also on the target list, and particular attention was paid to barges and tugs on the Seine in the first week of September.

The 12th TRS was reallocated in August to work with Patton's Third Army for its drive across France to the Seine and was given the vital role of checking bridges and roads for serviceability, and checking towns and woods for possible ambush sites. Patton was determined that nothing should slow his lightning advance. The Squadron flew 26 such missions in the first five days and could have done with the assistance of its sister unit from the 10th PRG; however, the 15th TRS still had to operate from Chalgrove as there was simply no airfield space in France for them. Nevertheless, one flight of the 15th

joined the 12th as the pace of operations continued, the F-6s flying dawn-to-dusk missions watching the flanks of the Third Army as it advanced. By 11 August the unit had moved forward to Rennes, being joined by the 15th TRS the following day.

The sterling work performed by the unit was recognised by General O. P. Weygand. who wrote: 'The spectacular successes achieved by the Third US Army in recent weeks would not have been possible without the prompt and accurate observation and reporting of the enemy disposition and movement, which was so efficiently provided by the 10th Photo Reconnaissance Group.'

The Polish fighter squadrons of the RAF were certainly maintaining the offensive spirit that they had first shown during the Battle of Britain and in the anti-V-weapon campaign. They were also taking part in the offensive sweeps over the Continent, and on 18 August the Brenzett-based No 315 Squadron flew 36 sorties. During one of these fighter sweeps the Squadron was operating near Beauvais airfield when they spotted 60 enemy aircraft – and promptly went in to the attack. By the end of the fight the Squadron had claimed six-

---

[1] As related in *Dancing in the Skies, op. cit.*

Right: A neat stack of P-51s on their return from a mission; 374th FS/361st FG. (Ken Delve Collection)

Left: Walter Konantz's first P-51 after its first mission. (Walter Konantz)

teen of the Fw 190s destroyed plus one probable and three damaged, although, sadly, the Squadron Commander, Sqn Ldr Eugeniusz Horbaczewski, flying Mustang III FB355, was shot down and killed after he had claimed three of his opponents. His combat career had begun with No 303 Squadron on Spitfires and continued through various campaigns until he took command of No 315 Squadron in February 1944, leading it through the V-weapon period, (he claimed four kills himself) and on into the offensive operations that, for him, ended on 18 August. He had scored 5.5 victories with the Mustang to bring his total to 16.5 destroyed plus one probable and one damaged.

For the RAF's No 122 Wing, the two months following D-Day brought intensive operations and they claimed 72 enemy aircraft, even though most tasking was against ground targets. One particularly good day for the Wing was 20 August, when Nos 19 and 65 Squadrons ran into twenty or more Fw 190s east of Paris and shot down nine of them, three falling to Flt Lt Lance Burra-Robinson. These were his first victories with No 65 Squadron, but he already had a number of air and ground victories whilst flying Mustang IIIs with No 122 Squadron. (The Wing returned to the United Kingdom the following month to become part of the escort force covering Bomber Command's daylight missions.)

By 23 August the Third Army was across the Seine and the Germans began to fall back to the next river line; sorties on 25 August reported large-scale rail movements of German forces in the Dijon–Besançon gap, and as a result of this intelligence XIX TAC units executed a 'rail cutting' plan to cut off this escape route and trap the German forces. The

Left: The 353rd FG peels off to land at Raydon. (Ken Delve Collection)

greatest land battle in late August was around the Falaise Gap, with Allied tactical air power smashing German armoured vehicles.

August proved to be a black month for the Luftwaffe as losses continued to rise amongst the fighter force and the effects of the Allied bombing campaign were becoming more evident. On 11 August Berlin ordered a restriction on flying within Luftflotte 3 because of the growing fuel crisis: fighters were permitted to undertake unrestricted operations only when required to combat Allied heavy bombers,

and all other flying was curtailed. The following month saw a major reorganisation of units which, along with the strong aircraft construction programme, meant that 1,260 single-engine fighters were allocated to the Defence of the Reich (a significant increase from the 850 on this task in April). The Strategic Bombing Offensive was having a major impact on German war industries and the defence of these industries was becoming critical. The stage was being set for some of the largest air battles of the war.

Meanwhile road and rail remained the main targets, and in mid-September – and in the face of Allied pressure – the German ground forces had no choice but to pull back, risking road travel by day: 'At 1515 the Squadron was airborne again on its greatest MT strafing expedition – the long awaited chance had arrived, German transport was pulling out of the Vimoutiers area and 19, like all the other squadrons in Normandy, sailed in and dealt von Kluge's elements a mortal blow. A total of 21 MT destroyed and 17 damaged was obtained on this one sortie.'[1] The

Far left: P-51 *Temptation*. Matthew Martin had to bale out of this aircraft on 5 December 1944 when the engine caught fire. He ended up as a prisoner of war. (Matthew Martin)

---

[1] No 19 Squadron ORB, 18 August 1944.

Squadron had not finished for the day, and after further sorties its claims had risen to 38 destroyed, 11 smoking and 42 damaged.

The Mustangs were soon being called upon to fly with 1,000lb bombs, but the initial sorties did not go well – there were instances of the bombs exploding during the dive and a number of aircraft were lost in this way. The arming system of the bomb was thought to be causing the problem but none of the experts could confirm this. During the investigation the aircraft reverted to using 500lb weapons.

Ground attack was, as already mentioned above, by no means an easy task. Apart from the risk from enemy action there was the problem of self-inflicted damage. It is essential when dropping bombs to avoid the fragmentation effect of the weapons – not always one's own but also those of others dropping in front, and there are numerous instances of aircraft being lost or damaged through such damage. The Mustang was particularly prone to damage when strafing as a percentage of bullets always ricochet and have a fair chance of striking the aircraft. The front end of the Mustang was vulnerable to such hits (unlike the somewhat more rugged P-47) and a number of aircraft were lost to this cause.

Other weapons were also being tested. In December the Mustangs of No 515 Squadron undertook 'bomb trials with 60lb HE bombs dropped into the sea to check whether the impact fuse of the long stick on the nose cap of the bomb is activated on contact with the water. It was found that the bomb detonated satisfactorily.'

September 11 was the first day for some time that the Luftwaffe rose in significant numbers to take on the attackers. One of the Allied missions that day was the third of the 'shuttle' raids, hitting oil targets at Chemnitz, before flying on to Russia, escort being provided by the 20th FG. Other oil targets were also attacked by other Divisions, and all came under heavy attack, the 'Bloody Hundredth's' (100th BG) B-17s being rescued by the 339th FG who shot down fifteen German fighters. The combined total of fighter claims was a record 116. Intense combats were also recorded over the next two days, and high scores once more cost the Luftwaffe fighter arm dearly.

As Bomber Command continued its series of daylight operations the need for

Right: Complete with two bombs, and sharkmouth design – a Mustang of No 112 Squadron at an airfield in Italy. Having flown Kittyhawks with the Desert Air Force since December 1941, the Squadron acquired Mustang IIIs in June 1944. (Ken Delve Collection)

fighter escort remained high, and in October a number of RAF Mustang units moved to Andrews Field for this work. The previous month No 234 Squadron had commenced its conversion to type and duly moved to Bentwaters to form another escort Wing along with Nos 64 and 118 Squadrons (the latter having acquired Mustangs in January).

Pounding the Enemy

The daylight bombing offensive was, of course, still in full swing and the fighter escort role being performed by the Mustang units – the majority of which were now equipped with the P-51D – remained crucial as the Luftwaffe was still present in large numbers. The aim of the fighters was to destroy the enemy and protect the bombers. Some units had particularly good days: on 25 August, for example, the 354th FG flew six fighter sweeps and ended the day with a claim for 51 enemy aircraft destroyed in the air and on the ground, a feat which earned the unit a Distinguished Unit Citation. This day's effort was a record for VIII Fighter Command and, indeed, the 354th ended the war as the most successful fighter unit with a total claims record of 956 kills (701 of which were air-to-air), 32 probables and 428 damaged – for the loss of 178 pilots.

The fighting capability of the P-51 was increased in the latter part of 1944 by the introduction of the Berger G-suit (to help counter the effects of G during a turning fight) and the K-14 gyroscopic gun sight: 'I moved the safety switch to the ON position for gun control and turned on power for the K-14 computing sight . . . my K-14 gunsight was working perfectly. I selected a 109 that happened to be in front of me . . . I kept the 109 in the sight from about 15 degrees to 0 degrees deflection and fired short bursts as I closed in. The 109 started to smoke, then it flamed and headed down . . . I came up behind the second 109, centred it in my K-14 sight, and fired a long burst . . . it started to tumble and smoke was pouring out and pieces were falling off . . . another 109 . . . I turned and pro-

ceeded to cut him off. When he was in range, as determined by my K-14 sight, I gave him a long burst. The K-14 sight was zeroed in perfectly . . .'[1]

The K-14, developed from a British sight, had been intended for bomber use but engineers at Bovingdon had suggested that it could be used by fighters. A number of sights were handed to the 357th FG for trial and one of their engineers, S/Sgt Idaho Augugliaro, devised a suitable mount for the P-51D. The Group's CO, Col Donald Graham, was impressed and in-

Top: An atmospheric 'men at work' photograph of No 213 Squadron's KH467. (Ken Delve Collection)

Above: A Mustang III of No 260 Squadron. Kittyhawks gave way to Mustangs in April 1944, by which time the Squadron was operating out of Cutella, Italy. (Ken Delve Collection)

[1] Rudy York of the 359th FG in Eric Hammel, *Aces Against Germany, op. cit.*

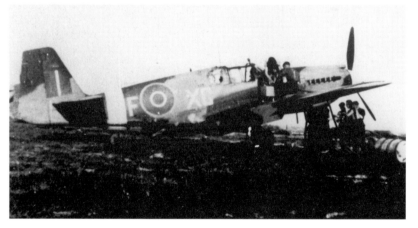

Top: P-51s of the 31st FG. (Roger Freeman Collection)

Above: Mustang I AG425 of No 26 Squadron, early 1945. (Andy Thomas Collection)

the legs and thus increase the pilot's G tolerance. The 4th FG had evaluated the British Frank Suit in March/April and found it unsatisfactory. By June the 339th FG had received a number of American Berger suits, which used compressed air rather than water, a type that was already being used by Ninth Air Force P-47 pilots. Initial impressions were favourable and Berger suits were issued to the 4th FG the same month. The G-3 suit had been developed from the 18lb Navy suit after tests at the Aero Medical laboratory at Wright Field: '. . . a pair of pneumatic pants weighing 2 lbs and containing air bladders which fill with compressed air from the airplane's vacuum instrument pump . . . several thousand G suits were shipped overseas to fighter units in 1944 and they achieved immediate popularity among the men who have to wear them.'[1]

Throughout 1944 the 'Little Friends' did a superb job of looking after their bombers, and although bomber losses remained high there was little doubt now that the Luftwaffe fighter force was being bled to death – especially in regard to pilot experience. There was no shortage of fighters from the production lines in Germany, but pilots, and aviation fuel, were becoming more difficult to obtain in sufficient quantity.

One of the major problems of high-level escort missions was that of cold – and the RAF suffered badly: 'Oh how dreadfully cold it was up there at 35,000 feet. We sat there motionless for over 3 hours in biting frost and no matter how many items of clothing one wore, the cold seeped through them into one's bones and marrow so that one's legs and arms felt like frozen logs . . . how we envied our American colleagues their electrically heated flying suits.'[2]

Others found the summer months somewhat frustrating: '. . . that summer of 1944 was a dry gulch for those of us eager to mix it up with the Germans. The real fun of combat was at the end of a day of ac-

structed that the rest of his fighters be modified. The 'Leiston mod', as it became known, was subsequently adopted by the other P-51 Groups and by late autumn the K-14 was well established.

The G-suit, designed to give pilots protection from the effects of G during high-energy manoeuvring, was another innovation entering service. With the onset of positive G the blood drains from the upper parts of the body (head first) and tries to end up in the legs. This causes 'grey out' and 'black out', leading to loss of combat effectiveness. The G-suit was designed to constrict the flow of blood into

[1] Commanding General's 3rd Report.
[2] Tony Jonsson, *op. cit.*

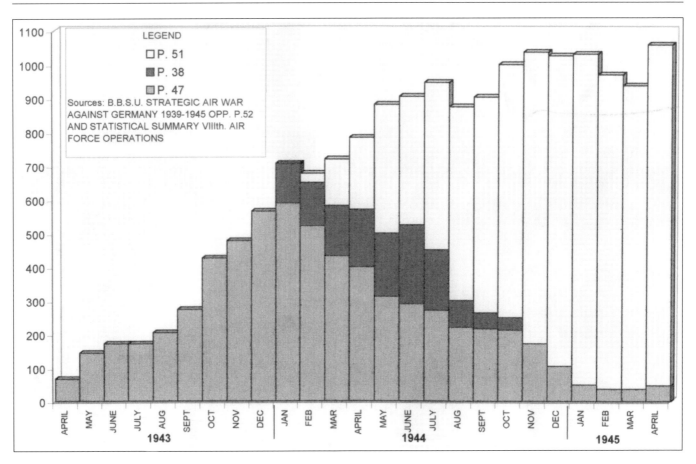

tion, when we'd sit around in the Nissen hut set aside as an Officers' Club, drinking scotch and eating spam sandwiches while chattering like a bunch of bluejays – refighting our dogfights or refining our high angle deflection shots that nailed a 109.'[1]

Mustang IV

The RAF began to operate the Mustang IV in September 1944, the first 30 aircraft being P-51Ds (with the V-1650-7 engine) from the Inglewood plant. However, the remainder of the production deliveries were P-51Ks from Dallas and were designated Mustang IVA by the RAF. Significant changes on previous variants included six 0.50in guns and a clear-visibility bubble canopy, and as this latter meant a narrower fuselage, a dorsal fillet was added to maintain the handling characteristics. The variant served with Fighter Command in the escort role and with the Desert Air Force, operating in Italy, for both escort and ground-attack duties.

Walter Konantz was airborne on 11 September as part of the 55th FG's escort group for B-17s of the 3rd Air Division raiding a synthetic oil plant in Germany. The sortie resulted in a somewhat hair-raising experience:

'Take-off and form up was normal and the three squadrons spread out in escort formation just at our rendezvous time with our bombers. I had noticed a bunch of tiny specks up ahead but without a closer look had dismissed them as P-51 escorts from another 8th Air Force fighter group. I had drunk a second cup of coffee at the Mess some three hours ago and the urge to get rid of some of this had become quite painful! The P-51 had a relief tube stored in a clip under the seat – a plastic cone with a rubber tube running out of the bottom of the airplane and venting overboard. In order to use this appliance, it was necessary to undo the seat belt and shoulder harness as well as the leg straps

[1] Chuck Yeager, *Yeager*, Century Hutchinson, 1985.

Left: A chart showing the changes in fighter equipment of the Eighth Air Force. The dominance of the P-47 had given way to that of the P-51 by May 1944, and by the end of the year virtually all squadrons had re-equipped. (Ken Delve Collection)

and parachute/dinghy combination and scoot well forward on the seat in order to "make the connection". I was in this position when I heard a voice over the radio . . . "Me 109s, here they come!" I looked up just in time to see 50 or 60 Me 109s streaming through our formation in a 45 degree dive with their guns firing. Fortunately none had picked me as a target but one crossed right in front of me firing at a Mustang below and to my left. These were the first enemy airplanes I had ever laid eyes on and buck fever caused me to roll over in a dive after the Me 109. He saw me coming and steepened his dive to the vertical. We were both now headed straight down from 24,000 feet in a wide open power dive. Both airplanes were very skittish from the extremely high speed and since I was not strapped in, the slightest movement of the stick caused me to leave the seat and hit the canopy above. We passed through a layer of slight turbulence and I felt like a basketball being dribbled down a court. The 109 was having as much trouble as me, his plane was bucking and skidding as both of us were nearing compressibility. At about 10,000 ft I initiated a steady 4g pull-out and the Me 109 started to pull out at about the same time, but before he had raised his nose more than 30 degrees his right wing ripped off through the wheel well and he spun into the ground in a matter of seconds. He had no time to get out before the aircraft impacted and exploded in a

wooded area. Just before I started my pullout I glanced at the airspeed indicator and saw the needle at 600 mph – 95 mph over the red line speed of 505. One of our pilots counted the fires on the ground after this huge dog fight and reported to the Intelligence Officer at debriefing that he had counted 30 fires on the ground. Our Squadron had claimed 28 Me 109s for the loss of two P-51s and my claim was allowed even though I had no camera film of the victory.

'After parking my plane, I had climbed out on the wing ready to jump down when my crew chief said – "Hey Lieutenant, better zip up your pants before you go in to debriefing."'[1]

On 10 October the Eighth Air Force underwent a reorganisation, VIII Fighter Command giving up its three Fighter Wings to the three Bombardment Divisions – the 65th FW to the 2nd BD, the 66th FW to the 3rd BD and the 67th FW to the 1st BD. The move was not as radical or restrictive as it might appear and the Fighter Groups still enjoyed great flexibility of action. October was a quiet month operationally, the air battles of September and the general impact of the bomber offensive on Luftwaffe capability having reduced the combat effectiveness of the enemy fighter force. There were, however, increasing reports of small numbers of jet fighters – and the occasional

---

[1] Walter Konantz, personal communication.

Right: Biggin Hill, February 1945: Mustang IV KH765 of No 154 Squadron. (Andy Thomas Collection)

P-51 success against Me 163s and Me 262s. Lt Urban Drew, for example, knocked down two of the latter as they took off from Achmer (this being the home of Kommando Nowotny, which had become operational in September as the first Me 262 unit). These 7 October victories were Drew's final scores of the war – bringing his total to six confirmed – as he left the 375th FS in early November to return to the United States.

October 18 saw Lt Godden of No 541 Squadron in FX952 on a four-hour sortie to photograph the Sorpe Dam – 'the first low level sortie for several years to penetrate behind the Ruhr'. His report was summarised in the unit ORB:

'Height 4,000 ft for Vatach 800 ft–3,000 ft for oblique. 1700 hours. Target Job 854 BC Sorpe Dam. Photos of Rhine at Rheinsbrohl factory at Dattenfeld, factory working at full blast. No photos of Bonn due to heavy smoke. Sorpe Dam – 5 runs. First oblique at 3,000 ft, verticals at 4,000 ft, discovering balloons close hauled, pilot came down to 800 ft and did further obliques of both sides of dam. On last run ran into point blank light flak – all tracer and very accurate. Pilot fired back. Pilot reports that dam not breached, that there appears to have been some seepage running from central crater into compensating basin. Pilot claims strikes on locomotive in Ludenscheid area.'

In October No 26 Squadron re-acquired a number of Mustangs – having given up the type in favour of Spitfires the previous March – and by December the ORB was recording: 'All pilots are now polishing up their Mustang flying after not having flown this type for six months.' An operational detachment was maintained at Coltishall, whilst in January the main part of the Squadron moved to Harrowbeer, although on 21 January it was on the move again – to North Weald.

The reconnaissance aircraft were encountering increasing numbers of enemy aircraft as the Allied advance pushed further into France. Losses began to mount, but the missions were of crucial impor-

tance and had to be flown. There were also too many instances of Allied fighters attacking the recce aircraft: for example, Lt Shaeffer of the 10th PRG was shot down by P-47s on 29 September.

At times the recce pilots had to improvise. One such occasion was on 20 October, when two 12th TRS pilots, Lt Donald Lynch and Lt Max Burkhalter, found a 280mm railway gun. They tried to call down artillery fire but had problems with the R/T, so, rather than lose such a valuable target, Burkhalter orbited over the artillery contact car to act as a radio relay whilst Lynch made dive attacks at the target and called the fall of shot. Some 70 rounds landed in the target area. Don Lynch was awarded the Silver Star.

The Allies launched the next phase of their offensive on 11 November. Air power was once again to the forefront of the plan, the various TacR units flying intensive operations in the first few days, although poor weather from 10 to 16 November proved somewhat restrictive. On 17 November aircraft of the 10th PRG reported over 300 trains 'east and west of the Rhine', indicating a major German movement of forces towards the Third Army zone of operations. One of the more successful missions flown that day was the visual recce of the Metz–Merzig–Sarrelautern area made by Lt Mingo Logothetis and Lt Max Burkhalter of the 12th TAC R. During their mission they reported:

Right: F-6D 44-13666: a good, clear photograph of the camera fit. (Ken Delve Collection)

Left: Walter Konantz shot down an Me 262 on 13 January 1945. This was the first such victory for the 55th FG. (Walter Konantz)

'Merzig marshaling yards ° full, seven engines with steam. Haze and smoke made observation difficult over Merzig. Photos taken at Q1391, small marshaling yard – five trains, no engines with steam up. Several oil tank cars in trains. L3101 one train headed east with five plus boxcars. Scattered vehicular traffic east and west along highways. Q3799 one train stationary, headed west with steam up. Five oil tank cars and several box cars. Q2495 entrenchment's and tank traps running north and south. L5012 train headed northwest, make-up undetermined. Q5996 steam coming from underpass, probably train at marshaling yards St Wendell – 1.3 full three trains with steam up. Q0875 photos taken of town. Q3789 enemy vehicles along side of road – stationary headed north. Q3369 train moving north with 10 plus box cars. Q9669 appears to be railroad siding or spur. U9974 convoy of 12 plus trucks, some with trailers, in village between Worms and Mainz. Five plus trains, unable to pinpoint due to weather. No flak or enemy aircraft encountered.'

All that from a single sortie! The amount of information flowing from the Allied reconnaissance units was simply amazing.

This was backed up by further missions the following day, and the intelligence assessment was that a Panzer division was being moved to the area; this was, indeed, to prove part of the build-up of German forces for the Ardennes counter-offensive. It was essential that a close watch be kept on German movements, and as part of this the 10th PRG was tasked in early December to 'provide coverage from Trier to Koblenz to Mannheim to Zweibrucken, and the areas near the battle zones were to be covered three times daily. In addition, four reconnaissance routes were to be flown twice daily covering the main railway lines and highways as far NE as Kassel.'[1]

'Lightweight Mustang'

Development of the P-51 continued, and in October the 'Lightweight Mustang' (P-51F/Mustang V) was under test by the A&AEE at Boscombe Down. The summary to the report on these tests stated that 'Brief handling trials have been com-

[1] Tom Ivie, *Aerial Reconnaissance – 10th PRG*, op. cit.

pleted on this aircraft (FR409) which is an experimental lightweight version of the Mustang. In general, the aircraft was found pleasant and easy to fly. Compared with the previous Mustang III and IV aircraft tested, there was an improvement in view, due to the use of a larger cockpit hood. There was also a marked improvement in take-off and climb performance, due chiefly to the reduced all-up weight.'

The total weight-saving was around 1,500lb – a significant figure when compared with the average loaded weight for a Mustang III of around 9,200lb. The report went into some detail regarding a range of handling and performance aspects of the aircraft. The conclusions were generally very favourable, the only significant criticisms being 'the heaviness of the rudder, causing lack of harmony with the other controls, and the large change of directional trim with speed and power'.

Memorable Mission

If October had been quiet, November was to open with a bang. On 2 November almost 700 B-17s in five waves headed for the Merseburg oil plants. The morning sorties by the 3rd Division had an escort of 400-plus P-51s, and these were soon engaged with over 100 enemy fighters, shooting down nineteen for the loss of one Mustang. A short time later it was the turn of the 1st Division, and their 200 P-51s, to encounter the enemy. The 352nd FG claimed 38 destroyed; 28 fell to the 328th FS, a new record, with their CO, Maj George Preddy, downing a Bf 109 to become the Eighth's leading ace (with a score of 24° plus five strafed). Other Groups were similarly engaged, and the day's score ended as the second highest to date at 134–3–25. American losses were relatively light – 26 B-17s and eight P-51s.

Jack Ilfrey recounted a memorable mission he flew with his wingman, Duane Kelso, with the 79th FS/20th FG on 20 November 1944:

'On this particular afternoon I led a flight of five P-51Ds to a rendezvous with two P-38 'Photo Joes', escorted and covered them while they took pictures over and around Berlin. It was our habit, after

Right: Work in progress on a 353rd FG P-51 and a P-47 in a hangar, 26 June 1945. (US National Archives)

Below: Maj W. Barley and *Double Trouble Two*, 352nd FS. (US National Archives)

escort, to hit the deck and get our kicks ground strafing targets of opportunity on the way back home to England. By this time we were secure in the knowledge that those P-51s made us feel like hunters in the skies over Germany. Our morale was high, during ground strafing, chasing or evading their fighters, during dog fights, just firing the guns.

'We spiraled down through a hole in the cloud and sure enough found plenty of trucks and other equipment heading towards the front lines. We were now heading in a westerly direction and at the same

Right: Honington, 22 February 1945: a P-51 of the 364th FG (44-15576) has returned with a 'significant amount of damage'. (US National Archives)

time sliding under a rather massive weather front. I had been busy shooting 'em up and didn't know exactly where we were. I told the boys to form up, let's get together and head for home. It was a little after 1600 hours so I set course for England, figuring that, because of fuel and the approach of darkness, we might have to land in France or Belgium. We were in good tight formation with me still trying to get my bearings when we came right up on Maastricht – still in German hands – and were given a hot reception. As we turned east to avoid the flak my wingman, Kelso, called that he had been hit and was losing power. We were around 7–800 ft in poor visibility but we were getting away from the front lines. I had just seen a cleared stretch which appeared to be a small emergency type strip. I pointed it out to him and told him to try for it and that I'd attempt to cover him. Knowing that we were almost out of ammo and low on fuel I told the other three boys that they were on their own.

'Kelso and I were picking up ground fire and I stayed as low to the trees as possible. He made a rather hairy wheels down landing, stopped right near the edge of the trees and jumped out. I was aware that he had been fired on while landing but I came in to land almost immediately – being fired on as well – God, what a hairy landing, dodging holes, muddy as hell but my airplane, *Happy Jack's Go Buggy*, made it. I taxied the short distance to where Kelso was waiting, set park brakes, jumped out on the wing, took off my chute and dinghy and got him into the seat. We immediately discovered that four legs were not going to fit and allow me full rudder control, so I stood up and got him to cross his legs – and then I sat down on his legs, head sticking up! So there I was, head and neck bent down, knees almost up to my chin and started a most hairy take-off. Almost castrated myself pulling back on the stick. For a second I thought we weren't going to make it, threw down some flaps and *Go Buggy* pulled up over the trees. We made a short hop to the airfield

at Brussels and I returned to Kings Cliffe the next day – to a not very friendly reception from the Group CO, Col Rau, who was of the opinion that Squadron Commanders should not risk themselves on such antics.'[1]

It was obvious by late 1944 that the war in the West was all but won and that, barring any unforeseen disaster, Germany would be defeated in early 1945. The situation in the Far East was not, however, as simple, and there was a need to revise the 'Germany first' policy and build up strength in the Pacific Theatre. As part of this general revision, a November 1944 review of aircraft supply reduced RAF orders for the P-51 from 785 to 605, and whilst this reflected RAF projections for 1945 aircraft requirements it was also partly due to an acute need by the USAAF for the type – especially for operations in the Pacific. A further change was made in Eighth Air Force fighter organisation this month, with operational training units being created within each combat Fighter Group: new pilots from the USA were allocated to their respective Groups rather than, as previously, the 495th and 496th FTGs. These latter Training Groups continued to function as sources of refresher training for Eighth Air Force pilots as well

Right: Aircraft from the 374th FS/361st FG, February 1945. (Ken Delve Collection)

[1] Personal communication.

Left: *Jersey Jerk* as part of the escort returning from Lutzkendorf, 9 February 1945. (Ken Delve Collection)

as 'processing' pilots for the Ninth Air Force.

As part of the Luftwaffe's development in the latter part of 1944, Adolf Galland, as Inspector of Fighters, '. . . evolved a plan by which, instead of fighter strength being used as heretofore dissipated by frequent weak attempts at interception, it would be built up to deal a series of concentrated attacks against the daylight raids. Galland was able to inform the Ops Staff that the fighter force was ready to undertake this operation, named *Der Grosse Schlag* (The Big Blow) in November. The few occasions, however, when it was possible during the autumn of 1944 to secure the large-scale employment of the fighter force did not bring the success which had been hoped for.'[1]

By mid-November the Luftwaffe's single-engine fighter force had grown to 3,300 aircraft as a veritable flood of new machines arrived from the now dispersed (and often underground) factories. The problems of pilots and fuel, however, remained acute. Paper numbers were no reflection of the real situation: on 21 November, for example, only two formations of fighters, of 170 and 180 aircraft, were airborne to intercept the American raids (700 B-17s plus 650 Mustangs), and, of these, only six and 30 aircraft respectively actually engaged the bombers. This was a day when the Luftwaffe had called for a maximum fighter effort. A few days later, on 26 November, approximately 400 German fighters were in the air to engage American formations around Hanover – and promptly lost 25 per cent of their number. Lt Jack Daniell of the 505th FS/339th FG was in his first combat, and claimed five Fw 190s. (He remained with the 505th to March 1945 but was unable to add to his score.) Despite the heavy losses, almost twice as many German fighters were active the following day, but it was evident that many of their pilots were inexperienced as they made little attempt at combat manoeuvres. The 357th FG promptly knocked down 30 of the group that they engaged; other Fighter Groups also scored highly and the day's tally rose to 98.

In July the RAF Mustang force had started escorting Coastal Command anti-shipping strikes, the first unit to undertake this task being No 315 Squadron. These missions were largely uneventful. December 7 proved to be the most successful day when the Squadron, operating from Peterhead and escorting a Beaufighter/Mosquito force to Norwegian waters, tangled with fifteen Bf 109s and Fw 190s near Gossen. Although one Mustang was shot down, the Poles claimed four Bf 109s and two Fw 190s destroyed plus a further two probables. The policy decision to escort such Coastal Command strikes had been agreed by Leigh-Mallory in January, although fears had been expressed as to the 'great strain to pilots flying single-engined aircraft for 3–4 hours at a stretch over the sea, the difficult weather conditions likely to be encountered and the navigation problems which the flights involved.'[2] The escort mission was to continue to the end of the war with various squadrons undertaking the task.

---

[1] *The Rise and Fall of the German Air Force*, op. cit.
[2] AHB Narrative, *Air Defence of Great Britain*, Vol. IV.

A good day for Nos 64 and 126 Squadrons was 4 May 1945, when they came across a group of U-boats near Kiel, which they promptly strafed, claiming five as damaged.

Battle of the Bulge

On 17 December 1944 the Germans launched a major offensive on a 70-mile front centred on the US First Army in the Ardennes. Twenty German divisions smashed through the thin American front lines and Panzer spearheads were soon exploiting the breakthrough. The initial German success was also a major failing of Allied intelligence as it caught the Allies completely by surprise. Intensive air operations were flown by both sides and numerous air combats took place.

The reconnaissance squadrons were heavily tasked but also became involved in a number of fights – with some success. John Hoefker of the 15th TRS, already a rarity in the recce world by being an ace, claimed 3½ (although the two Bf 109s were not confirmed). Two weeks later he was being chased by P-47s (another 'misident') and whilst avoiding the American fighters was shot down by flak. Having reached the ground in one piece, he was then shot at by Allied infantry!

Two days after the start of the offensive the weather turned foul. Part of the German plan was to seek a period of bad weather in order to negate the overwhelming Allied air supremacy, although major fighter reinforcements had been moved to the area, over 20 Gruppen (1,200 aircraft) having been transferred from Reich Defence duties. However, the need for air reconnaissance meant that pilots had to carry on. On 21 December Capt Travis of the 10th PRG volunteered to fly a mission to the Bastogne area. The cloud base was only 50ft and the visibility 100yds, but somehow he managed to locate and record both German and American positions – and earned a well-deserved Silver Star. The following day Patton's counter-attack reached the area. It was not until 23 December that the weather finally cleared enough for the Allied aircraft to play a significant role in the developing battle. Air power was by no means the sole Allied element that caused the failure of the German offensive but it was certainly very significant. By 26 December the Germans had started to fall back, their most advanced spearheads having fallen just short of the River Meuse.

Attacks from Italy

The Axis forces were under pressure not only from the offensive in the West but also from the south as the advance up Italy continued. Once again tactical air power was playing a crucial role, with both American and RAF units flying Mustangs in this theatre. Four Fighter Groups re-equipped with P-51Ds in spring 1944, the 52nd with the Twelfth Air Force and the 31st, 325th and 332nd with the Fifteenth. Long-range bomber-escort missions were flown from April onwards, the first major operation taking place on the 21st of that month when the 31st FG escorted B-24s to attack the oil refineries at Ploesti in Romania. It was a good day for the Mustangs and they claimed 17 destroyed, seven probables and 10 damaged for the loss of two aircraft, the mission earning them a Distinguished Unit Citation. Other escorts were flown against the same target, the destruction of the vital Ploesti oil installations being given a high priority by the Allied planners, and a number of these saw the attackers fly on to bases in Russia, including, as related above, 'shuttle' missions flown from the United Kingdom.

The MTO (Mediterranean Theatre of Operations) acquired its first P-51 ace on 23 April when Frederick Trafton (308th FS) shot down three enemy aircraft (to add to his existing tally of two) whilst on escort duties to Wiener Neustadt. After downing the third one he was shot down and taken prisoner.

Aircraft of the Fifteenth Air Force flew their first Operation 'Frantic' (shuttle bombing to Russia) mission on 2 June, Lt Col Chester Sluder leading the escort for

Below: *Denver Belle* of the 364th FG showing combat damage, February 1945. (Ken Delve Collection)

the B-17s; the P-51s of the 325th FG landed at Piryatin. On 'Frantic II' (22 July), the 31st FG escorted P-38s of the 82nd FG (as bombers) to Poltava; three days later they attacked the airfield at Midec. The 307th FS also strafed a convoy – and fifteen minutes later spotted a formation of Stukas near Jaroslev and downed 27 of them.

The Mustang was also operating from Italy in the TacR and interdiction role. In July 1944 No 112 Squadron gave up its Kittyhawks (having flown the type for much of its time with the Desert Air Force in North Africa and on into the Italian campaign). The Squadron history (unpublished) records that 'Operations in Mustangs did not start until July 5, but the previous four days were very busy in testing the new aircraft and looking for snags. These snags included canopies flying off and bombs failing to release correctly.' It continued a few days later with:

'Bombs continued to hang up on the 14th, one on the first mission and one on the second. This led to one pilot, Fg Off Newton, spending a couple of nerve-racking hours in the air trying to get rid of it. Flying in FB287 the bomb was without a fin and consequently it was armed; this made it impossible for Fg Off Newton to land and he was ordered to bale out. The pilotless aircraft circled him a couple of times and then hit the sea and exploded.' The problem with the bombs was to continue throughout July and a number of 'experts' arrived to try and devise a solution.

The RAF had been increasing its Mustang strength elsewhere in spring, No 260 Squadron giving up its Kittyhawks in April for Mustang IIIs and No 213 Squadron replacing its Spitfires with Mustang IIIs in May. The former moved to San Angelo in late May and the latter to Leverano in July.

In July the 332nd FG (the famous 'Tuskegee Airmen', a coloured unit) had begun operations with P-51s, having flown P-39s and P-47s. They were to acquire a reputation for sticking to their bomber charges like glue, a principal hammered home by the CO, Lt-Col Benjamin Davis: '. . . your job is to keep enemy fighters away from the bombers. Your job is not to shoot down enemy fighters and become an ace.' The unit nevertheless notched up a high score, the strafing of Romanian airfields

on 30 August, for example, bringing 83 claims.

As part of the overall Allied strategy it was decided that an amphibious force, supported by airborne landings, should assault southern France. The air element of Operation 'Dragoon' included a number of Mustang units. On 14 August, for example, No 112 Squadron moved to Rosignano in order to fly escort cover for a Horsa glider assault.

On 18 August 1944 the 31st FG were part of the escort on a bombing mission to the oilfields at Ploesti, Romania. Bob Goebel was on that mission and it was not long before combat was joined with a group of Bf 109s:

'"Border Black Leader, break left," I called – I saw about half of them turn away from us, and the rest followed Tommy and his wingman. As I got partway around, I caught sight of them again. I could see that they hadn't closed on Tommy, and they didn't seem to be turning hard. I whipped up into a wingover and came barreling down in the opposite direction, picking out the nearest one. I waited until I couldn't miss, and then cut loose with all six .50s. I poured a steady hail into him at very close range. The pilot left the 109 immediately.

'Pulling up slightly, I made a quick check around me and spotted another one low and ahead on the left. I was still at max throttle and had come down below 10,000 ft, so I was really moving. I closed on him very fast, almost on the deck, and I got strikes all over him with the first burst. I held the trigger down for another second when, suddenly, the cockpit canopy whipped off and he came hurtling out. When I looked around, I was alone in the sky. I had no idea of where my wingman was and only a vague idea of where I was. As I reduced my throttle and prop settings and checked my fuel, I tried to raise Tommy on the radio but without success. I set power for a climb back up to altitude and began making sharp turns every ten seconds or so to clear my tail as I climbed.

'BANG! The aircraft shuddered. I broke right by reflex as I went to full power. Then I sneaked a peek back. Sure enough, there were two 109s coming hard with black smoke pouring out of their exhaust stacks from the water injection. I continued my max-rate turn, and then we went through some violent gyrations, but they didn't seem to press the attack. They broke off the engagement, probably assuming that I would be more than a little relieved and willing to do the same. Logic was on their side; I should have jumped at the opportunity to break off the fight 600 miles from home, low on fuel and ammo. No chance! My adrenaline really flowing now, and I was determined to have a go at them.'

Bob Goebel caught up with the 109s and managed to shoot one down before he ran out of ammunition. He made it safely back to San Severo 'running on fumes'. Between 29 May and 28 August Goebel was credited with the destruction of eleven enemy fighters, plus one probable – all Bf 109s.

As in northern Europe, airfield strafing had become an increasing part of the Mustang's role. For example, the 4th FS, having completed an escort task on 29 August, found an airfield packed with 100 or more Me 323s. They used up all their ammunition and caused havoc amongst the German gliders. Two days later the parent Group, the 52nd FG, was awarded

Right: Maj E. Bankey with *Lucky Lady VII* of the 364th FG, 23 March 1945. Bankey ended the war with his P-51 score at 8.5 enemy aircraft destroyed. (Ken Delve Collection)

used their bombs on 20 barges that they found there; two barges were destroyed and two badly damaged. The formation then split up and Red Section flew north, train hunting in the Padua–Vicenza area, and later to Istrana and Treviso. By the time they returned to base at 0850 they had 11 engines destroyed and one damaged. Blue Section under Flt Lt Hearn went to the Udine area and claimed 17 locos destroyed.'

During this sortie Sgt Jones, flying HB925, was shot down by flak and was picked up by ASR Walrus: 'Sgt Daniel and Lt Lund took-off at 1000 to cover the rescue and at 1025 saw a Walrus land and pick up the pilot. The Walrus was being shelled and it found that it could not take-off, so a Catalina was called in. The Walrus was taxying around and the Catalina, which was behind it, could not get it to stop. The Catalina asked the two Mustangs to do a beat up of the Walrus to bring it to a halt.' This was accomplished and Sgt Jones was duly transferred to the Catalina.

November saw little change in the activities of the RAF's Mustang units in Italy, rail and road targets being the favoured prey. A number of squadron records make reference to dropping 'fire bombs' (napalm) from 100–150ft at about 300kts in a dive, but there is little comment as to the effectiveness of the tactic.

The squadrons flew a number of operations over Yugoslavia, often in support of Balkan Air Force medium bombers. No 213 Squadron, for example, operated from Biferno from mid-July.

'Bodenplatte'

As 1945 opened there could be little doubt that the Luftwaffe was 'on the ropes'. There appeared to be no shortage of aircraft, but trained and, even more crucially, experienced pilots were in short supply. Nevertheless, the Luftwaffe fighter force in the West played one more card – a massive attack by 1,000 aircraft against Allied airfields in Europe in an attempt to blunt Allied air power. The great Luftwaffe

a Distinguished Unit Citation for operations over Romania on 31 August 1944.

By September the major effort was being expended in attacks on the enemy lines of communication in Italy – and especially the rail network. Operation 'Strangle' had been designed to throttle the German supply lines and had been in operation for some months, and, with stalemate on the ground, even greater efforts were made to destroy enemy re-supply and reinforcement routes.

In September the Mustang IIIs of No 112 Squadron flew 712 operational sorties (1,040 hours), dropping 363 tons of bombs and firing 179,540 rounds of ammunition. The diary records that 9 September was a particularly good day, the Squadron claiming thirteen locomotives, one 1,200-ton ship, one Ju 88 shot down by Flt Lt Hearn, five aircraft destroyed on the ground (one He 111, one Ju 52 and three SM.79s) and a further thirteen aircraft damaged on the ground. The attacks against rail communications increased as the weeks went by, and the No 112 Squadron book records that '. . . 28 locos were clobbered before breakfast on October 21 by another long range recce of Northern Italy by Red and Blue Section. Taking off at 0630, all the aircraft flew direct to the Adige River and

Left: A 353rd FG P-51B – 43-6800? – on 1 January 1945, having returned with no tail. (US National Archives)

offensive of New Year's Day 1945, Operation 'Bodenplatte', was an unmitigated disaster for the Germans. This attempt to cause fatal damage to the Allies' tactical air power by destroying it on the ground met with only limited success, but the Luftwaffe itself lost a large number of aircraft and pilots. Although the attacks were made early in day, a number of Allied aircraft were already airborne. For example, at Gilze Rijen No 268 Squadron had an aircraft damaged on the ground whilst it was taxying out, but of those already airborne on TacR sorties Flt Lt A. Mercer shot down a Ju 88 near Utrecht whilst Flt Lt J. Lyke claimed one of the Fw 190 escorts.

One of the greatest successes of the day fell to the 352nd FG, which was airborne when the Germans appeared and engaged 50-plus enemy aircraft, claiming about half of them for no loss. Lt Col John Meyer's 487th FS did particularly well, Meyer himself shooting down two Fw 190s. (He was to end the war with 25 confirmed victories, all but three of them in a P-51.) The unit received a Distinguished Unit Citation for its actions.

On 13 January the now-famed 55th FG scored its first victory over the Me 262. Walter Konantz relates the story:

'The 55th FG was on a freelance area support mission instead of our usual bomber escort missions. We were also trimmed down from the usual 50 planes to just 37 P-51s. The 338th Squadron had just three flights totaling 12 planes. The three squadrons spread out to search for targets of opportunity. The 338th, having destroyed on the ground at Giebelstadt airfield just a week before, headed for this field to see if there were any left. The twelve Mustangs were circling the field at about 5,000 ft, planning our strafing routes and picking out targets on the ground.

'At this point I saw a plane taxiing onto the runway and was surprised to see him take off. I would have thought we had been seen and the tower would have advised him to park the plane and seek shelter. I called out the now airborne plane but no-one else saw him. He continued climbing, made a 180 degree turn and came back directly under me headed in the opposite

Left: Pilots of the 353rd FG wish each other luck before another mission. (US National Archives)

direction. I did a tight 180 and ended up about 200 yds behind him. At this point, he had built up enough speed that I was no longer closing on him even though I was at full throttle and had made a diving turn behind him. The new K-14 gyroscopic gunsight had only been installed in this plane a week earlier and I had never fired the guns with this sight before. It worked perfectly and the German plane, now identified as an Me 262, was saturated with nearly 40 hits. He made no evasive action whatsoever, possibly the pilot had been hit. His left engine burst into flame and the Me 262 [made] a slow descending spiral and crashed about 2 miles from the airfield.

'I still had some ammunition left so I headed back towards the airfield and picked out a twin-engined plane as a strafing target and commenced my pass. The other Mustangs had already strafed and all the flak gunners were alert and ready for me. Light flak was coming from all directions. I continued my pass until I got within range of my target and saw that it was a burned out hulk from last week. I did not fire my guns but kept very low until I passed the boundary of the field. Somewhere on the pass, a single small calibre bullet came into the cockpit from the left side and cut a 6 inch groove in my jacket sleeve and struck the radio control box on the right side of the cockpit – this put my radio out of commission. I headed west looking for any Allied airplanes I could follow back to England and eventually met up with a P-47 who took me to his base at St Trond, Belgium.'[1]

The following day was one on which the Luftwaffe attempted a major defensive effort as the US bombers headed for Derben, Magdeburg and Stendal. Sweeping ahead, the 357th FG picked up JG 300's 100-plus fighters forming up to attack the bombers and ploughed into them. In the ensuing mêlée the Mustangs claimed 56 for the loss of three – a new record for the unit. By the end of the various air battles that day the Luftwaffe had lost 90 aircraft. It was the last great air battle over Europe:

---

[1] Walter Konantz, personal communication.

Right: The groundcrew had to battle with the English weather to keep the fighters serviceable. 353rd FG, 10 January 1945. (Ken Delve Collection)

Left: No 26 Squadron, from North Weald, March 1945. Aircraft 'L' was flown by Flt Lt R. E. Pope, 'E' by Flt Lt A. F. Crosley and 'D' by Flt Lt G. D. Sutcliffe. (Ken Delve Collection)

'The fighter defences for strategic defence had been whittled down to the bone to support operations in the East and a heavy daylight attack on Magdeburg on February 14 could only be countered by a meagre 100–130 sorties, while assaults on Dresden and other targets on the two following days could be met with only negligible opposition. Deep penetration daylight raids during the remainder of the month continued to be only weakly opposed.'[1]

January had also seen the first P-51Ks join the squadrons. This Mustang variant was built at the Dallas plant for the British and Australian market and was basically a D model with a redesigned canopy, giving more headroom, plus a change of propeller to Aeroproducts instead of the Hamilton; indeed, some pilots thought the K models were slightly inferior to their D models.

The majority of the operational sorties being flown by the No 26 Squadron detachment out of Coltishall were 'Big Ben' missions, the code-name given for operations

against the V-2 ballistic rocket. Whilst it had been possible to intercept the earlier V-1 rockets, the ballistic V-2s were unstoppable, and the only possible tactic was to attack the missiles at their point of launch. A great deal of air effort was expended on standing patrols sweeping likely launch areas.

Reconnaissance had always been an important element of the bomber campaign, both pre-attack to acquire intelligence of the target and post-attack for damage assessment. Such reconnaissance assets were always in short supply, some being dedicated to individual Commands or Groups and others, such as the TacR Mustangs already considered, being of a somewhat more general nature. The growth of the German air defences in the latter part of 1944 had taken an increasing toll of these missions, and although a number of sorties took advantage of fighter escort – having to land at the fighter base for a co-ordination brief – this was not consid-

---

[1] *Rise and Fall of the German Air Force, op. cit.*

Below: A Mustang IV of No 442 Squadron. The unit re-equipped from Spitfires to Mustangs in March 1945 and began flying bomber escort sorties in early April. (Ken Delve Collection)

ered to be an ideal solution. Thus, in November 1944 HQ Eighth Air Force and 325 Reconnaissance Wing formulated a plan to equip the 7th PRG with its own P-51s for fighter escort work. Selected ground crew went to the 355th and 356th FGs to learn how to service the P-51, and in early January a group of pilots went to Warton to convert to the P-51 and, in due course, to fly the Mustangs to the Group's base at Mount Farm.

By the end of the first week of January fourteen Mustangs were in place and the pilots were on a gunnery course; in addition, four experienced fighter pilots were detached to Mount Farm – Capt L. Z. Dizette (355th FG), Capt D. M. Williams (20th FG), Lt E. L. Gimbel (4th FG) and Lt R. G. Goldsworth (357th FG). The first escort mission was flown on 13 January, four P-51s of the 22nd TRS, led by Maj Oscar Johnson, covering an F-5 photo mission. To the chagrin of the P-51 pilots, no enemy aircraft were seen. A shortage of reconnaissance aircraft and an increased level of tasking led the Eighth Air Force to approve the modification of a number of P-51s with a K-25 camera in an oblique position behind the pilot. Three such aircraft from the 358th FS/355th FG, escorted by three P-51s, flew a mission to the Politz oil refinery on the Baltic coast on 21 January. This target was heavily defended by flak and the pilots also saw a number of enemy fighters, including Me 262s.

The following month the 25th TRS, now based at Denain/Pouvy, also began P-51 operations, the first escort mission being flown on 3 February by Maj Hubert Chirldress and Capt Robert Florentine as escort to the F-5 Lightning of Lt John Saxton on a mission to photograph Rhine bridges.

Wide-Ranging Remit

Meanwhile the land battle in the Low Countries continued in the face of stiff German resistance. Allied air power was proving decisive on numerous occasions

and often a single aircraft could make all the difference. The TacR squadrons had a wide-ranging remit and amongst the tasks they were undertaking was that of finding suitable targets for the large numbers of Allied fighter-bombers that were 'on call'. In one such instance, on 14 January 1945, Capt Edward Bishop of the 10th PRG was on an artillery-spotting mission in Belgium when he observed a column of enemy tanks approaching Houffalize. He called a fighter-bomber unit in to the attack but they were driven off by intense flak, and he therefore called down artillery fire on the flak defences so that the fighter-bombers could make their attack.

The Eighth Air Force's Scouting Force was proving invaluable in helping the bomber force reach its targets in the face of poor winter weather – but also managed, from time to time, to take on the enemy more directly. Such was the case on 6 February, when the 355th FG (2nd Scouting Force) '. . . observed three Me 163s at Bielefeld flying at 1230 hours, 24,000ft, heading west north west. At Magdeburg they ran into 100 Me 109s flying west north west, more than 50 in each formation, flying at 15,000ft. The first formation was hit by a four-ship flight of the Scouting Force with claims of 5–1–0 (the entire lead flight). In the melee that followed, the remaining fighters joined in. However, the enemy aircraft seemed to lack co-ordination as they broke formation, split-s'd to the deck in a number of instances, [and] engaged in dog-fights amongst themselves. No enemy aircraft were see to approach the bombers.' Lt-Col Brooks was awarded a DSC for his 'courage, aggressiveness and contribution to the success of the bombing mission on this day'.[1]

Operation 'Clarion' was launched on 22 February, a concerted offensive against German road, rail and river traffic, with strategic and tactical aircraft ranging far and wide and the P-51s putting in a maximum effort. Near Berlin the 435th FS (479th FG) ran into sixteen Me 262s and the fight was soon on. The Mustangs of-

ten operated with their fighter-bomber colleagues, the USAAF squadrons working with the P-47s and the RAF units with other types such as Typhoons; ORBs frequently record comments along the lines of '. . . led Typhoon fighter-bombers to the target and then photographed the results'.

The TacR pilots were determined not to waste any sorties. Fg Off J. Bowskill of No 268 Squadron was airborne in FR921 on 26 February for an 'Arty/R' sortie: '. . . having failed to get any response from the ground station he went to a TacR fre-

[1] 355th FG Operational Journal, in *Fighting Scouts of the 8th Air Force, op. cit.*

Above: Mustang III FX889 with sliding hood. The aircraft served with Nos 122 and 315 Squadrons. (*FlyPast* Collection)

quency and asked if there was any task for him to do. In response to a request from the Contact Car, in exceptionally bad weather which forced him to fly at zero feet over the battle area, he found and accurately pinpointed six heavy MT vehicles filled with infantry and other information of first-rate importance to the Army.'[1] For this sortie Bowskill was awarded an immediate DFC.

The previous day, 25 February, 20th FG ace Capt Charles 'Tink' Cole made his final sortie, ending up as a PoW:

'It was a dull, dreary, high-overcast day that Sunday, February 25, 1945. The 20th Fighter Group had been assigned to the Magdeburg area for strafing and targets of opportunity. This was to be my first mission with the 55th Fighter Squadron. The week before, Colonel Robert Montgomery, our group commander, had called me into his quarters and told me that he was transferring me from the 77th Fighter Squadron, with which I had flown some 240 combat hours, to the 55th as their new operations officer. I voiced my objection, but in vain. I was to report to the 55th the next day and, in addition, the colonel said

[1] No 268 Squadron ORB.

I was flying too much and I was to cut down on missions, flying only one in four or five.

'I had been on the ground all week, so I decided this Sunday would be a good time to break in with the 55th. I set up the squadron flight with me leading the lead flight (Sailor White), 1st Lieutenant Schuyler Baker leading Yellow Flight, Captain Dick Fruechtenicht leading Red Flight, and Captain Ron Howard leading Blue Flight. Typically, a squadron on a combat mission was made up of four flights – white (lead flight) a yellow flight, a red flight, and a blue flight. There were four aircraft in each flight, making a total of 16 aircraft in the squadron. White and Yellow Flights made up the lead section, and Red and Blue Flights made up the second section.

'We found a couple of trains and put them out of commission while cruising around at 1,000 feet above the ground. However, due to the poor visibility, Fruechtenicht and his entire two-flight section lost me and my lead section while we were strafing trains and other ground targets. While still looking for targets, we came across a German aerodrome with four Fw 190 fighters on the take-off roll and the rest of the squadron lined up waiting to get airborne. I let the four aircraft get airborne, and then I went after the leader. His two-ship element had broken off to the left and his wingman followed them, so the leader was alone.

'In a few seconds I found myself in a tight Lufbery circle at 500 feet above the ground, staring across the circle at the German pilot and wondering how I could get the advantage and enough lead on him to shoot him down. For the moment, we were evenly matched, but then I remembered that if I lowered 10 degrees of flaps, I could increase my angle of attack and turn my P-51 in a tighter circle. This I did, and, sure enough, I began to turn a tighter circle and started to get a lead on the Focke Wulf. Apparently the German saw what was happening and decided to try a reversement. I saw his ailerons move and

knew what he was going to try. I was ahead of him. When he completed the reversement, I was waiting and had a good lead on him. I gave a short burst with my guns and he snap-rolled into the ground. Of course, we were only 500 feet above the ground and this is not much room for maneuvering a fast fighter aircraft.

'I turned and dropped my left wing so I could get a clear view of the crashed Fw 190 and take pictures with my hand-held camera for confirmation purposes. As I completed the turn and looked up, an Fw 190 suddenly appeared in front of me. All I had to do was grip the trigger to activate the guns, which I did. I apparently caught the Fw 190 in the converging cone of my guns, which I had set at 2,000 yards. The plane just blew up. Just getting airborne like they did, they must have had a full fuel load and, with the main fuselage tank situated mid-airplane, beneath the pilot, a hit in this area would be disastrous, which it was.

'I flew through the parts of this plane and was about to pull out when I saw another Fw 190 about to belly-land in a field. I couldn't resist not helping him belly in. All I had to do was drop my nose, line up my gunsight, and give him a burst, which I did, and he crashed.

'I had started a turn and climb to gain some altitude and get away from this area when another Fw 190 appeared in front of me. I turned to get a lead on him and fired my guns. Again, I must have hit the pilot. As he started to turn away, the Fw went into a snap-roll and snap-rolled into the ground. After I shot him down, I looked around and could see nothing but large German crosses on airplanes. I decided it was time to get the hell out of there. I could not see or find any of my squadron. I set course for England and was thinking about my good fortune when my instrument panel just blew apart, leaving nothing but twisted metal and broken glass.

'My first reaction was to bale out I didn't know how badly the airplane was damaged, or how much time I had to leave it. I

Right: The Mustangs of No 213 Squadron operated from Biferno as part of the Balkan Air Force. (Ken Delve Collection)

opened the canopy, unhooked my belt, and stood up to dive over the side. It was then that the connecting cord on my headset jerked on my head and caused me to think, "Wait a minute!" I then realised that the aircraft was still flying and the engine sounded okay. I thought, "Hell, settle back down and fly this bird out", which I started to do.

'I looked around, but there wasn't any other aircraft in the area. This was a phenomenon that always mystified me. I had been in dogfights before where one minute the air was full of airplanes, or so it seemed, and in the next few minutes there wouldn't be an aircraft in the sky. Where they all went so quickly, I'll never know. Not having a compass or any other instruments, I guessed at a heading that would get me back into France or England. About this time my wingman, Major Maurice Cristadoro, a green member of the 20th Group staff, joined me, and we kept flying in a westerly direction. After about 10 or 15 minutes I noticed sparks underneath the cowling and then I realised the burning sensation that I had on my face was coolant that had flowed back into the cockpit and where the glass from the instrument panel had hit me in the face; the coolant caused a stinging sensation.

'It was shortly after this that the engine froze up and I shut it down to prevent a fire. I looked around, found a field that looked good and set up a straight-in approach and belly-landed the bird. After the bird came to a stop, I stood up to get out and it was then I realised that I had not refastened my safety belt. I got out of the cockpit, took off my chute and left it and the dingy in the cockpit. All this time my wingman was circling overhead and I thought, "He is waiting for me to clear out and then he will strafe the bird and burn it up", so I left the plane and headed for the woods. Then I saw Cristadoro heading for England. I wasn't about to go back to the bird and destroy it. I took off my G-suit and my .45, dug a hole and buried them. I didn't want the G-suit to fall into enemy hands since it was new in our service and I didn't know whether or not the Germans knew anything about a G-suit or how it worked. I got my little escape compass out and checked it to see if I was headed in the right direction. I was, and I thought as long as I am in this forest I will keep going and then tonight maybe I can hook a ride on a train headed west. I kept walking and as long as I was in the forest I was safe. After a while I came to the end of the forest and there was nothing but small, scrub cedars and another forest about 2000 yards away. I got down on my hands and knees and started to crawl through the scrub bushes.'[1]

---

[1] 'Tink' Cole, 20th FG Association newsletter, via Jack Ilfrey.

Shock Waves at 600mph: P-51 Compressibility Trials

'Major Fred Borsodi, test pilot, making a high-compressibility dive from 40,000 ft in a P-51D over Wright Field , saw a ripple move over the wing towards the trailing edge as the plane's speed increased and then move slowly forward again and disappear as the aircraft slowed down in coming out of the dive. He was the first man to see a compressibility shock wave on an aircraft wing. He made another high-speed dive and brought back pictures to prove his claim. Visual discovery of the shock wave was accidental in that the purpose of the series of 32 compressibility dives flown by Major Borsodi was to determine stability characteristics of the P-51D at high Mach numbers and establish a safe Mach number limit which should not be exceeded by other pilots.

'Not satisfied when he learned that compressibility began to make an aircraft shudder and shake at a Mach number of .76, Borsodi continued his tests until he reached .86 when the coolant radiator, oil cooler and hydraulic line cracked from the intense vibrations. At this Mach number he was flying at a true airspeed of approximately 640 mph – believed to be the fastest instrumented flight ever made. His dives revealed that a pilot can encounter the effects of compressibility (usually first noticeable as vibrations or tail-buffeting) and safely slow down his aircraft, and that the greatest danger lies in rapid pull-outs from dives in which high acceleration forces (G) will rip off wings and tail.

'By trimming the P-51D nose heavy, prior to entering the high-speed dive, Borsodi was able to keep the aircraft under control at all times. Tendency of the aircraft to porpoise during the dive was prevented by holding the control stick firmly; efforts to compensate for porpoising only intensified the danger.

'General effects of compressibility on the P-51 include vibrations and tail-buffeting, followed by porpoising tendency, slight heaviness of the ailerons and tail. Tail heaviness should be trimmed out; the stick should be held as nearly stationary as possible. Cutting power seems to have little effect, but helps in reducing speed. The AAF Board of Orlando makes the following recommendations to avoid compressibility – (1) Do not exceed airspeeds corresponding to three-fourths the speed of sound at the altitude at which dives or maneuvers are to be carried out. (2) Avoid violent use of ailerons. (3) Never roll into a vertical dive above 30,000 ft. In this altitude, speed may be increased so rapidly that the critical speed may be involuntarily exceeded. (4) At high speed at altitude, use controls gently as if the aircraft were near a stall. Do not be in too much of a hurry to recover from a dive because high-G forces will cause entry into the compressibility range above 20,000 ft and much more easily than below 20,000 ft.'[1]

[1] Report, ACSEA Weekly Intelligence Summary No 78, 13 May 1945.

The monitoring of road and rail traffic remained critical, not so much now to watch for German reinforcements but rather to spot when they were trying to pull back and establish new defensive positions – German columns on road and rail made ideal targets. With the major Allied ground offensive taking place in the north, Montgomery having persuaded General Eisenhower to allocate resources to his 'war winning' push to the Rhine (Operation 'Market Garden'), operations by the Third Army had slowed to a near halt, although Patton was pushing towards Prum and Bitburg in what has been termed his 'creeping offensive'. On 3 March Trier (on the Moselle) fell and the push continued towards the Rhine at Koblenz, and on 15 March the 15th TRS moved to Trier/Evren airfield in order to remain close to the battle zone. The race was now on to cut off

the escape routes over the Rhine, and so the TacR units were tasked to check regularly the status of the bridges – all of which were now heavily defended with AA guns and with a strong Luftwaffe presence.

Contact with German jets was not a frequent occurrence for the Mustang pilots, especially when the jet in question was an Arado Ar 234 reconnaissance bomber. One of the few aerial victories scored over this type was made by Capt Don Bryan of the 328th FS/352nd FG on 14 March 1945. Bryan was on his second tour with the Group and was already an ace (his score standing at twelve, plus one shared); he had also seen, and attempted to catch, Arado bombers a number of times before. On this particular day he was flying P-51K 44-11628 (PE-J):

'As we were coming back towards the Rhine River from the east on March 14, I

Right: No 213 Squadron Mustangs escorting Beaufighters to a target over Yugoslavia. (Ken Delve Collection)

saw an Arado crossing directly in front of us, north to south, from my right to my left. He seemed to be flying toward the newly completed engineer bridges around Remagan. A group of P-47s was over the bridges, providing aerial cover, but I decided to try to get him. I broke away from the bombers and started chasing him. By then, however, I was way back from him; it seemed like a million miles. As I turned to my left to follow, the Arado turned to his right and crossed the Rhine from due east to due west. When he made the turn, I saw my chance and tried to cut him off by turning obliquely to my right inside his turn. I did cut him off, but he outran me again and crossed the river. Then he made a second turn and followed the course of the river directly towards a floating engineer bridge. There was no possibility I was going to catch him. Instead of trying to follow him, I turned to the NE so I could head him off as he came off his run on the bridge. I figured the SOB had to go home sooner or later.

'Sure enough he made a diving south-to-north attack right along the roadbed of the floating pontoon bridge. When he pulled up he turned to his right onto east. If he stayed on course he would have to cross my line of flight . . . Instead of wait-

ing until he got in front of me, I dove down and commenced my attack. I wanted to be right on top of him as he flew by me. I rolled to the right, almost over onto my back, and started my dive. I was trying to keep him in sight. As he flew past, I don't think he was any more than 100 yds from me. I then rolled fully left. He was flying flat and I was in a full 90 degree bank at the time I hit him. There was no need to lead him. It was just point and pop. I did some good shooting for once in my life. I saw strikes on both of his engines. I knew he was not getting away from me. I then rolled into a normal position and fell in right behind him. His engines were dead; he was slowing down and I was throttling back. I had all the time in the world to poke at him with my guns.

'I glanced back and saw that my entire squadron was right behind me. Behind it was the rest of the 352nd FG. And behind our Group I could see a great many P-47s. I just stayed there, right behind the Arado, squirting bullets at him now and again. He finally rolled to his right and flew directly in.'[1]

Already an ace whilst flying P-47s with the 328th FS prior to its re-equipment with P-51s, Don Bryan was CO of the unit from January to April 1945. Three further Ar 234s were shot down the same day, one by a Mustang and two by P-47s of 56th FG. A number of Mustangs had arrived at the latter's Boxted home as consideration was given to converting the 56th – much to the consternation of these Thunderbolt die-hards. In the event they held on to their P-47s to the end of the war.

March 12 saw No 19 Squadron as part of an escort force: 'Another show was laid on escorting 44 Mosquitoes to the Kattegat area. The weather was misty to start with but cleared up as the target area came up. The Mosquitoes rendezvoused with us over base at 1320 and set course out to sea. Unfortunately there was a layer of 10/10 over the Kattegat, and the Mosquitoes chose to patrol above it, so there

---

[1] *Aces Against Germany*, op. cit.

was no strike, no ships being seen. They turned and set course for base and as everyone was settling down to go home, and were passing Lista to the south of Norway, F/Lt Butler leading White Section saw some aircraft passing him head on. The visibility was bad down on the sea, making it hard to identify the aircraft, but they turned out to be 10 Me 109s. A dog fight started at once, Green and Tonic Sections also being attacked by three others. Unfortunately, White 2, S/Ldr M. R. Hill, was shot down in the melee. Also Green 2, P/O Overy, was shot up in the first bounce and got some shell splinters in the back; however, he got back safely and is now rapidly recovering. The Squadron destroyed one and one probable, the CO getting the destroyed and F/Lt Butler the probable. This brings the Squadron's total to 143° destroyed, 40 of these since D-Day.'[1]

March also saw RAF Mustangs involved in one of the most dramatic raids of the war – an attack on the Gestapo HQ, the Shell House, in Copenhagen on 21 March. Three Mustang squadrons, Nos 64, 126 and 234, escorted the Mosquitos to the target.

On the night of 22/23 March Patton's forces finally crossed the Rhine at Oppenheim. The No 268 Squadron ORB recorded for 24 March: '. . . the long awaited offensive by the British Army to cross the Rhine started today. In brilliant summer-like weather the Squadron flew six TacR, three Arty/R and two flak-spotting missions.' A heavy air effort was tasked to support the offensive, almost 2,000 American bombers and hundreds of fighters attacking German airfields or, in the case of the B-24s of the 2nd Division, dropping supplies to Allied ground forces. It was a busy day and some fighter Groups flew three sorties.

Late March had generally been a quiet period for the USAAF fighters. A mass raid on Berlin on 15 March had elicited little Luftwaffe response and only one German fighter, an Me 163, was shot down. Four days later the 78th FG mixed with the Me 262s of JG 7 with no result; a short while later they came upon a group of 50 Bf 109s forming up and in the ensuing battle claimed 32–1–13 (plus two passing Ar 234s) for the loss of five Mustangs. It was

[1] No 19 Squadron ORB.

Ninth Air Force Statistics

The following table is a Ninth Air Force summary based upon the USAAF Form 34A returns and gives the 'Claims against enemy aircraft for the period Oct 16, 1943 to May 8, 1945.'

Enemy Ac	P-51 air	P-51 gnd	F-6
Do 20			3–0–0
Do 217	4–1–3	1–0–1	1–0–0
Fw 44	1–0–0		
Fw 56	1–0–0		
Fw 190	271–2–117	57–0–26	55–7–19
Ju 52	1–0–0	2–0–3	2–0–0
Ju 87	2–0–0	3–0–11	14–1–0
Ju 88	5–1–12	42–2–26	5–0–1
Ju 90		1–0–0	
Ju 188	1–0–0	1–0–0	1–0–0
Ju 288		1–0–0	
He 111	4–0–1	37–0–20	3–0–2
He 115		0–1–1	
He 126 [sic]		1–0–0	1–0–0
He 129 [sic]	3–0–0	0–0–6	
He 177		2–1–3	
He 280			1–0–0
Me 109	376–29–129	45–1–17	40–5–16
Me 110	48–8–32	9–1–2	3–0–2
Me 163		6–0–2	
Me 209	2–1–2	0–0–2	
Me 210	2–4–0	5–0–0	0–0–1
Me 262	7–2–12	1–0–1	0–2–2
Me 410	22–1–20	5–0–0	
Storch			2–0–0
P–47[1]			1–0–0
Misc	1–0–0	38–1–66	5–0–2

[1] Recorded as a captured aircraft; for obvious reasons 'real own goals' are not included in such statistical listings. The author was unable to find a similar summary for VIII Fighter Command.

'Venerable', 'to co-operate with French warships on naval bombardment of the Atlantic pockets. R/T tests were carried out with the *Dusquesne* [sic] and *Lorraine* in Plymouth harbour.' Dummy shoots were carried over the next few days as procedures were tightened up and practised; finally, on 13 April, the Squadron moved to Cognac/Château Bernard ready for Operation 'Venerable' to commence two days later. The first shoot took place on 15 April: 'Spotting for naval bombardment of Point du Grave [mouth of the Gironde] with *Dusquesne* and *Lorraine*, dawn to dusk flew 56 sorties, some pilots having flown three. On the whole the ships were a little erratic.' Similar missions were flown throughout April, culminating on the 30th:

'32 operational sorties flown with *Dusquesne*, the early sorties had a certain amount of R/T trouble but by lunch time things were going well and some good shoots were carried out, despite the usual erratic gunnery of the French ships. No flak was seen and the operation proceeded smoothly until late evening when *Dusquesne* blew out a gun barrel and flying ceased. By this time French ground troops had made steady advances on the Isle D'Oleron and air operations ceased to be of further help.'

A great deal of work was carried out in co-operation with forward air controllers: 'The Contact Cars with our armoured Division had many requests for air observation [4 April], 80% of which were successfully filled, and specified bridges were reported 'up' or 'demolished', several gun positions and road blocks were pinpointed.[1]

On 7 April the escort fighters shot down 59 enemy fighters and it was thought that the majority of these belonged to Sonderkommando Elbe, a German suicide unit created to ram enemy bombers in a last desperate act to force 'unacceptable losses' on the Americans. They appear to have rammed eight bombers, but this was their

suggested that the presence of the Me 262s had been intended to decoy the escort P-51s into dropping their fuel tanks and thus reducing their combat time, leaving the bombers vulnerable to follow-up attacks.

Operation 'Venerable'

The Allies continued to advance towards the German heartland, but at the same time operations were undertaken to clear pockets of enemy resistance in France. On 5 April the Mustangs of No 26 Squadron were placed on standby for Operation

Left: A photograph of two P-51Ds of the 332nd FG, Fifteenth Air Force, taken in April 1945 from a No 104 Squadron Liberator. (Andy Thomas Collection)

---

[1] No 268 Squadron ORB.

one and only mass effort. Most German losses were now being suffered on the ground as the fighters strafed airfields at every opportunity: the figures for 10 April set a new record, with 284 German aircraft claimed as destroyed (105 of these by the 329th FG). A week later, on 16 April, the fighters were hunting in south-east Germany and Czechoslovakia and during attacks on airfields claimed 752 aircraft, the top scorers being the 78th FG with 125 destroyed and 86 damaged. Capt Robert Ammon (339th FG) accounted for eleven destroyed, although subsequent records credit him with nine. The P-51s also suffered, 34 aircraft falling to ground fire. A further 200 German aircraft were destroyed on the ground in the same area the following day.

The air war was, however, winding down, and a ban was imposed on strafing missions: there was little point in accepting such Allied losses with the war nearly over. April 25 saw the last bombing raid mounted by the Eighth Air Force, the 1st and 2nd Divisions attacking various targets:

1. 1st Division:	307 B-17s + 188 P-51s to Pilsen airfield and Skoda works.
2. 2nd Division:	282 B-24s + 203 P-51s to rail facilities at Bad Reichenhall and Hallem, plus Traunstein transformer station.
3.	19 P-51s sweep Prague/Linz area.

Few enemy fighters were encountered, the only confirmed victory being that by Lt Hilton Thompson (479th FG) whilst escorting the B-24s to Traunstein. Thompson spotted an Ar 234 and shot it down near Reichenhall. This proved to be the last confirmed Eighth Air Force fighter score.

Italy

The Allied advance in Italy had been very slow. The final offensive of 1944 had taken Ravenna and Bologna but a German counter-stroke on 26 December in the Serio val-

---

A-36 Tasking, Twelfth Air Force, January 1944[1]

Jan 5 Gun positions, Mignanu and Monte Porchia
6 Gun positions in Cervaro–Monte Trocchio area + rail targets
7 Guns, trucks, rail in Cervaro–Aquino–Cassino area
8 Rail targets S of Rome
9 Rail targets S of Sumona
10 Comms targets N of Rome
11 Guns and defences in Ceravaro–Monte Trocchio
12 Avezzano rail yard + rail targets Cisterna di Latina and Rome area
13 Rail yards at Isolla del Liri, Valmontone and SE of Frosinone + Formia docks
14 Anzio harbour + San Guiseppe
15 CAS in Piciniso and Atina areas
16 Rail at Cecian and S of Sienna
17 Anzio, Avezzano and Tarquinia
18 Atina and Minturno areas, petrol dump at Pignataro Interamna
20 Bridge at Viterbo + CAS for 36th Div attack across Rapido
21 CAS in battle area + Velletri and Minturno
22 Support Anzio landings by cutting l-o-c
23 Cover Anzio landings + Vallescorsa, Fundi and rail at Sezze
24 Cover Anzio landings
25 Civita Castellana, Itri and Velletri
26 Harass road and rail + fuel dumps in Ceprano–Priverno area
27 Rail and bridges at Poggio Mirteto, Cescano, Ciampino
28 Road and rail in Cassion–Vicenza–Velletri areas
29 Anzio beachhead + l-o-c targets
31 Targets E of Anzio

[1] Based upon 'USAAF in World War Two: Chronology', issued by the Office of Air Force History.

---

ley prevented any further advance. There could be no further Allied ground advance until spring, and the planners began to look to a late March/early April 'jump-off'. In the meantime, Allied air power was tasked to prepare the way. Although the strategic bombers were still heavily involved in attacks on Germany, the tactical elements went after targets in and around the German front lines.

The Twelfth Air Force continued to provide direct support to the ground units as well as taking an active part in attempts to sever all lines of communication to the German front-line forces. The A-36s were active on such tasks virtually every day, the range of which can be appreciated from the accompanying statistical summary for January 1944.

The Fifteenth Air Force ranged over much of Europe as part of the Allied bombing strategy of hitting Germany from all sides, and the P-51s were kept busy on escort duties in addition to their tactical roles. On 24 March the 332nd FG flew the longest escort to date – a 1,600-mile round trip with B-17s to the Daimler-Benz tank works in Berlin. The 'Tuslegee Airmen' shot down three Me 262s over Berlin, the jets falling to Lt Roscie Brown, Lt Robert Williams and Lt Samuel Watts, with another two Me 262s and an Me 163 as probables – for the loss of three Mustangs.

However, on 9 April the spring offensive was launched and air power – both strategic and tactical – was once more employed on a massive scale. The tactical squadrons, including the Mustangs, were allocated to CAS operating under ground control from control cars ('Rover David' and 'Rover Frank' for No 112 Squadron).

The war in Europe ended on 8 May 1945, but on that day not all German pilots seemed willing to surrender. Allied aircrew were warned to be ready for trouble whilst Luftwaffe aircraft were being flown to surrender points. The final combat of the war took place that evening when Lt Robert Little of the 12th TRS shot down an Fw 190. Five enemy aircraft had bounced his Section.

The war in Europe was over but Japan was fighting on. Within weeks of VE-Day the decision was taken to keep three P-51 Groups (the 55th FG, 35th FG and 357th FG) as part of the Occupation Force for Germany; all other fighter Groups would return to the United States, where some would retrain for deployment to the Pacific Theatre. The Mustang Groups moved to bases in Bavaria during July. By autumn most of the Groups based in the United Kingdom had left for home. The final closure ceremony took place in February 1946 when VIII Fighter Command HQ said farewell to Honington.

Right: A No 213 Squadron Mustang strafing a train in Yugoslavia, 21 April 1945. (Ken Delve Collection)

4

THE PACIFIC THEATRE

The year 1944 also saw a major increase in the employment of P-51s in the CBI and Pacific theatres. The 311th FG of the Tenth Air Force had received various P-51s and A-36s in the latter part of 1943 and by October was supporting the US-Chinese advance on Myitkyina. The F-6s of the 8th PRG were also active in the same area, providing vital reconnaissance in what was, up to the siege of Myitkyina, a fairly fluid situation. By the autumn Mustangs had also formed elements within the 68th (23rd FG) and 69th (51st FG) Composite Wings operating initially in south-west China but later taking part in operations in French Indo-China and Burma. Fighter escort, counter-air operations (especially airfield strafing) and ground attack missions kept all the P-51 units fully occupied into 1945 as Japanese air and ground forces remained strong. The Allied advance was, however, inexorable both in the CBI theatre and in the Pacific.

The first attack on Formosa by units of the Fourteenth Air Force took place on 23 November 1943 when fourteen B-25s, escorted by eight P-38s and 'eight battle worn but newly-arrived P-51As' attacked airfield targets. The P-51s claimed five

Above: Maj-Gen Claire L. Chennault plus P-51 crews. (US National Archives)

Left: P-51Cs of the 3rd Air Commando flying out of Gainsville, Florida, 6 September 1944, prior to deploying to the Far East. (John Sutherland via Bob Eason)

enemy aircraft in aerial combat plus a further four during ground strafing – a good start to Mustang operations.

The first few months of 1944 were fairly quiet for the China-based units whilst the Japanese concentrated on their offensive in Burma and on building up for the next phase in China. In March 1944 the 51st FG gave up its P-40s in favour of P-51Bs and Cs. On 17 April an offensive was launched by the Japanese in Hunan Province, although this soon changed its axis of advance towards the Tung Ting Lake area. As part of the air effort in support of Chinese troops, the 23rd FG flew over 500 sorties – despite poor weather – and managed to claim a number of aerial victories in addition to the primary ground support task. It was, however, to little avail and the Japanese advance continued; the American fighters had to withdraw from various airfields as they became threatened.

On 8 August Hengyang fell and it seemed that American air power, still primarily P-40s, could do little to save eastern China from collapse. Air reinforcements were slow in arriving as the 'Germany first' policy continued to deprive other theatres of resources, but, as mentioned above, a change of policy was already under way.

In June the 118th TRS had arrived in-theatre, establishing its HQ at Chengkung and being attached as a fighter unit to the 23rd FG. Its first operations were flown on 18 June and for the remainder of the year, in common with all the P-51 units, it was kept very busy. One of the most remarkable days for the 118th was 23 December, when Lt-Col Edward O. McComas became the Fourteenth Air Force's only 'ace in a day'. The Squadron, led by McComas, flew from Suichuan to skip-bomb the Wuchang-Hankow ferry terminal; having successfully attacked this target the pilots strafed Wuchung airfield, claiming at least two aircraft. McComas then spotted six 'Oscars' above the airfield and went after them, claiming one. A little while later he saw nine 'Oscars' at Ehr Tao Kow airfield preparing to take off. Diving down to attack, he quickly destroyed four of the Japanese fighters. McComas had been CO of the 118th since September 1943; his first aerial victory was scored on 16 October when he shot down one 'Tojo' and damaged another in the Hong Kong area. His score rapidly rose, and by the time of the 'ace in a day' incident he was already an ace, having claimed eight enemy aircraft destroyed. He ended the war with a score of 14 destroyed, one probable and one damaged, all the claims being made whilst flying a P-51C – his usual aircraft being *Kansas Reaper*.

At the end of August 1944 the three P-51 squadrons of the 311th FG transferred from the Tenth to the Fourteenth Air Force and moved to the Chengtu area (although the 530th FS did not actually arrive from India until 21 October); when it moved, the Group still included a number of A-36s on its strength. Late August also brought a renewed offensive by the Japanese Eleventh Army towards Canton, Kweilin and Linchow. As the advance continued, the Americans lost valuable airfields and the task of air power became increasingly difficult.

Kweilin became one of the key bases, and various units, including the 68th Composite Wing, operated from this now vital airfield. Japanese pressure continued, however, and it had to be abandoned on 13 September, the 118th TRS moving to Liuchow and the Chinese-American Wing to Peishiyi, and the 74th FS operating from Kanchow until the last possible moment.

The major air effort remained that of ground support, but a number of strategic missions were also flown, such as an attack on Hong Kong on 16 October by B-25s and B-24s escorted by P-51s (the mis-

sion on which Edward McComas had scored his first victory). The P-51s dive-bombed shipping and only one aircraft was lost from this highly successful attack:

'. . . we arrived down in the Hong Kong area and the first thing I know I see three enemy aircraft up there that I couldn't identify. I knew they were Japs but I'd never seen the type before. We called them out and turned into them, and as we pulled up into them, why, they went straight up and I could see we were going to stall out so I bent it over. These guys came right down on top of us and shot down the three guys who were with me, and they chased me all the way down to 8,000ft, which was the altitude I needed to get back over some hills. I swear I believe the Jap was trying to overrun me in a dive. His tracers were really going by me head. When I got back I talked to the Old Man, telling him about this new type Jap fighter (which was later identified as a Zeke 52) . . . the good part of this story is that all the guys actually got back.'

The Chinese began a counter-offensive on 22 October, supported by American air power, although this rapidly stalled and the Japanese were moving forward again within a week. In recognition of the changing strategic situation, at the end of Octo-

Right: A pair of Air Commando P-51s airborne over Burma. (US National Archives)

124

Left: Top Fourteenth Air Force ace Lt-Col Edward McComas. General Chennault gave him a P-51D. (US National Archives)

ber the CBI theatre was split in two – China and Burma-India – although this had little immediate impact on the fighter units. By November the Fourteenth Air Force's 36 squadrons included 32 fighter units, many of which were equipped with the P-51. The Chinese-American Composite Wings operating in Central China south of the Yellow River included the 3rd and 5th FGs.

The 311th FG was intensively engaged from November, the first operations being against rail targets in northern China – including attacks on critical bridges. The Mustangs also escorted medium bombers, primarily B-25s, to similar rail targets; for example, on 9 November the Group escorted B-25s to the Kaifeng rail yard, during which they engaged a number of 'Oscars' but were only able to claim one damaged. The score of enemy aircraft rose later in the month when Lts Field, Arasmith and Reed of the 530th FS each claimed a

'Nate' on 17 November, with Field claiming a further two 'Nates' the following day (whilst other Squadron pilots claimed a 'Tojo' and an 'Oscar'). Liuchow was evacuated on 8 November and the P-51s in this part of the theatre concentrated most of their attention on either road sweeps or attacks on airfields. The 75th FG were having a particularly hectic time, engaging twenty enemy aircraft over Hengyang on 12 November, losing four but claiming four with two others probable and six damaged. Both the 75th and 76th were also busy attacking ground targets, including skip-bombing railway tunnels. The Japanese offensive paused in early December to re-supply but re-started on 10 December and had soon linked up with Japanese forces in French Indo-China. The remaining elements of the Fourteenth Air Force were isolated in what was left of eastern China. It was certainly a period of crisis.

December 18 was a particularly good day for the Mustangs when 42 P-51s strafed airfields around Hankow. The 311th put in claims for 16 destroyed, four probables and seven damaged both on the ground and in the air, for the loss of one aircraft. Three days later the Group went after rail targets near Tsingpin and claimed nine locomotives – plus five 'Nates' over Tsinan, these falling to Lts Pearson and Sharp. Tsinan airfield was attacked by twelve aircraft on 26 November, and although six of the Mustangs were damaged by ground fire they claimed the destruction of twenty bombers and ten fighters. This routine was set to continue into 1945.

New Guinea

The Japanese advance through New Guinea, with its serious threat to Australia, had been held and by spring 1944 the Allies were leap-frogging their way back up the north coast, supported by Fifth Air Force units. One of those units was the P-47-equipped 348th FG ('Kearby's Thunderbolts'). The first P-51s destined for this unit had arrived at Port Moresby in early summer but it was not until early the following year that the type entered combat with the Group, by which time the 348th had added the 460th FS to its existing three units (the 340th, 341st and 342nd). Late summer saw the Group as part of the air element for the invasion of the Philippines and by early December all four squadrons were operating from various bases in the islands.

As 1944 opened, the Tenth Air Force was still heavily involved with operations in the Myitkyina and associated areas, the 311th FG's A-36s and P-51s being engaged primarily in anti-airfield work and attacks on Japanese supply and troop areas. The

Below: February 1945: a P-51 makes its way to shore. (US National Archives)

P-51 Tasking, 311th FG, January 1944

Jan	1	11 A-36 + 15 P-51, Myitkyina airfield
	2	30 A-36/P-51, Loilaw bridge area
	3	22 A-36/P-51, Sahmaw area supply dumps
	6	? A-36/P-51, ground support Sumprabum/Taihpa Ga
	7	19 A-36/P-51, Nanyaseik supply dumps
	8	21 A-36/P-51, bridge at Hopin + rail attacks
	10	12 ac, Loilaw area, bridge, barracks and dumps
	11	36 ac, large camp and stores
	13	10 ac, Lalawng Ga, Maran Ga and Shaduzup, Myitkyina airfield
	17	?, Shaduzup, Ngamaw, Sahmaw
	18	17 ac, dumps and barracks at Sawnghka
	19	26 ac, targets on road Ngamaw Ga to Maingkwan to Mashi Daru
	20	40+ ac, dumps along rail from Maingkwan to Mashi Daru
	21	27 ac, Sumprabum and Kamaing
	22	28 ac, Kumnyen-Ngamaw Ga, Suprabum
	23	28 ac, dumps at Kamaing and Mogaung

accompanying statistics, from the Tenth Air Force summary of operations statistics, show the Group's activities for January 1944 and provide a good indication of both the intensity and nature of the work.

In August the 311th FG transferred to the Fourteenth Air Force.

China-Burma-India-Pacific Operations

In a post-war study, General Kenney wrote: 'The European show did not like the B-24 or the P-38 and P-47; they preferred the B-17 as a bomber and P-51 as a fighter. I told Arnold I was not that particular. All I wanted was something that would fly. I thought that I would get somewhere with this argument.'[1] Although the P-51 was slow to appear in this theatre of the war, numbers rapidly increased.

The first Mustang presence in the South West Pacific Area (SWPA) had been the F-6Ds of the 82nd TRS operating from Morotai at the end of 1944, and it was not until March 1945 that the first fighter groups, the 348th and 35th, arrived in-theatre with the P-51D.

The appearance of the P-51s in the SWPA at the beginning of 1945 caused the Theatre intelligence staff to issue an iden-

tification brief: '. . . the plane's outstanding characteristics are the square contours of the wings and stabiliser in plain [plan?] view, the rectangular fin and rudder assembly in side view, the bubble canopy which is raised above the straight, smooth line of the fuselage, the full dihedral of the wings and the prominent, centrally placed air scoop beneath the fuselage in front view, and the in-line engine.'[2] The brief must have helped as there are very few recorded instances of 'own goals' in air combat in this theatre.

The 341st FS was the first of the 348th FG units to re-equip, and it flew its first missions on 6 January. Heavy tasking and a shortage of equipment meant that conversion training often included operational sorties. Luzon was invaded on 9 January and Allied progress was rapid, each move being supported by as much air power as could be made available.

The Mustangs were soon making their presence felt, scoring a new record within SWPA when, on 11 January, they shot down seven enemy aircraft in a single mission. The extract of the Squadron combat report was included in SWPA Intelligence Summary No 256:

'On 11 January 1945, six P-51s took off at 0800 on armed recce and photo mission to Appari and road south through Belete [sic] Pass. Four P-51s were ordered to return to Leyte after being airborne a short time. One element continued on mission and at approximately 1015, flying at 500 ft on a heading of 360 degrees south of Tuguegarao airdrome . . . they observed 13 bogies above them flying a heading of 180 degrees at 3000 ft. The P-51s made a 180 degree climbing turn to 3500ft.

'The bogies were recognised as 11 TONYs, one TOJO, and one BETTY bomber flying a stepped up V of three elements, formation on each side of the BETTY with the BETTY leading the formation. The Captain and

---

[1] General Kenney in *USAF Warrior Studies – General Kenney Reports*, Office of Air Force History, Washington, 1987.
[2] SWPA Intelligence Summary No 255.

127

Lieutenant closed on the enemy formation and first engaged the enemy over Cabagan. The Captain closed on the element leader and his wingman of the enemy's third element on the left, and fired a burst into both TONYs causing them to explode in mid-air.

'The P-51 Flight Leader and his wingman then closed on the enemy's second element on the left side of the V formation, each P-51 firing a short burst into each of the two TONYs, causing both of them to explode and burst into flames. The Lt then closed on the wingman of the first element on the left side, fired a short burst and the TONY exploded. This Tony's element leader broke left and disappeared into the cloud layer after his wingman was shot down.

'The enemy's formation broke up at this time into elements to counterattack. The Lt made a 180 degree turn and observed a TONY flying head-on at him, firing as he flew at the P-51. Although the Lt returned fire, the TONY did not break, and appeared to be bent on ramming the P-51. The P-51 dropped slightly below the oncoming TONY, fired into its underside, causing it to disintegrate.

'Meanwhile the P-51 Flight Leader had moved to the right side of the enemy's formation as it started to break up into ele-

ments to counterattack and closed, firing on the wingman of the enemy's second element on the right side. This TONY exploded. The P-51 Flight Leader then dived below the BETTY and pumped a long burst into the underside of the fuselage. The right wing root caught fire, the bomber went into a dive, crashed and exploded in flames.

'The Captain passed under the BETTY and pulled up in a sharp left hand climbing turn. At this point, the P-51 Flight Leader observed a TOJO firing a 60 degree deflection burst at him. The P-51 Flight Leader pulled his plane into a tighter turn and the TOJO skidded under the P-51 and disappeared in the cloud layer.

'The Captain then dropped down on the enemy's first element on the right which was trying to get away. At approximately 800 ft altitude the P-51 Flight Leader closed on these two TONYs from dead astern. A short burst into the enemy's element leader caused it to explode. The TONY's wingman broke down and to the right. The Lt followed him down and as the TONY leveled off at approximately 300 ft the P-51 Flight Leader fired another short burst. The TONY began to smoke and started to dive towards the ground. It leveled off before hitting the ground, skidded along the surface of the earth on its

Right: Lingayen, 27 April 1945: the 386th Air Service Squadron repair depot. (US National Archives)

Left: 2nd FS/2nd Air Commando P-51Ds take off for another Burma mission. (Walter Eason)

belly, exploding in a burst of flames before it came to rest.

'The second Japanese pilot shot down opened his canopy and waved his arms as though he were waving to friendly aircraft. Both pilots believed that the Japanese mistook the P-51s as friendly TONYs.'

Amazing Combat

One of the most amazing combats took place on 11 January when a pair of F-6s from the 82nd TRS took off from Mindoro on an armed reconnaissance of the northern part of Luzon looking for Japanese airfields:

'The leader was the Squadron Commander, Capt William A. Shomo. His wingman was 2nd Lt Paul M. Lipscomb. Flying at 200 ft, just SW of Baguio, they

suddenly saw about 200 ft above them a twin-engined Jap bomber, escorted by 12 of the latest-type Jap fighters. They told me afterwards they figured it must be some very important General or Admiral being evacuated back to Japan. Neither of them had ever been in combat in their lives, but they figured you had to start sometime and here was a wonderful opportunity. Shomo, with Lipscomb hugging his wing, climbed to the attack and opened fire. Either the Nips didn't see them before the shooting started or they mistook the P-51s for some of their own aircraft. It was probably the first time they had seen a Mustang as it had arrived in the Theater only a week or so before.

'Shomo promptly shot down the bomber while Lipscomb destroyed a fighter. The

fight was now on. The Nips had broken formation and now tried to get re-formed and do something about the two hornets that seemed to be swarming all over them, but they just weren't good enough. In addition to the bomber, Shomo got six fighters, while Lipscomb shot down four fighters. The remaining two Japs left a high speed for the north. The kids flew around taking pictures of the eleven wrecked and smoking Jap planes on the ground and then headed back home.

'I made Shomo a Major and put in a recommendation to MacArthur for a Congressional Medal of Honor. Lipscomb I recommended for a Distinguished Service Cross and promoted to the grade of First Lieutenant. Their awards came through a few days later.'

William Shomo was flying F-6D 44-14841 *Snooks 5th* when he scored his 'Betty' and six 'Tony' record on 11 January. Contrary to the Kenney report, Shomo had been in combat before, claiming a 'Val' the previous day.

The primary task of the Fifth Air Force in the early part of 1945 was to isolate the Luzon battlefield and support the ground forces. By February three of the four squadrons of the 348th FG converted to the P-51 (the 460th FS converting in March), thus giving the Fifth a variety of P-51 units – the 348th FG, the 3rd Air Commando and the 71st TRG (82nd and 110th TRS). The 3rd FS (Commando) and 4th FS (C) of the 3rd Air Commando had been operating from the Philippines since late 1944:

'On February 15th one of our P-51 fighter pilots from the 3rd Air Commando shot down one of our own DC-3 transports and earned a decoration for the job. He was returning from a mission against Formosa when he saw the transport circling with the wheels down for a landing at an emergency field on one of the Batan Islands, north of Luzon and about halfway to Formosa. The islands at that time were occupied by the Japs. The P-51 pilot had to decide whether it was one of our own planes that was lost or a Jap-built DC-3

with American insignia. He flew up alongside and satisfied himself that the pilot was not a Jap. He then dived in front of the transport to keep it from landing at the Jap-held strip. The pilot of the transport circled again and again started to glide in for a landing. The P-51 pilot then decided on a desperate measure. Lining his sights on the left engine of the DC-3, he poured a burst of machine-gun fire into it and knocked the engine out of commission. The transport pilot promptly ditched the plane in the ocean and the occupants got into their rubber boats.

'The P-51 pilot then called Lingayen for a Catalina rescue plane and settled down to see that no-one came along to bother the rubber boats. Luckily a Catalina was already on the way to the general area to pick up another fighter pilot who had been forced down in the water a few hours before. In a short time the Catalina arrived

Right: Capt Louis in his aircraft, showing the American flag on the tally list, reflecting his shooting down, as ordered, of a C-47. (US National Archives)

Left, upper: Final briefing for a 2nd FS mission. (Walter Eason)

Left, lower: S/Sgt Joe Banyas loading rockets on to a P-51D of the 2nd FS in Burma. (Walter Eason)

and picked up the crew and passengers from the DC-3. Among them were two nurses and two Red Cross girls on their way to Lingayen. The pilot had run into bad weather and gotten lost. He was getting short of gasoline and thinking that he was in friendly territory had decided to land.

'The P-51 lad already had painted on the nose of his airplane seven Nazi swastikas and one Italian insignia, which he had earned in the European Theater, as well as a Jap flag for a victory in the Pacific. He added an American flag in memory of his latest exploit. I awarded him an Air Medal.'[1]

Having flown P-38s in Europe, Lt Louis Curdes had been forced down by mechanical trouble in Italy and made a prisoner of war, but he escaped and made his way back to Allied lines. Later he requested a transfer to the Pacific Theatre and in August 1944 joined the 4th FS (C) within the 3rd FG (C) (the designation of the Air Commando units). His first victory was a 'Dinah' on 7 February, followed by the DC-3/C-47.

The tactical reconnaissance squadrons received F-6Ks in February 1945 to supplement, and in some case replace, their F-6Ds. On 3 February Manila was taken by US forces and the major effort was now concentrated on seizing Bataan and Corregidor. Ground attack sorties, from

'barge-busting' to napalming Japanese positions, were interspersed with long-range (eight-hour) escort missions shepherding B-25s. The latter were, however, the exception and the 348th FG spent most of its time attacking ground targets, the Japanese line of retreat along Metropolitan Road and the Balete Pass receiving much attention in March and April.

The final assault on the Japanese pocket at Luzon took place in mid-May and the fighter types were fully involved in fighter-bomber operations during this period. Indeed, the 348th received a commendation for its work.

Between late June and mid-August all Groups moved to new bases on Okinawa and Ie Shima, (a small island off Okinawa), the 348th moving to the latter location in late June having ceased operations around the Philippines on 20 June. The first sweep over Japan was made on 16 July when fifteen aircraft of the 340th FS escorted B-25s to Miyakojono, Kyushu. The P-51s each carried a single 500lb bomb, these being dropped on a bridge. A similar mission was flown by the 342nd two days later, but the raids on Japan were then interrupted by a phase of attacks on coastal targets around Shanghai. However, Japan was back on the board by the end of the month. It was not until 1 August that the Group claimed an enemy aircraft over Japan, at least two 'Franks' falling to the 460th FS that day. On 4 August a flight of 340th P-51s shot down all four Zeros that they encountered whilst flying SAR cover for a PBY. The final operational sortie was flown on 12 August by fifteen Mustangs of the 340th FS, during which the aircraft attacked a number of small ships.

China

As 1945 opened, the Fourteenth Air Force maintained the pressure on Japanese forces in China, airfield attacks and the destruction of the rail network occupying the majority of the effort. Tsinan was

[1] General Kenney, *op. cit.*

Left: A 4th FS/3rd Air Commando Mustang. (Roger Freeman Collection)

again the target on 3 January, with the 311th FG's P-51s claiming eight 'Oscars', two 'Topsys', one 'Sally', one 'Lily' and one unidentified aircraft destroyed on the ground, although nine of the attackers were damaged by ground fire. The fighters also engaged a formation of 'Oscars' over Sinsiang and claimed two probables and three damaged. Two days later they were involved with at least a dozen 'Oscars' in the same area and shot down five for no loss. Twenty Mustangs of the 74th FS and 118th TRS hit airfields in the Shanghai area on 17 January and put in claims for 65 aircraft, most of them destroyed on the ground in what was becoming a familiar pattern for such attacks. By this time the Chinese counter-offensive was getting into its stride. Wanting was captured on 20 January and a week later the ground forces linked up with the Chinese 38th Division, re-opening the 'Burma Road' land route from India to China.

January 25 was another successful day, 530th FS pilots claiming 35 aircraft destroyed on the ground at Lantienchang and Nanyuan plus three 'Nates' and two 'Oscars' in aerial combat, again for no loss. Similar operations continued until mid-February, the 530th 'Yellow Scorpions' flying their last mission from Sian on 14 February and moving to Kwanghan the following day to rest and train replacement pilots. In the period from 7 November, when these operations had commenced,

the Squadron claimed 37–27–45 in the air and 130–22–29 on the ground, plus 517 locomotives and various other ground targets – an incredible achievement. The 'rest' period, however, was cut short and in March the Squadron was tasked with attacking airfields on Okinawa as part of the pre-invasion 'softening-up' process. The first operation was flown on the 24th, six Mustangs strafing three airfields and claiming two aircraft. The same targets were hit the following day, but this time the Mustangs ran into 20-plus Japanese fighters, mainly 'Tojos'. Lt Read shot down one 'Tojo' and one 'Oscar', and the Squadron claimed six others damaged. One Mustang was lost, and the pilots reported that these Japanese pilots were of a much higher calibre than those encountered in China.

Below: Maj John Herbst, 23rd FG. (US National Archives)

Above: The 2nd FS take off for the longest mission of war – to Bangkok – led by Bob Eason in *The Hungry One*, 15 March 1945. (Walter Eason)

On 14 February Lt-Col Levi Chase had led Mustangs of the 1st Squadron, 2nd Air Commando, to bomb Japanese positions in Pakokku whilst Maj Pryor led aircraft of the 2nd Squadron against other targets. With these sorties the 2nd Air Commando commenced its operational career in support of the Fourteenth Army in Burma. The fighter elements of the 2nd Air Commando had been activated in April 1944 and, equipped with P-51Cs, had been under intensive training in Florida from May to October, the training concentrating on close air support and interdiction missions, often at long range. In October they prepared to move to India, finally arriving in December and initially becoming established at Kalaikunda. However, it was soon decided that the fighter units were to move to the Burma front, and so in January they collected new P-51Ds, and a few F-6Ds, from Karachi and moved forward to Cox's Bazaar on the Arakan front, where they came under the operational control of the RAF's No 224 Group. As part of the air support plan for the Fourteenth Army's planned offensive to reconquer central Burma, the two squadrons became part of the First Provisional Fighter Group in support of IV Corps. The offensive was launched towards Meiktila on 14 February, and on a daily basis until 6 March the Mustangs provided fire support to the ground forces.

Hunting the Japanese

From early March onwards the role changed to that of hunting down the Japanese Air Force in the air and, more particularly, on the ground. The first such mission took place on 7 March, an escort to B-24s attacking Martaban port, but no enemy aircraft made an appearance. The following day the Mustangs strafed Mingaladon and Hmawbi airfields near Rangoon, Lt-Col Chase and Capt Eason each claiming aircraft hit on the ground, although very few Japanese aircraft appeared to be present. Escort missions on 9 and 11 March brought no action, and in order to make an effective strike on their elusive enemy Lt-Col Chase decided to attack the main airfield at Don Muang, Thailand. This was a bold move as it would involve a 1,500-mile trip, but Chase was able to convince Eastern Air Command that it was both possible and desirable to launch such an attack. Intelligence sources confirmed the presence of substantial numbers of Japanese aircraft at Don Muang and the mission was scheduled for 15 March. Forty Mustangs, twenty from each squadron (see panel overleaf), left Cox's Bazaar mid-morning, each aircraft equipped with two 110gal drop tanks. Three hours later the formation reached Ayuthaya, where the two squadrons split, the plan being for the 1st Squadron to hit the airfield from the north, followed a few minutes later by the 2nd Squadron from the west. On the final run-in to the target Chase saw two 'Oscars' at about 1,000 feet and he and his wingman, Lt Hadley Dixon, shot these down whilst the rest of the 1st Squadron approached Don Muang in line abreast, the plan being for each pilot to strafe whatever appeared in front of him. The airfield was crowded with aircraft and all the Mustang pilots claimed scores, Lt Bob Spann being credited with two destroyed and five damaged. An unfortunate 'Sally' bomber drifted over the airfield and was promptly pounced on and shot down by Maj William Buxton and Lt William Holman.

Chase had now arrived and called the Squadron to make a second run, which many did just prior to the arrival of the 2nd Squadron from the north-west. They, too, had a successful run over the target, some pilots turning back in for a second attack. The mission was an unqualified success, with the squadrons being credited with twenty destroyed, four probables and eighteen damaged. The only sad note was the loss of Capt Modine, who was shot down and killed by flak over the target. The units received a Distinguished Unit Citation for this mission. The average flight duration was 6hr 45min, and half the pilots wore the new G-suits. None complained of fatigue, but some took benzadrine just before reaching the target area.

Japanese airfields in Burma and Thailand were attacked on a regular basis by the Mustangs, targets such as Mingaladon, Zayatkwin, Chiang Mai, Prae, Moulmein and Hmawbi featuring on an almost daily basis during March. A dawn attack on the 26th against Hmawbi was a success – but at a cost: the Mustangs of both Lt-Col Chase and Maj Pryor were hit by ground fire and both pilots ended up in enemy territory, Chase in a forced-landing and Pryor by parachute. A daring rescue bid was launched when Bob Eason and Bobby Spann flew two L-5s to the area, escorted by a pair of P-51s, to try and pick up the downed pilots. Chase was safely picked up but Pryor had landed in a

Composition of Don Muang Raid, 15 March 1945[1]

Pilot	Aircraft	Claims
1st Fighter Squadron:		
Lt-Col Levi Chase	'85 *Smiling Jack*	1 air, 2 gnd
Lt Hadley Dixon	'63	1 air
Lt William Gadow	'11 *Mary Jane*	
Lt Dale Grastorf	'53 *Lady Esther II*	
Capt William Marshall	'21 *Nancy*	2 gnd
Lt Bert Lutton	'61 *Peggy Jane IV*	1 gnd
Lt Edwin Harkins	'31	1 gnd
Lt Herman Lyons	'57 *Son of a "B"*	1 gnd
Lt Col William Buxton	'19 *Baby Girl*	° air, 1 gnd
Lt William Holman	'59 *Jackie*	° air, 1 gnd
Lt Bob Spann	'45 *Big Gas Bird*	7 gnd
Lt Robert Smith	'43 *Rosali*	2 gnd
Capt Warren Modine	'15 *Barbara*	Crashed
Lt Roger Morrison	'25 *Pot and Dot*	2 gnd
Lt Harold Hettema	'35 *The Pasadena Kid*	2 gnd
Lt Dean Wimer	'55 *Butch*	2 gnd
Capt W. Robert Eason	'17 *Queen Bee; Anna Belle V*	2 gnd
Lt Richard Fishburn	'27 *Drone Bee; Miss Francis*	2 gnd
Lt Robert Cason	'37 *Lazy Be*	2 gnd
Lt Benjamin Lundberg	'47 *Buzzin Bee*	2 gnd
2nd Fighter Squadron		
Lt-Col Roger Pryor	'14 *Weak Eyes Yokam*	2 gnd
Lt B. J. Mayer	'20 *Cheese Cake Chassis*	
Lt William Wilson	'22 *Hatchet Face*	1 gnd
Lt Charles LeFan	'18 *Ash Kan Wilkse*	1 gnd
Remaining pilots, Flight composition not known:		
Maj William Grosvenor	'34 *Earthquake McGoon*	2 gnd
Capt Albert Abraham	'50 *Adam Lazonga*	1 gnd
Capt Edward Atha	'88 *Available Jones*	1 gnd
Capt Glen Charpie	'72 *Hairless Joe*	
Capt Julian Gilliam	'64 *Repulsive J Repugnant*	
Capt Sherard Sorenson	'30 *Sir Cedric Cesspool*	
Lt Robert Beck	'26 *Hamfat McGoon*	1 gnd
Lt Dorman Beckner	'56 *Duchess – Lil Abner*	
Lt LeVerne Donner	'70 *Tombstone Jake*	1 gnd
Lt John Harris	'52 *Clamlike McSlop*	1 gnd
Lt Robert Heisick	'40 *Cyclone McGoon*	1 gnd
Lt Paul Kent	'68 *J Swineface McCarpetbagger*	1 gnd
Lt Edward Pearle	'74 *Miss Margie Lue; Rebel Gal*	1 gnd
Lt Edwin Pike	'36 *Pretty Boy McGoon*	2 gnd
Lt Tom Tesla	'54 *Lonesome Polecat*	1 gnd

[1] Details via Bob Eason.

Top: Mustang IV KM730 en route from Barrackpore to Allahabad. It was intended to equip an SAAF Wing for operations against Japan, but this did not become effective before the end of the war. (Andy Thomas Collection)

Above: A P-51 being given a 150-hour inspection at Clark. 25 June 1945. (Ken Delve Collection)

wooded area and the L-5s could not reach him; he was taken prisoner by the Japanese.

The Allied advance continued towards Rangoon, and although the 2nd Air Commando flew a number of ground support missions its primary task remained that of destroying the Japanese Air Force. Thus April saw a continuation of the missions to airfields in Burma and Thailand, although not without loss: three Mustangs went down to ground fire during the 9 April attack on Don Muang, for example, although all three pilots were picked up by the Thais and interned. The final mission into Thailand was flown on 29 April when sixteen aircraft attacked Koke Khathiem and eight attacked Nakhon Sawan, a number of aircraft being destroyed at the former location. The final airfield attack was mounted against Moulmein on 2 May, after which the 2nd Air Commando supported the Allied assault on Rangoon, the final wartime mission being flown on 9 May.

In just over two months of operations the Mustang squadrons of the 2nd Air Commando had claimed 60 enemy aircraft

Left: An engine change for a 310th FBS aircraft at an 'advanced base in the Philippines'. (US National Archives)

destroyed, the majority of these on the ground. Although the P-51 had been criticised for its vulnerability in the ground attack role, Lt McGinnis Clark of the 1st FS (2nd Air Commando) had cause to be grateful for the rugged nature of his Mustang during a strafing mission on 23 April:

'Capt Bill Marshall led his flight on a strafing mission that morning about 80 miles north of Rangoon. Lt Clark was strafing a truck at an altitude of about 50 ft when the truck suddenly veered off the road into a field. Lt Clark turned to fire on the truck when suddenly a telegraph pole appeared immediately in front of his plane. There was no way to avoid the pole; he hit it and sheared it with his port wing. The plane ricocheted off the pole and was nearly flipped upside down. As the plane righted itself he could see parts of the pole, some of the cross arm, and wires, hanging from his left wing. This debris soon fell off. Altitude was gained gradually until a more comfortable 2,000 ft was reached. The plane flew at a max speed of about 150 mph. With Lt Eddie Harkins as escort, Clark headed north looking for a British-held strip. Clark landed *The Hungry One* at Lewe I whilst Harkins flew back to Cox's Bazaar to alert repair personnel.'

S/Sgt Ted Uley was one of the repair crew: 'Sgt Hutchinson and I got our equipment together, including sheet metal material for the wing and enough rivets to get it into flying condition. After repairing the wing, the plane was pre-flighted but a rough engine indicated a change of plugs was needed. The replacement plugs were no better so the old plugs were cleaned and the carburetor readjusted. Here was an airplane that had hit a telegraph pole and surely must have been knocked out of alignment. We were not sure that the landing gear should be retracted but we felt that the plane could and would fly.'[1] Lt Clarke cleared the trees at the end of the strip – just – and flew back to Cox's Bazaar.

---

[1] *World War Two Air Commandos*, Vol. II.

Right: A formation of 318th FBG Mustangs over Ie Shima. (Ken Delve Collection)

Another Mustang force commenced operations in this theatre when the decision was taken to base B-29s in the Marianas to attack the Japanese homeland: the escort for these bombers was to be provided by Mustangs based on Iwo Jima, some 660 miles from Japan. On 7 April 1945 a force of B-29s escorted by 108 P-51s of VII Fighter Command attacked the Nakajima-Musashi factory, each P-51 having a 165 US gallon drop tank under each wing. This was the first occasion on which land-based US fighters appeared over Japan. To all intents and purposes it signalled the end, although there was much hard fighting yet to be done and the Mustangs were invariably at the forefront of the air effort.

By spring 1945 most of the missions being undertaken by the 23rd FG were

Right: P-51s strafing Japanese 'Nicks'. (US National Archives)

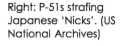

ground strafing. Ed Bollen was with the 75th FS when it took part in such a mission, along with the 76th FS, led by Lt-Col Ed Rector:

'We approached Shanghai at about 10,000 ft and when about 20 miles out started a high-speed descent. At this time the four groups split with each going to their assigned airfield. Our group headed to Lunghwa with only five aircraft. A flight of three were to strafe the airfield while Capt Harper and I flew top cover to protect them from any fighters . . . when were

about four miles out I spotted a fighter over the airfield at about 4,000 feet . . . I called him out to Harper and we started an immediate climb towards it . . . I started a diving turn to the left pulling into range about the time he had completed 180 degrees of turn. I was now on a westerly heading which put me up-sun from him. This placed me in a 90 degree deflection shot and in relation to his aircraft I was aiming straight down into his cockpit. I pulled the proper lead and fired three short bursts. All three hit in and around

Below: An unidentified location in the Pacific, but a very atmospheric photograph showing a variety of aircraft types. (Ken Delve Collection)

the cockpit. We were using API ammo which gave little flashes of light when they hit. As I completed the third burst I was so close that I had to break off the pass and pulled into a steep climb to get into position for another attack. As I climbed, I lowered my left wing to see what he was doing and saw that I had shot his left wing off at the root and that he had baled out.'[1] The victim had been a 'Raiden' flown by Lt Masatsake Hayasaki.

Over Formosa

The SWPA Intelligence Summary for 14 April 1945 included reference to P-51 operations over Formosa:

'The unspectacular and reluctant type of air opposition the Japanese are currently offering Allied units over Formosa is exemplified in the following squadron narrative:

'"At approximately 1500, three enemy aircraft were sighted flying at 4,500 ft just SE of Kilan. Red Flight was flying about 4,000 ft heading due north; three enemy aircraft were spotted about 2 o'clock high, heading SE. Red Flight climbed to 5,500 ft. The enemy aircraft, consisting of one Nick and two Zeke 52s, were flying a vic formation, with the Nick leading. When the enemy sighted our fighters they echeloned to the right, with the Nick on the left. When our fighters approached within range, the Nick made a sharp turn to the left, the Zeke on his right made a gentle turn to the left and the other Zeke went straight ahead.

'"Capt F. made a pass from above and directly astern of the Zeke on his extreme right. About 200 yards away the Zeke turned about 90 degrees to the left and Capt F. made a pass and fired about a one second burst, observing hits all along the fuselage and cockpit. The Zeke did a Split S and when he straightened up, Capt F. fired a three second burst and the Zeke blew up in mid air, the pilot was seen to bale out.

'"Capt F. then dove on a second Zeke who in turn pulled up allowing Capt F. to make a head-on pass, firing a one second

burst, but observing no results. At this time, Lt C., the No 3 man, who had been going 120 degrees to Capt F., went down through the clouds and observed a Zeke which was going 180 degrees to him. Lt C. turned left with the Zeke and approached head-on. Lt C. fired a one second burst from 30 degrees about 50 yards away. The Zeke was seen to burst into flames and passed directly in front of Lt C. Lt P., the No 4 man, saw the Zeke crash into the ground. Lt P. was able to make a pass on the Nick from 90 degrees. He fired a two second burst, hits were observed on the cockpit and Lt C. saw the Nick burst into flames and crash into the ground."'

The ACSEA Weekly Intelligence Summary included an extract from a report that had first appeared in the Fourteenth Air Force Intelligence Summary entitled 'Psycho-Analysis of a P-51 by a Japanese Squadron Leader'. The Japanese airman is reported to have inspected a wrecked P-51 shot down during a raid on Ching-Tao and then given his impressions of the American aircraft to a newspaper:

'After having examined the plane, Squadron Leader Hatzu-Ki pointed out the merits and demerits of the P-51 in a conference with newspaper men. "Construction of the aircraft places stress on the protection of the pilot rather than on the machine and thus manifests the national characteristics of the American people," he stated. Pointing to the difference between the actual aircraft and the American exaggerations about it, he concluded this was an ordinary type, nothing above the standard of the fighter aircraft of the world.

'He said, "The P-51 was manufactured by the North American Corporation before 1944 and had been used by the American forces in Chungking for about one year. Wreckage of a B-29 which I saw in Kyushu in Japan was much better than this type so far as quality and process of manufacture is concerned. Due to shortage of materials, the quality of American aircraft is

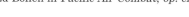

[1] Ed Bollen in *Pacific Air Combat, op. cit*

falling off, even more than is indicated by this P-51.

'"There were four machine-guns on the plane merely of 12.7mm calibre – no 20mm cannon as exaggerated in American propaganda. The windproof glass in front of the cockpit was thick. The back of the cockpit was covered with a bulletproof steel plate. This shows the essential characteristic of the American people, because were no such safety protections on the aircraft, no American pilot would dare fly it.

'"There was no armoured protection on the machine (such as engine etc.) so that any if any part of the machine were hit the aircraft would fall quickly. With a sturdy landing gear and a large tail, the plane is quite stable, but this indicates the inferior skill of the pilots. Technically speaking, the landing gear should be light in weight and the tail should be small in size to be efficient. The landing gear is as sturdily constructed as that of the training aircraft, shows that American pilots without sufficient training and hours' practice were not proficient.

'"The engine (Allison V-5 type) was not very good either in design of in construction. Owing to material shortages, the Americans have used a great number of substitutes, such as artificial rubber, silk, etc.; also, they do not use paint. Thus generally speaking, this aircraft is worse than the Jap fighters."'[1]

A typical week for this early summer period was that for 20–26 May, as summarised in the ACSEA intelligence review and reproduced in the accompanying panel.

The 35th FG had arrived on Okinawa and sent 48 aircraft on a sweep along the west coast of Kyushu as far as the naval base at Sasebo. The only enemy air activity was three floatplanes, and these were quickly shot down, the one despatched by Capt Richard Cella being credited as the first official victory over Japan. 'That evening the Japanese radio announced

[1] ACSEA Weekly Intelligence Summary No 78, 13 May 1945.

P-51 Mustang Activity, SWPA, 20–26 May 1945

May 20	81 ac	Marikina area
	111 ac	Balete Pass
21	95 ac	Marikina area
	69 ac	Balete Pass (with A-20s)
	28 ac	Cagayan Valley (escort B-25s)
	33 ac	Acopi Place
22	83 ac	Kina area
	92 ac	Balete Pass (with A-20s)
	15 ac	Santa Fe area (with A-20s)
	12 ac	North Luzon (with B-25s)
23	12 ac	Ipo area
	127 ac	Balete Pass
	63 ac	North Luzon (with B-25s)
24	167 ac	Balete Pass
	66 ac	North Luzon
25	117 ac	Ipo area
	58 ac	North Luzon
26	106 ac	Ipo area
	48 ac	Balete Pass
	67 ac	North Luzon

Below left: Capt John Vogt of the 318th FG being strapped into his aircraft by S/Sgt Fay Lear at Ie Shima. (US National Archives)

Below: The 35th FG on the break over Yontan, Okinawa, 27 July 1945. (Ken Delve Collection)

that we were so hard up for airplanes and pilots that we were using flimsy training type P-51 Mustangs piloted by young American girls in our operations against Formosa.'[1]

According to the intelligence report for 30 June 1945, 'A total of 91 P-51s, attacking Hyakurigahara, Shimodate, Kasumigaura and Katori aerodromes on June 23 had 90 encounters with unidentified, unaggressive planes, of which 19 were destroyed, two probably destroyed and 13 damaged, with the loss of three P-51s (two pilots were saved). The Mustangs also destroyed 13 planes on the ground, probably destroyed 12, damaged ten, in addition to inflicting severe damage to the hangars at Shimodate.'

The 'Zeke 52' had been encountered by American aircraft on numerous occasions, but it was not until July that a comparative performance trial was carried out against the aircraft, the 'opposition' being provided by a P-38, P-47 and P-51. The aircraft had been captured and had in due course been rebuilt by the Technical Air Intelligence Centre (TAIC) and given the number TAIC 7 ('4340). An extract of the report was contained in the ACSEA Weekly Intelligence Summary and the relevant sections for the P-51 are reproduced here:

'The Japanese Zeke 52 aircraft is an all-metal low wing single-seat aircraft of conventional appearance. It is powered by a Nakajima Sakae 31A twin row radial engine. Armament consists of two fixed synchronised 7.65 machine-guns forward and one 20mm fixed automatic cannon in each wing. The Zeke's high rate of turn, general manoeuvrability, and good flight characteristics are its most desirable combat

---

[1] General Kenney, *op. cit.*

features. Poor performance, weak arma- ment, high control forces at high speed, and excessive vulnerability make it an undesirable combat aircraft.

'The P-51 was 80 mph faster at 10,000 ft and 95 mph faster at 25,000 ft. Due to advantages in speed, acceleration and high-speed climb, all three Allied fighters were able to maintain the offensive in in- dividual combat with the Zeke 52, and to break off combat at will. The Zeke 52 is greatly superior to all three Allied fight- ers in radius of turn and general manoeu- vrability at low speeds. The pilots of Al- lied fighter aircraft should take advantage of high-speed performance when engag- ing the Zeke 52 in combat; speed should be kept well above 200 IAS during all com- bats, 'hit and run' tactics should be used whenever possible, and following the Zeke through any continued turning maneuver must be strictly avoided.'[1]

The same month an interim report was also issued of a partial trial against a 'Tojo'; this Tactical Flight Test was reported in SWPA Intelligence Summary No 282 (as with the 'Zeke' report, only those ele- ments concerning the P-51 are included here):

'A short tactical test flight of a Tojo, P- 51, F6F and Seafire shows the Tojo to be a formidable air adversary. The Tojo had

[1] ACSEA Weekly Intelligence Summary No 88, 27 July 1945.

Right: P-51 *Mickey* at Clark Field, Luzon, 25 June 1945. (US National Archives)

Left: A Fourteenth Air Force P-51 pictured from the C-47 it was escorting at the time, 27 August 1945. (US National Archives)

been recovered and repaired by the TAIU at Clark Field.

'Only one speed run at 5000 ft was made. The cockpit of the Tojo became excessively hot due to the fact that the blast tubes were closed, not allowing proper cooling.

	'Tojo	P-51
'RPM	2600	2750
'Manifold pressure	38"	49"
'Airspeed	275mph	not given

'Full power was not applied to the Tojo due to the fact that the engine was new and had very little slow time. War Emergency power on the Tojo at 5000 ft is 41.7" and 2650 RPM, and it is believed that an IAS of 300 mph could be attained at that altitude and power setting.

'The initial acceleration of the Tojo was very good and it was able to compete with the P-51. All Allied aircraft were able to rapidly pull away in a dive. Initial zoom climb of the Tojo was better than any of the Allied planes. The Tojo was able to gain and maintain an angle of climb better than the Allied planes. Slow airspeed (140–150 mph) caused the P-51 to overheat. The Tojo could draw a lead on all of the Allied aircraft at slow speeds and low power settings; however, this advantage rapidly decreased as speed was increased.'

So the basic advice was the same as for the 'Zeke' – don't get involved in a slow speed turning fight!

July saw three main operational areas within SWPA – Honshu-Kyushu, Formosa-Ryukyus and Luzon – with almost daily operations against a variety of ground targets, including lines of communication and airfields. The P-51s had an almost 'free run' as regards air opposition, but ground fire continued to cause losses.

The P-51 had been late arriving in the Far East theatres of war, but by early 1945 numbers had significantly increased and by spring it was playing a major part in the air war. For the latter months of the war with Japan the P-51 was able to dominate the sky in the same way that it had over Europe.

5

POST-WAR MUSTANGS

The post-1945 period brought a very mixed fate for the P-51. The RAF quickly disposed of its Mustangs, partly in response to the 'contract' arrangement of Lend-Lease under which the vast majority of the later variants were acquired, and which required purchase, return or disposal of the aircraft. Most units maintained an operational training programme up to the days prior to their disbandment or re-equipment, and, sadly, tragedy occasionally struck. Having suffered few losses in the latter months of the war, No 112 Squadron had a 'Black Thursday' on 26 July when it lost five aircraft and pilots. A formation of nine had taken off from Lavariano for a reconnaissance sortie; two returned to base with engine problems and the others proceeded to carry out various operational procedures. At one point they descended into a valley for 'strafe practice' but the weather closed in and it became obvious that the sortie would have to be aborted. Only two aircraft made it out of the valley; the other five hit the ground.

Although the jet era had begun, development and evaluation of the P-51 continued, both as a combat type in its own right and as a platform for aerodynamic and systems trials. Indeed, although reference has been made from time to time to various operational trials, there has been no space in this book to cover all aspects of the diverse involvement that the P-51 had with such work. However, the mention of jets makes it worth noting a trial that took place at Wright Field

Above: 'AK'-coded Mustangs of No 213 Squadron. (Ken Delve Collection)

using 44-7253 fitted with a pair of PJ31-1 aeropulse engines, attached through the bomb shackles. The report of 27 July 1945 concluded that 'the action of the jet exhausts on the tail of the airplane is considered to have caused excessive vibration of the airplane, especially the pilot's compartment. This may have been aggravated by the lack of synchronisation of the firing of the two jet engines.' What was not stated was the actual purpose of the trial installation.

More power and improved aerodynamics had led to numerous instances of compressibility effects, and a number of trials were undertaken to investigate this phenomenon. For example, 'A Mustang III, KH505, was allocated to RAE for high speed research, and this showed up some unpleasant compressibility effects, and indeed the aircraft was eventually lost in failing to recover from a high Mach No dive, killing the Canadian pilot, Sqn Ldr E. B. Gale.'[1] The accident occurred on 25 May 1946.

On 4 October 1946 Air Proving Ground Command at Eglin issued its report on the 'Service Test of the P-51H Airplane'. Three P-51H-1 aircraft were used (44-64169, 44-64170 and 44-64171) and one P-51H-5 (44-64395). The first of the H-1 aircraft was tested with a special fuel (ANF-33) with a

Left: Mustang IVs (plus Tempest VIs) of No 213 Squadron. (Ken Delve Collection)

water injection system, but 'the performance data obtained cannot be considered as typical of the subject airplane because this fuel was never authorised for standard use'. However, comparisons were made with water injection and standard fuel in the H-5 aircraft included in the evaluation. The evaluation had been ordered as a Priority One task in June 1945, but with the ending of the war the urgency appears to have been removed. The general recommendations of the report were that:

'a. The P-51H airplane without water injection is considered an acceptable but not a desirable replacement for the P-51D type airplane.

'b. If the V-1650-9 engine is released for war emergency power ratings of greater than 67" Hg manifold pressure, the P-51H airplane [can] be considered a desirable replacement for the P-51D.'

Three 'test missions' were flown – escort, fighter strike and fighter-bomber strike. The escort mission recorded a radius of action of 945 miles (allowing, as with all these test missions, a 40gal fuel reserve). The fighter strike, with six 5in HVAR (High Velocity Aircraft Rockets)

---

[1] Eric Brown, *Wings of the Weird and Wonderful.*

and two 110gal external tanks, gave a radius of action of 925 miles. The radius of the fighter-bomber strike mission, with the aircraft armed with six rockets and two 500lb bombs (and thus no external tanks) was greatly reduced at only 365 miles.

An armament report was prepared at the same time, with the three aircraft used for the evaluation mounting six .50 machine guns, three in each wing, and an underwing rocket installation. The general conclusion was that the 'armament installation of the P-51H airplane is functionally reliable and operationally suitable for service use'. The rocket tests included salvo firing from 10,000ft in a 20-degree dive at 320mph, no problems being recorded. However, it was remarked that the inboard guns tended to jam under high G (an old P-51 problem).

The importance of the water injection system for the P-51H's performance, and the difficulties suffered with this system during the evaluations, led to a further series of tests in December 1946. These employed ten P-51H aircraft at Patterson Field to 'secure satisfactory operation of the water injection system and the Simmonds' Boost Control as installed on P-51H airplanes'. Various modifications were made during the tests, such as increasing the water pump pressure from 19 to 22psi, installing a water by-pass line to alleviate air pressure to the boost control, and changing the size of the bleed hole in the water regulator. These had the desired effect and the system proved to be both reliable and efficient, producing war emergency figures of 80in Hg boost.

The final series of P-51H tests took place in early 1947, the report being dated 29 August, and involved P-51H-5 44-64388 being 'winterised' for cold weather functional tests: 'It was concluded that at extreme low temperatures the hydraulic fluid used became too viscous to operate the landing gear system, that certain hydraulic seals, valve cases, hoses, shock mounts and insulations were unsatisfactory. Also that the landing light, gunsight, machine guns and gun camera all failed to function satisfactorily. Further tests and development [must] be conducted to improve or replace these defective components.' Cold weather conditions – in temperatures down to –60°F – were to be experienced by the Mustangs in their next war, Korea.

Air National Guard

The ending of the Second World War not only slowed down (and in many cases halted) the development, testing and trials of aircraft such as the P-51, it also saw them being disposed of in vast numbers. The Mustang rapidly left US front-line service as jet types became available. The formation of Strategic Air Command in March 1946 led to major organisational changes, which included SAC's acquisition of two P-51 Groups, the 33rd FG (58th, 59th and 60th Squadrons) and, in August, the 27th FG; a third Group (the 82nd) was added later to give SAC a total of over 200 Mustangs by mid-1947. It was, however, a short-lived period as the P-80 soon began to replace the P-51 and fighter units were moved from SAC to Air Defense Command.

However, in America the Mustang found a new lease of life with the Air National Guard, and it soon became the most widely used type with that organisation. The Guard was created following an announcement in January 1946 by the Army Chief of Staff that National Guard air units were to be activated to 'provide a reserved component of the Army and Army Air Forces of the United States, capable of expansion to immediate war strength, able to furnish land and air units for service anywhere in the world'. Fiscal Year 1946 saw the approval of twenty Fighter Groups and 62 Fighter Squadrons, along with five Composite Groups; squadrons in the West and Midwest regions were each to be equipped with 25 P-51Ds. It was one of these units, the 120th FS in Colorado, that, on 30 June 1946, became the first Guard unit to receive Federal recognition.

Right: Mustang 44-64180 carrying an interesting slogan, with the PF-180 serial under the tail. (*FlyPast* Collection)

Right: The Air National Guard was a major post-war user of P-51s, as here with P-51D-30NA 44-74825 of the California ANG. (*FlyPast* Collection)

Right: A North Dakota ANG P-51. (Ken Delve Collection)

Growth was slow, in part due to budget constraints and transfer requirements, but in FY 1947 some thirty squadrons received P-51Ds. There was, of course, no shortage of aircraft (or indeed of the other fighter type, the P-47, that Guard units were acquiring) and likewise there was no shortage of trained personnel, air crew or ground crew, willing to join the new units.

On 18 September 1947 the United States Air Force was formed and the Guard now became the Air National Guard (ANG); in the same Fiscal Year a further nine P-51 units received Federal recognition, but in the same year the ANG also received its first jets. Within a few years these would bring about the demise of the P-51, but not before a major upsurge in activity with the outbreak of the Korean War in 1950. On 11 June 1948 the USAF introduced a change in the aircraft designation system, with F-for-Fighter replacing P-for-Pursuit, and so all the Mustangs instantly became F-51s rather than P-51s.[1] By FY 1949 the original plan for the ANG ORBAT had been fulfilled, and, although four more P-51 units had been recognised, jets continued to replace Mustangs in some units. This re-equipment programme was, however, reversed in many cases in 1950 as part of the reorganisation brought about by the Korean War. In addition, as discussed below, the Guard was called upon to hand over a number of P-51s for USAF use.

Twin Mustang

This is, perhaps, the best place to consider one of the most unusual derivatives of the P-51, the F-82 Twin Mustang. The need for an escort fighter to accompany bombers, especially B-29s, on long-range sorties in the Far East theatre had led to the consideration of various factors, including that of pilot fatigue. A long sortie, seven or eight hours in duration, put a strain on single-seat pilots that could affect their combat performance. One possible solution was a two-pilot fighter, and North American proposed to achieve this by joining together two of their highly effective P-51s. giving twin-engine reliability and performance and providing for two pilots. Four prototypes were ordered by the USAAF on 7 January 1944 under the XP-82 designation. The first flight took place on 15 April 1945, the aircraft being based upon two P-51Hs but with various modifications such as an extra 57in section in front of the tailplane unit and strengthened outer wings to allow for the carriage of drop tanks. Major changes had to be made to the centre section where the two aircraft were joined, and a new undercarriage system was devised. The first two prototypes were powered by two Packard Merlins (a V-1650-25 and a V-1650-23 to give 'handed' rotation and thus reduce the torque problem. The aircraft was assessed as having a maximum speed of 482mph at 25,000ft. The third prototype, the XP-82A, was powered by two Allison V-1710-119 but this, along with the fourth aircraft, was cancelled. Nevertheless, the USAAF was convinced that the P-82 had potential and so an initial order was placed for 500 aircraft under the designation P-82B. The first aircraft left the production lines in spring 1945 but only twenty had been completed before the war with Japan ended in August – and the USAAF began its cancellation of projects, including all the remaining P-82s. None of the aircraft entered squadron service, but they were used for a series of trials and evaluations.

The first post-war defence budget, however, made provision for 250 Twin Mustangs for use as escort fighters and night fighters; 100 of the former, designated F-82E, were ordered in December 1945 and 150 of the night fighter variants (F-82F and F-82G) the following autumn. In the meantime the first evaluation reports were being published:

'The P-82C night fighter is a twin-engine, twin-fuselage airplane, powered by

Right: The second prototype XP-82 Twin Mustang, 44-83887, over Southern California in 1945. (Ken Delve Collection)

---

[1] However, for the purposes of this book the change in designation has been ignored and the aircraft will continue to be given its better-known P-51 designation.

two Packard-built Merlin V-1650-23 and V-1650-25 engines. In appearance the airplane resembles two P-51s joined by the center wing section and the horizontal stabiliser and elevator. The pilot's cockpit is in the left fuselage and the radar operator's cockpit is in the right fuselage. Five hundred [and] ninety-four gallons of fuel are carried internally in wing panel fuel tanks. The radar set is installed in a nacelle which is suspended under the central wing section and extends forward to a point even with the propeller spinners. The airplane is armed with six fixed caliber .5-inch machine guns in the center wing section, and is equipped with wing racks to carry bombs, chemical tanks, drop fuel tanks or rockets. With full internal fuel and ammunition, take-off gross weight is approx 20,000 lbs. The P-82D is identical to the P-82C except that it is equipped with the AN/APG-1 radar set.'

These introductory comments were made in the an Air Proving Ground report dated 19 December 1947 and entitled 'Comparative Test of Night Fighting Equipment in P-82 Aircraft'. The report concluded that '. . . the P-82C and P-82D aircraft are not satisfactory for night fighting operations because of limited field of view, impairments to night vision (exhaust flare, instrument glare and muzzle flash), obstructed view of the flight instruments, undesirable landing characteristics, inadequate landing light, a nose-down change of trim when the guns are fired, excessive aileron forces and poor deceleration.'

The tests had their origin in a letter dated 11 July 1945 for the 'combat suitability of the P-82 Night Fighter'. In mid-1946 the two aircraft, 44-65169 and 44-65170, arrived, along with an amplification of the evaluation rationale: '. . . the tests and evaluations are based on an assumption that the P-82 will be a more suitable night fighter than a day fighter. One hundred of the day fighter version of the P-82 have been ordered, but presently available performance data indicates that this type of aircraft may not be particularly adaptable as a day fighter. If such is the case, it may be advisable to convert all P-82s to night fighters.'

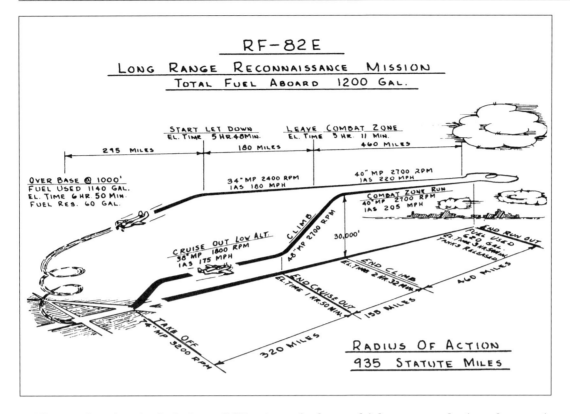

The evaluation included 27 GCI missions using an A-26 as a target, with various intercept approaches and with the target using varying degrees of evasion:

'Results of these missions indicate that the P-82 airplane is capable of making satisfactory interceptions from stern, beam and head-on initial approaches, and that its limitations in making these interceptions are primarily limitations of the radar equipment. The P-82 proved capable of following the target airplane in mild and moderate evasive action, but because of the visual limitations cited above, it was limited to an approach path below and to the right of the target airplane. It was found that the P-82 was not able to follow an A-26 airplane which was employing maximum evasive action (80 degree banks, sharp reverse spirals, steep climbing and diving turns); in every case the radar set jumped contact as soon as the target airplane commenced to take maximum evasive action, However, it is the opinion of the testing personnel that evasive action of this sort will rarely be encountered in tactical situations. The P-82 was able to follow and close with a B-29 target airplane which was employing the maximum evasive action of which it was capable. The poor deceleration of the P-82 was a disadvantage in all these missions. Close co-ordination was required between pilot and radar observer to avoid overshooting the target airplane.

'NORTH AMERICAN P-82

'Since the jet airplane has entered the aviation field, the fighter plane with reciprocating engines has been nearly forgotten – however, the Army Air Forces has [sic] not overlooked the P-82 Twin Mustang. The performance and battle record of its predecessor, the P-51, in itself is enough to cause much consideration to be given to this airplane. This twin engine, twin fuselage, low wing fighter is the most versatile of its type ever built. The Government has purchased twenty production items to date. These articles are designated as P-82B airplanes and employ Packard built Rolls-Royce engines with a two stage, two speed supercharger and driving a four bladed eleven foot Aeroproducts full feathering propeller. Each engine develops approximately 2300 hp at

Left and right: Two charts from a USAAF report showing mission profiles for the RF-82. (Ken Delve Collection)

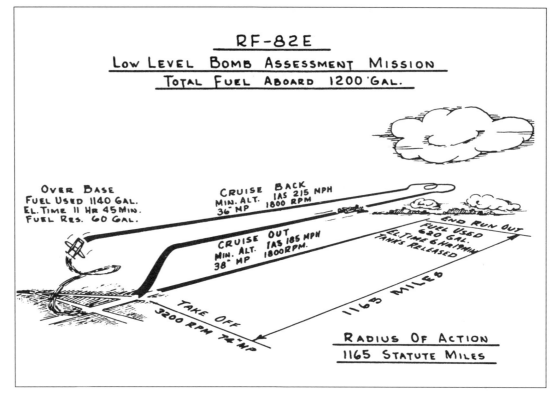

RF-82 E
LOW LEVEL BOMB ASSESSMENT MISSION
TOTAL FUEL ABOARD 1200 GAL.

OVER BASE
FUEL USED 1140 GAL.
EL. TIME 11 HR 45 MIN.
FUEL RES. 60 GAL.

CRUISE BACK
MIN. ALT. IAS 215 MPH
36" MP 1800 RPM

CRUISE OUT
MIN. ALT. IAS 185 MPH
38" MP 1800 RPM.

END RUN OUT
FUEL USED 620 GAL.
EL. TIME 6 HR 1 MIN
TANKS RELEASED

TAKE OFF 3200 RPM 74"MP

1165 MILES

RADIUS OF ACTION
1165 STATUTE MILES

its highest ratings. The frontal arrangement is designed for minimum air resistance. This plane can climb close to 7,000 feet a minute and approaches a top speed of 500 mph. Its versatility can be illustrated as follows:

'*Interceptor* – the right hand cockpit of the airplane is so designed that the canopy can be removed and a special piece of fairing slid in its place so as to produce a clean right fuselage. Also, in this version the bottom of the wing can be cleared of bomb racks and shackles since no external tanks or rockets will be required.

'*Attack Fighter* – for this version an eight gun nacelle is hung from the midsection ... Each gun in the nacelle has 400 rounds of 50 caliber gun ammunition available. This would give the operator fourteen forward firing 50 caliber guns for attacking and strafing purposes with no external fuel. The airplane in this version would have a yardstick range of approximately 1900 miles.

'*Fighter-Bomber* – airplane in this version can carry two 2,000 lb bombs, one under each wing, and with a full complement of internal gas can attain a range of over 1500 miles. External fuel either on the center section or outboard of the bombs could be carried in addition thus increasing this range.

'*Long Range Escort Fighter* – for this version two 310 gallon tanks can be carried on the bottom of the center wing and with the 600 gallon internal fuel a yardstick range of almost 5,000 miles can be obtained at an average airspeed of approximately 240 miles per hour A long range version has been suggested which would carry four 310 gallon external tanks and tanks behind the pilots and in the ammunition bay. It could attain a range of close to 7,000 miles.

'*Long Range Fighter* – with no external fuel, external bombs or guns, the airplane with 600 gallons internal fuel has a yardstick range of approximately 2,500 miles with an average true airspeed of 240 mph and remaining in the air 9.34 hours.

'*Photographic Reconnaissance* – a nacelle for the center wing has been designed by North American Aviation which can accommodate all type cameras required by the Army Air Forces to make this airplane a photographic type. This nacelle could be added or taken off at the pilot's convenience converting the airplane easily into any configuration listed before. In other words a standard configuration of the airplane with this nacelle added makes it automatically the reconnaissance type.

'*Night Fighter* – the Army has already built the P-82C and P-82D airplanes which are versions of night fighters. Tests to date prove the airplane to be very satisfactory in this condition. The P-82C contains the SCR-720C air interceptor equipment similar to that used on the Northrop P-61 for the purpose of locating enemy airplanes on an indicator in the right hand or radar operator's cockpit. The high speed of this airplane over any that has been built to date in the night fighter category will prove its additional versatility. Included in this airplane is the AN/APN-1 radio altimeter which aids in blind landing approaches and over water flight. This altimeter indicates the ex-

act distance above land or water and not above sea level. The P-82D is identical with the exception that it contains AN/AFG-1 radar search equipment instead of SCR-72C.

'*Rocket Fighter* – with design gross weight, this plane can carry twenty five 5" rockets suspended under the wing.

'The latest version of the P-82 airplane is known as the P-82E and will have provisions for Allison V-1710-143 and V-1710-145 engines. New additions also include the rapid type N-3 caliber gun, pilot ejection, newly designed fire extinguishing systems and a partially redesigned cockpit. It is probable that quite a few of these airplanes will be built as night fighters after the tests on the P-82C and P-82D referred to above are completed.'

The following May the evaluation team at Eglin issued another report on the P-82, this time to 'determine if the AN/APG-

Right: P-82B 44-65176, coded 'PQ-176'. (US National Archives)

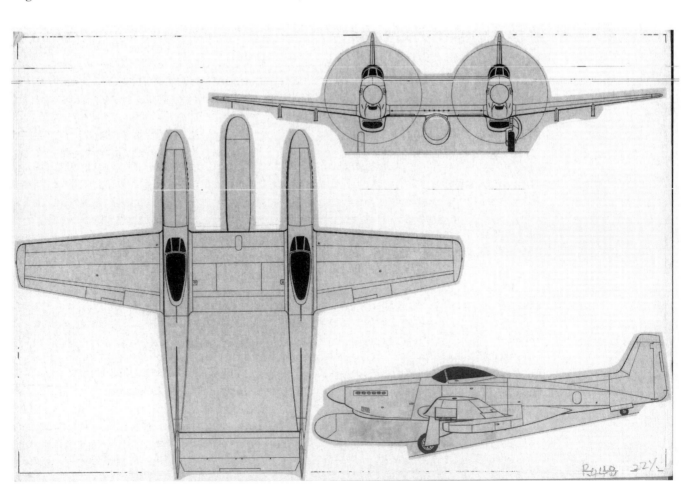

1 is suitable for blind firing of fixed guns, to determine the effect of vibration caused by firing the .50 armament of the P-82 on the radar screen and to determine muzzle blast effect of the guns on the radar nacelle'. A P-82D was used for these tests from March 1947 to the date of the report in May 1948 and the results were not promising. It was concluded that firing the guns blurred the radar screen and also damaged the radome; furthermore, the radar could not be used for 'blind fire' except from dead astern of an non-evading target!

The P-82E had duly entered service with Strategic Air Command's 27th FG (522nd, 523rd and 524th Squadrons), the first aircraft being accepted at McChord AFB, Washington, in March 1948. However, the service life of the type was very short and by mid-1950 the 27th FG had re-equipped with F-84Es. Production of the night fighter Twin Mustangs resulted in three variants – 91 F-82Fs with AN/APS-13 radar, 45 F-82Gs with SCR-720C radar and fourteen F-82Hs, winterised versions of the F-82G for service in Alaska.

Amongst the units to acquire the type was the 449th based at Ladd Field, Alaska. The unit detached aircraft to Marks AFB, Nome, in order to fly patrols in the Bering Strait, the growth of the Cold War and heightened tension with the So-

viet Union meaning that this geographical region, where the US and Russia were adjacent, took on added strategic importance. Indeed, whilst operating from Nome in June and July 1950 the F-82s were tasked with flying 'near' Soviet territory to take reconnaissance pictures. The radar operators used hand-held cameras for the task and the aircraft operated in pairs. By July the Russians had moved a number of fighters into the area and these started to respond to the American reconnaissance flights, although no actual engagements were recorded. It was, however, decided to terminate this type of mission. The unit re-equipped with F-94s at the end of 1950.

A report from Eglin dated 8 September 1949 concluded that '. . . the F-82 type aircraft can be modified for PR and would be a suitable interim, medium range, reconnaissance type. An F-82 modified for photo use would be suitable as an interim reconnaissance aircraft for all types of low altitude recce, 15,000 ft precision mapping, and tri-metrogen charting up to 30,000 ft altitude. The RF-82 aircraft possesses a more desirable speed/range combination factor for tactical and low altitude strategic reconnaissance than the standard RF-80 aircraft.'

One aircraft, 44-65172 (FQ-172), had been fitted with a detachable pod for the

Left: F-82G Twin Mustang general arrangement.

153

trials. Nothing, however, came of this development. The last F-82H was withdrawn from service in 1953 – but that is moving ahead of the story somewhat, and it is time to step back a few years and look at the Mustang's role in the Korean War.

The Korean War[1]

On 25 June 1950 North Korean forces crossed the border into South Korea and the first trial of strength with the Communist world began. It was a trial that Western leaders were determined to win, and, under the auspices of the newly established United Nations, a coalition was put together to repel this invasion. The major military part of this UN coalition would be provided by the United States, but other countries would play a role in both the ground and air wars; indeed, it was the Australians who first activated a P-51 Mustang unit in-theatre. No 77 Squadron RAAF was mobilised for action at Iwakuni, Japan, on 30 June 1950 and the unit was soon flying patrols along the North Korean coast. No 77 also suffered the first combat loss when, on 7 July, Sqn Ldr G. Stout flying A68-757 failed to return from a mission, having probably been shot down by ground fire. Although there was seen to be a need for piston-engine

fighters in-theatre to counter the piston-engine North Korean aircraft – some of the American jets having proved unable to engage the slow(ish) and highly manoeuvrable Communist types such as the Yak-9 – it was in the ground attack role that the Mustangs were to expend most of their effort in Korea.

Having left the Second World War with an enviable combat record, the P-51 was still viewed as an effective all-round aircraft, even though a closer examination of its wartime record would have shown its vulnerability to ground fire. However, when the call came in 1950 for piston-engine aircraft there was no other choice than the P-51 as this type was still serving in large numbers with the ANG; other types with better ground-attack capabilities, such as the P-47, were simply not available in quantity. At this stage the ANG had 764 P-51Ds on strength, and 145 of these were acquired by the USAF, shipped to Alameda in California and then sent on to join the Far East Air Force (FEAF) for operations in Korea. Many of these aircraft were then replaced in ANG

[1] The author is very grateful to Robert F. Dorr for permitting the reproduction of extracts from his article *Korean War Operations*, featured in the *FlyPast* magazine special issue entitled *Mustang*, published in November 1997.

Left: The 35th FG in Korea, January 1951. (US National Archives)

service by P-51Ds and P-51Hs taken out of storage and overhauled. The aircraft carrier USS *Boxer* arrived at Yokosuka, Japan, on 23 July with its cargo of Mustangs, and a number of F-80C squadrons began to re-equip – the 35th and 36th FBS (Fighter Bomber Squadron) of the 8th FBG (Fighter Bomber Group), the 39th and 40th FIS (Fighter Interceptor Squadron) of the 35th FIG (Fighter Interceptor Group), and the 12th and 67th FBS of the 18th FBG. Prior to this, two other 'units' had, notionally at least, acquired Mustangs for operations in Korea. As part of the re-equipment programme for the ROKAF (Republic of Korea Air Force), the United States had agreed to provide a number of aircraft, including, under the 'Bout One' Project, ten Mustangs. Lt-Col 'Bud' Biteman recalled the project:

'President Truman authorised the immediate transfer of ten F-51s to the totally under-equipped ROKAF. Those ten Mustangs were gathered from wherever they could be found at US bases in Japan. Their condition [was poor]. Half of the instruments and navigation radios had been removed. Major Dean Hess and his crew, code-named *Bout One Project*, flew those '51s to Taegu for delivery to the ROKAF and one of their first steps was to paint the ROKAF markings to cover those of the USAF. Hess's people were supposed to train the ROKs, but since [the South Korean] pilots had never flown anything more sophisticated than a T-6, after a few

Right: A No 2 Squadron SAAF Mustang with a typical ground attack load of rockets. (Ken Delve Collection)

Right: Flt Lt Ross Coburn RAAF preparing for his first sortie from an advanced base, November 1950. (Ken Delve Collection)

Left, upper: 18th FBW line-up, 13 July 1951. (US National Archives)

Left, lower: P-51s of the 18th FBW and No 2 Squadron SAAF parked near the RP store, November 1951. (Ken Delve Collection)

Below: 18th FBW aircraft taxi out past a set of tanks possibly being used for napalm, July 1951. (US National Archives)

frustrating attempts at leading inept pilots into combat, Hess and his people told the ROK pilots to stand aside, and the *Bout One* pilots flew all of their initial combat missions.'

Biteman was also involved with the Dallas Provisional Squadron, which had been formed from volunteer ex-P-51 pilots of the 18th FBG – the 'Squadron' had no aircraft and the original intention was for these to be acquired upon arrival at Taegu. In the event, however, a shortage of aircraft meant that the 'Bout One' and Dallas Provisional organisations were combined under the command of Capt Harry Moreland. Another of the pilots involved was Lt Daniel James, and he recalled:

'Bout One pilots were given the choice of remaining with us in the new unit, or return[ing] with Dean Hess to Japan to scrounge additional pilots and equipment in order to establish his F-51 ROKAF training programme which was based near Masan. Most of their pilots elected to remain with us and fight the war, rather than become involved in the training programme with the ROKAF. When our two provisional units joined forces, we were renamed the 51st Provisional Squadron and we retained the original ten "Truman Gift" F-51s which had been flown to Taegu by Hess's people. We retained the "51st Prov Sqn" title until the 18th Fighter Bomber Group and its 67th Fighter Bomber Squadron moved north from Clark Field to rejoin the fray on approx August 1, 1950, when we were re-absorbed into the 18th and again renamed 12th Fighter Bomber Squadron. We continued to fly the remainder of those ten original relics until the arrival of the *Boxer* with its load of wonderful, "new," completely equipped National Guard Mustangs.'

The F-51s were not the only Mustangs available in-theatre, however; indeed, the F-82Gs of the 347th Fighter (All Weather) Group were, at the outbreak of war, the only fighters with the range to operate over Korea from bases in Japan. In June 1950 the three squadrons of the Group were at different locations: the 4th F(AW)S was at Okinawa attached to the Twentieth Air Force whilst the other two units, both within the Fifth Air Force, were in Japan, the 68th F(AW)S at Itazuke and the 339th at Yokota. However, all three squadrons were reunited as the conflict erupted and by 26 June were flying patrols over Inchon to protect shipping. An air evacuation took place from airfields near Seoul on 27 June and the F-82s provided low-level air cover, high-level cover being provided by F-80s. Enemy aircraft made an appearance, and in a series of combats the F-82s claimed three destroyed and one damaged – the first aerial victories for the USAF in the Korean War. A Yak-9 was the first to succumb, shot down by 1st Lt 'Chalky' Moran of the 68th, and this was followed by a Yak-11, downed by another 68th pilot, 1st Lt William Hudson. The other victory was over an La-7 by Maj James Little of the 339th; his colleague Lt Walt Hayhurst damaged another.

With the need to apply the maximum amount of air power to the ground war, the F-82s were soon being used for night interdiction, usually armed with HVARs to accompany the six .50 machine guns. Lt Richard Davis of the 339th Squadron recalled one such mission early in the war:

'We were to annoy the North Korean troops with our ten 5in HVARs and machine guns. Heading from Seoul towards Kaesong, at 20,000 ft, between 0200 and 0400 hours, we were supposed to be the only Allied aeroplane in the sky. Suddenly, just north of Seoul, the tail warning radar alarm sounded. The radar scanned about 4,000 ft to the rear of the aircraft and if the beam hit anything a red light would come on just above the gunsight and a door-bell type alarm would sound, very loud, just behind the pilot.

'Sometimes the alarm would sound if we forgot to inactivate the system before landing, when the beam hit the ground behind us. On this occasion, the bell really scared us (Chester Caleb was radar observer on this mission) and we made some real tight 360-degree turns while scanning the forward-looking radar screen, but could detect nothing. The warning ceased and we decided there was nothing to do but continue with the mission.

'As soon as the warning sounded, I had raised the red spring-loaded cover over the gun-firing switch, and switched to combat position. When we resumed our mission I

Right: 1st Lt Jack Lightner of the 12thFBS/ 18th FBG. Lightner was killed in action on 7 September 1950. (Robert F Dorr)

Below: RAAF Mustangs line up for another sortie. (Ken Delve Collection)

Below right: P-51s of the Republic of Korea Air Force, May 1951. (Ken Delve Collection)

forgot to safety the switch and – inevitably – about 5 minutes later I inadvertently touched the hair trigger on the stick. All six 'fifties blasted away – Noise . . . Flame . . . Tracers came from between the props. For a moment I thought someone was on my tail shooting. As soon as I realised what had happened, I turned the switch off and sheepishly explained to Chet. To say that he was upset would be an understatement!'[1]

Mustang operations were in full swing by August, and on the 5th of that month Maj Louis Sebille, commander of the 67th FBS, was awarded the Medal of Honor (the first such award to a member of the USAF) when he crashed his aircraft into a concentration of enemy troops. Although escort missions for bomber attacks, including B-29 sorties, were being flown, the major task was rapidly becoming that of supporting the hard-pressed ground forces, and as a result losses began to rise. The CO of No 77 Squadron RAAF, Wg Cdr Lou Spence, was shot down near Anangni on 3 September. A few days later 1st Lt Jack Lightner of the 12th FBS was shot down whilst attacking North Korean tanks. His flight of four Mustangs was led by 1st Lt Robert Blank, who recalled:

'During the attack, Jack Lightner destroyed two tanks and three trucks, and

[1] Walter Thompson, 'F-82: Killer over Korea', *Air Enthusiast*.

damaged another medium tank. We were being fired upon. Jack never said his aircraft had been hit. After expending all of our ammunition, the flight joined up for the return trip to Japan.

'We passed the coast of Korea and were about 20 miles out over the sea at an altitude of 7,500 feet when Jack called me and said his aircraft was on fire in the engine. He immediately turned around and headed for the coast as an auxiliary air base was located about 5 miles east of Pusan, Korea.

'I turned with him and flew 50 feet away and was giving him advice and encouragement over the radio. His engine quit entirely after only about 3 or 4 minutes and his plane began to lose altitude in a glide. I repeatedly told him to bale out no lower than 2,000 feet and that I would circle until a rescue boat could pick him up. Jack said he was baling out. The canopy was released, but Jack seemed to be having

difficulty getting out. He never had a chance to pull his ripcord to open the 'chute. He struck the water just behind the aircraft. I believe he was killed instantly . . .'

The UN landings at Inchon in September received heavy air support. The US X

Left: The shooting down of an Il-2 by an 18th FBW Mustang (Lt-Col Ralph Saltsman?) over Korea, 20 June 1951. (US National Archives)

Right: F-82 dispersal, January 1951. (US National Archives)

Below: P-51s operating from Chinhae. (US National Archives)

Corps' amphibious assault took place on 15 September, and a co-ordinated assault allowed the UN forces to break out of the Pusan area and, by 26 September, re-take Seoul. UN forces crossed the 38th Parallel on 1 October and within a week Mao Tse-tung was calling for 'volunteers' to resist 'the imperialists'. With the offensive taking on very much the doctrine used by Allied forces in the latter part of the Second World War, the integration of tactical and strategic air assets was a key element. By early October two of the main Mustang bases were K-3, used by the 35th FIG, and K-9, used by the 8th FBG, whilst Kimpo became a major base for the 51st FIG.

The complexion of the conflict changed in November with the direct intervention of Chinese forces – a massive ground assault with the support of jet fighters such as the MiG-15. Early on a patrol of four 18th FIG Mustangs near Yalu was 'bounced' by MiG-15s, but no damage resulted to either side.

On 16 November No 77 Squadron moved to Konan North in order to be closer to its ground targets and over the next few weeks was heavily engaged attacking what seemed to be endless columns of Chinese and North Korean troops and equipment. The Chinese launched a major offensive in December and pushed the Allies back. The enemy advance rolled on and the squadrons were forced to abandon their airfields and retire to the Pusan area. Mustangs were also being operated by the sole South African Air Force (SAAF) squadron in-theatre – No 2 ('Flying Cheetahs') Squadron. By the middle of November this unit had moved into K-24, near Pyongyang in North Korea, but the Chinese advance soon meant that this airfield, amongst others, had to be evacuated. The enemy advance continued through the winter of 1951 and Allied air power became critical in attempts to stem the advance, or at the very least secure the safe retreat of Allied ground forces.

Losses to ground fire remained high, the South Africans suffering a number of such losses in the early part of 1951 but also, on 1 March, establishing a new record for the 18th FBG by destroying seven vehicles and two tanks (and a number of troops) in 32 sorties – though with the loss of two aircraft and pilots. The RAAF Mustangs were withdrawn on 6 April 1951 when No 77 Squadron went to Japan to re-equip with Meteor F.8s and then return to the conflict. More Mustangs arrived in-theatre in 1951 with the activation of the 67th TRG equipped with RF-51Ds, this unit undertaking a variety of reconnaissance and associated tasks.

The Mustangs rarely came across any air opposition, but on 20 June 1951 Lt-Col Ralph Saltsman of the 18th FBW was able to take on an Ilyushin Il-2:

'. . . heard that a classified mission was planned for early morning take-off from K-16 [Seoul airport], so I flew up to that base from K-10 [Chinhae] at about 5.00am to participate. Apparently, our intelligence agencies had learned that the North Koreans planned to invade the island of Senmido, which was about 3 miles off the western coast of Korea and 75 miles south of the Yalu River. Allied forces apparently had a radar installation on the island.

'I was leading *Baker* Flight in the squadron led by Capt Ed Rackham. As we arrived over the area at about 7.00am at 12,000ft, we spotted six enemy aircraft of the Sturmovik type, circling below us.

'Rackham told me to attack them. When we reached the trailing aircraft at about 6,000ft the rear gunner opened fire on me. I took a position astern and below the aircraft, which appeared to be an Il-2, thus positioning my aircraft out of the gunner's view. Raising my nose I fired about 800

Left: Mustangs of No 2 Squadron SAAF strafe a train in Korea. (US National Archives)

Right, top: *Old Nadsob* taxying on a waterlogged part of the airfield. (Ken Delve Collection)

Right, centre: Capt Weldon Wilson and S/Sgt Gordon McRea carrying out gun harmonisation on an 18th FBW Mustang, May 1951. (Ken Delve Collection)

Right, bottom: Australia licence-built P-51s in the latter part of the war. This is A68-565. (Ken Delve Collection)

rounds of .50-caliber into the bottom of the enemy aircraft.

'It started to smoke. But as I repeated the attack, my windscreen became covered with oil, which limited my visibility to a small part of the left side. Unable to maintain visual contact with the enemy aircraft, I broke off the attack.'

The year 1951 saw mixed fortunes. The UN forces stemmed two communist advances (in January and April) and in May began their own offensive. By the summer it was clear that all sides were in favour of a ceasefire and negotiations at Panmunjom were given fresh impetus. It was not to prove that simple, however, and the war dragged on into 1953. By 1952 the run-down of Mustang strength in Korea was well under way; in December No 2 Squadron SAAF gave up the type after over two years of operations, during which it had flown more than 10,500 sorties for the loss of 74 aircraft and 34 pilots.

Worthy of note whilst considering the Mustang's role in the Korean War is that on 10 October 1950 a large number of ANG units were activated for 21 months' service, with further squadrons following the next year. These units were primarily designated to take the operational role of regular USAF units that had deployed overseas, although eighteen units stayed under State control to supplement local air defence. The last ANG units were released from the active service commitment on 12 December 1952, and the majority had returned to State control by that month.

The Korean War ended with the Panmunjom Armistice of 17 July 1953, and although Mustangs were to take part in other conflicts, the Korean venture was the last large-scale operational employment of the type. However, the P-51 remained the main fighter type within the ANG. In 1953 some 65 units were equipped with P-51Ds and P-51Hs in the FIS or F-B role, with a further four TF-51D-equipped TR squadrons. This was in some ways a slightly artificial picture as a number of units had been scheduled for re-equipment with jets,

Air National Guard Units: Mustang Period

101st	Massachusetts	133rd	New Hampshire	167th	West Virginia
103rd	Pennsylvania	134th	Vermont	168th	Illinois
104th	Maryland	136th	New York	169th	Illinois
105th	Tennessee	137th	New York	170th	Illinois
107th	Michigan	138th	New York	171st	Michigan
108th	Illinois	139th	New York	172nd	Michigan
109th	Minnesota	141st	New Jersey	173rd	Nebraska
110th	Missouri	142nd	Delaware	174th	Iowa
111th	Texas	146th	Pennsylvania	175th	South Dakota
112th	Ohio	147th	Pennsylvania	176th	Wisconsin
113th	Indiana	148th	Pennsylvania	178th	North Dakota
115th	California	152nd	Rhode Island	179th	Minnesota
116th	Washington	153rd	Mississippi	181st	Texas
118th	Connecticut	154th	Arkansas	182nd	Texas
119th	New Jersey	155th	Tennessee	185th	Oklahoma
120th	Colorado	156th	North Carolina	186th	Montana
121st	District of Columbia	157th	South Carolina	187th	Wyoming
123rd	Oregon	158th	Georgia	188th	New Mexico
124th	Iowa	159th	Florida	190th	Idaho
125th	Oklahoma	160th	Alabama	191st	Utah
126th	Wisconsin	162nd	Ohio	192nd	Nevada
127th	Kansas	163rd	Indiana	194th	California
128th	Georgia	164th	Ohio	195th	California
131st	Massachusetts	165th	Kentucky	196th	California
132nd	Maine	166th	Kentucky	197th	Arizona

but aircraft were in short supply. The pace of such re-equipment did, however, increase the following year, by the end of which Mustang strength numbered 288 aircraft in eight Fighter Interceptor Wings (FIW), whereas jet strength had risen to over 1,000 aircraft. By FY 1957 (i.e. 1956) the P-51D phase-out had been completed, the final departure being the last two Mustangs of the 167th FS in the latter part of the year, one to the Air Force Museum and one to Post 20, American Legion (Charleston).

International Career

The post-war period also saw the P-51 begin an international career, the type serving with over twenty air forces from Australia to Cuba and Uruguay. With a number of these it saw further combat. It was with countries of Latin and South America that the P-51 had its final usage, again seeing combat service with some. In the case of the Dominican Republic, the

last aircraft were not retired until 1984. This late period of usage of the P-51 meant that the warbird market had a source of aircraft and spares. Space precludes a detailed consideration of the overseas operators.

Australia

On 29 April 1945 CAC Mustang A68-1, the first licence-built P-51 for the RAAF, took to the air at Fisherman's Bend, the pattern aircraft being P-51D 44-13293. First deliveries took place in June, but few aircraft had entered service before the end of the war. Some 80 of the CA-17 (Mk 20) had been delivered by the middle of 1946 (and served as A68-1 to A68-80). The RAAF had also received almost 300 P-51Ds and Ks from the USAAF, but these were not operational by the end of the war with Japan either. The Mustang Wing, No 81 (Nos 76, 77 and 82 Squadrons), did, however, deploy to Japan as part of the Occupation Force.

Left, upper: S/Sgt Pleasant Bigger repairs the gun sight on an F-82, Korea, February 1952. (US National Archives)

Left, lower: A 35th FIW aircraft undergoing gun harmonisation. (US National Archives)

Additional aircraft were built as the CA-18, the batches comprising fourteen CA-18 Mk 22s (A68-81 to A68-96) as reconnaissance aircraft, 26 CA-18 Mk 21s (A68-97 to A68-120) in the fighter role, 66 CA-18 Mk 23s (with the Merlin 70) and a final batch of fourteen CA-18 Mk 22s (A68-187 to A68-200). In August 1946 the first Mk 20s went to No 75 Squadron at Williamstown, No 78 Squadron at the same base acquiring aircraft the following month. Six regular RAAF squadrons operated CAC-built Mustangs between 1946 and 1952, in which year jet types began to enter service. The CA-18s were also used by five reservist Citizen Air Force squadrons.

A number of Australian Mustangs have survived either in museum collections or as active aircraft on the warbird circuit.

Bolivia

The FAB (Fuerza Aérea Boliviana) acquired its first Mustangs, two P-51Ds and a TF-51D, in July 1954 from the American Aeronautics Corporation. The first aircraft never made it to its new home, crashing in Ecuador on 19 October, but the remaining two, including the TF-51, arrived in Bolivia in February. A fourth aircraft was ordered in November to bring the FAB back to the original strength of three, all four having come from a batch of ex-RAAF aircraft acquired by American Aeronautics in 1953. In late 1960 Bolivia received eight further Mustangs from Uruguay when that country replaced the type with F-80Cs. This meant that the FAB now had a sufficient number of aircraft, and adequate spares support, to operate its Mustangs on a more regular and effective basis. With the support of the American government, others were acquired in 1966, the next batch comprising six (including two TF-51s).

Part of the reason for the increase in American support was the Bolivian struggle against communist rebels within the country, including, in 1966–67, a significant campaign against Che Guevara in the Rio Grande area. The Mustangs played an active part in the spring 1967 campaign against this group, and it was during this period that the aircraft were given their 'shark-mouth' (actually meant to represent a tiger mouth) markings. That same year Bolivia was one of the countries destined to receive the re-manufactured Cavalier version of the P-51. Under Project 'Peace Condor', nine of these aircraft – including three to TF standard – went to Bolivia. The Mustangs were operated by Grupo

Right: A trio of RCAF Mustangs. (*FlyPast* Collection)

in the case of the P-51s as advanced trainers. It is believed that by the mid-1950s all the Mustangs were grounded. China may well prove to be a source of P-51 airframes in the future.

Costa Rica

In January 1955 the United States sent four F-51Ds to bolster the diminutive Costa Rican Air Force because of tension with Nicaragua, these aircraft later being paid for under the Reimbursable Aid Program (RAP). By August 1958 only two were left in service, and although the Air Force was keen to acquire more – an offer of the Indonesian aircraft was rejected on American advice, as was a similar offer from Panama the following May – no further acquisitions were in fact made. The two aircraft were sold to a US dealer in March 1964 as N617OU and N6169U. One of the ex-Costa Rican P-51Ds, ex-44-73339, is currently operated by Intrepid Aviation at North Weald in the United Kingdom.

Cuba

The new regime of Fidel Castro in 1959 attempted to acquire aircraft from a wide range of sources to build on the rather weak composition of the Fuerza Aérea Rebelda which had been established in May 1958. It appears that one Mustang (44-74505/N68DR) was 'smuggled' into the country in mid-1958, appearing as FAR 401. A further two P-51s were acquired in a similar way. Attempts to acquire additional P-51s were unsuccessful, and the three aircraft that had been operated by the FAR in the latter part of 1958 remained in service for an unknown period. The three P-51Ds flew their first combat operations on 18 November 1958.

Dominican Republic

In 1947 the Fuerza Aérea Dominicana sought combat aircraft and at first acquired a number of P-38s, along with a selection of American pilots for whom post-war civilian life had proved somewhat uninspiring. In mid-1948 the first six P-

Aereo No 2 at Colcapirua until 1978, when they were replaced by T-33As. Six of the surviving aircraft were sold to Northwest Industries of Canada.

Canada

RCAF squadrons had operated Mustangs within the RAF order of battle during the war (see above), and after 1945 these units returned to Canada. However, an additional 100 ex-USAAF P-51s were acquired in 1945 for fighter units, and these remained in service until replaced by jet types in the early 1950s. The last units to give up their Mustangs were the six auxiliary squadrons in 1956.

China

From 1946 to 1949 a batch of P-51Ds, reported to be around 50 aircraft, was used by the Chinese Nationalist Koumintang forces during the Civil War. With the victory of Mao Tse-tung's communist forces, the re-formed military, the PLA, continued to use a number of ex-American types,

Left: Camouflaged Mustangs of the Dominican Air Force. (FlyPast Collection)

51s were obtained, being mainly 'out of work' air racing aircraft. One aircraft was lost on its delivery flight but the remaining five entered service as '401 to '405. By November 1948 only four were airworthy, and two of these had no guns; another aircraft was lost the following month. In the early 1950s the Dominican Air Force was trying to acquire jets, but in an effort to expand its front-line strength it took advantage of a very good deal and acquired 32 ex-Swedish Air Force P-51Ds; in October 1952 these aircraft formed the 1st Escuadron de Caza. Some sources list ten ex-USAF P-51Ds, to Cavalier standard, which went to form part of Grupo de Caza Ramfis (named after Ramfis Trujillo, the dictator's son). In June 1963 Mustang strength was 31 F-51s, but by November 1969 the number of Mustangs had greatly diminished and the Escuadron de Combate comprised seventeen Mustangs and six Vampires.

El Salvador
The US mission of the 1950s recommended that the El Salvador Air Force acquire the FG-1D Corsair as its primary fighter type – which they promptly did, at the bargain price of $8,700 per aircraft. However, in 1968 the Air Force replaced a number of its Corsairs with, initially, six Cavalier IIs (also acquiring two TF-51Ds). Growing tension with neighbouring Honduras led to an expansion of the Air Force, including the acquisition of a further twelve F-51s. At least one aircraft was lost in the 'soccer war' with Honduras, during which time the aircraft were primarily operated from Ilopango, Santa Ana and San Miguel, with a number of mercenary pilots also flying the Mustangs. The Mustangs were disposed of in 1975 to finance new aircraft purchases.

Guatemala
An American military mission of mid-1945 had the task of reorganising and re-equipping the Guatemalan military, and one of the aircraft supplied under MAP was the F-51D, six being delivered in 1954 (three

in July and three in December). A further 24 aircraft were acquired over the next seven years, including a single TF-51D. During the late 1950s the FAG operated a four-ship display team, *Los Machitos*. Tragedy struck in January 1972 when three of the Fuerza Aérea Guatemalteca's Mustangs collided during an aerobatic display. The type remained in service until 1976, when it was replaced by the Cessna A-37B.

Haiti
In 1951 Haiti acquired four P-51Ds from Aircraft Sales Ltd of Dallas, the first two aircraft being delivered in April and the others in July.

Indonesia
Indonesia established its independence after the war and by 1949 was being given military assistance by Holland, including the handing over of the P-51s that had been used in the Netherlands East Indies. These aircraft went to form No 1 Squadron of the Indonesian Air Force. Indonesia remained a troubled region, and the following year the Mustangs were in action supporting operations against rebels on the island of Ambon (South Moluccas). The Mustangs remained in service to the mid-1960s. During the Confrontation with Malaysia they escorted B-25s on leaflet-dropping missions; there was little actual shooting during the period, the RAF having bolstered its air strength in the region.

Israel
When Israeli independence was declared in May 1948, the new state was surrounded by aggressive Arab enemies determined upon its destruction – and possessing strong, well-equipped armed forces. The Israelis had little in the way of military muscle, the air force being particularly weak as it included only eleven fighters (six Bf 109s and five Spitfires). During the latter phases of the War of Independence the fighter strength was increased in a number of ways, and four P-51Ds entered the inventory.

Right: Parked and ignored in a corner, Honduran P-51s await their fate. (Ken Delve Collection)

The IAF was very much the cutting edge of Israeli defence and had to be at constant operational readiness, not knowing when one of the adjoining Arab countries would strike next. In 1951 simmering problems with Syria broke out into conflict. On 5 April the IAF was called upon to mount an attack upon the police fortress at El Hama, and this was carried out by four Spitfires followed by four P-51s led by the Squadron CO, Meir Rolf. The Mustangs were tasked to hit adjacent bunkers and a tented encampment in a fifteen-minute assault with RPs and guns. The Spitfire attack was recorded as 'poor'; the Mustangs, however, 'were more accurate. Their rockets hit the bunker and burned the tents. Syrian light machine gun fire was directed at the planes to no avail, and no aircraft were scrambled towards the Israelis.'[1]

It was considered by many Israeli planners that conflict with Egypt was inevitable at some point in the 1950s, and a great deal of planning effort was expended devising suitable strategies. In typical Israeli fashion these involved pre-emptive attacks against Egyptian air power – to destroy enemy air capability on the ground – as well as air support for ground forces.

All offensive aircraft were included in the airfield attack plan (Operation 'Slope'), the Mustangs being allocated targets such as Kabrit, Fayid and Abu-Sueir airfields. The long-expected conflict came in 1956 with the Suez Crisis, but the nature of this war meant that the pre-emptive attacks on Egyptian airfields would not be required: the British and French would take care of Egyptian air power as part of their offensive to seize control of the Suez Canal. This is not the place to become embroiled in the arguments concerning the political machinations of France, Israel and Britain over Suez, suffice it to say that the Israelis were able to attack Egyptian ground forces in Sinai, the Anglo-French task force intervened to protect the Canal, the Americans gave no support (moral or otherwise) to their Western Allies and Russia threatened to intervene – all of which combined to bring the conflict to an untidy end, although Israel had achieved major gains.

For the Mustangs, one of the most unusual tasks during this short conflict was that of cable cutting. On 29 October the squadron commanders attended a brief-

---

[1] Col E. Cohen, *Israel's Best Defence*, Airlife, 1993.

ing, following which the first P-51 sorties were flown. Aviation historian Shlomo Aloni wrote an excellent account of these missions, from which the extracts here are taken:[1]

'The devised tactic was for the P-51 to tow a 164ft (50m) long steel cable with a weight at its end, the purpose of the weight being to aerodynamically balance the cable. The steel cable was attached to the target towing hook of the P-51. The pilot was expected to fly low enough for the steel cable to cut the telephone lines – while at the same time avoiding hitting the ground. This in itself was a demanding task, especially over the desert terrain of Sinai. To test the scheme a simulated telephone line was constructed near Hatzor air base and the testing was entrusted to 116 Squadron, an emergency P-51 unit based at Tel-Nof air base and mainly staffed by the Flying School instructors. The unit CO was Maj Itshak *Tsahik* Yavneh, the CO of the Flying School, and he appointed Lt Amitai *Shafan* (Rabbit) Hason as the cable-cutting test pilot. The whole affair was regarded as top secret and most of the unit's pilots, including several of those who eventually flew the operational cable-cutting missions, did not know the exact nature of Lt Hason's flights.

'Soon, however, it became evident that the aerodynamic behaviour of the cable was not satisfactory, so instead of a single weight at its end several weights were distributed along the cable. This also meant that if a portion of the cable was torn off there would still be enough left to allow the pilot to complete his mission. The greatest difficulty was to fly at the right altitude: if the pilot flew too low he lost the cable, if he flew too high he caused no damage to the telephone lines. During the tests it became evident that the steel cable could cut the telephone line but was a 'one shot' device. The successful multiple cutting of the telephone lines – a prerequisite of the planning – was yet to be achieved.

'THE FIRST MISSION

'On October 29, the 116 Squadron Mustangs were to be the first IDF/AF aircraft to fly "offensive" missions against Egypt. Two telephone line targets were designated for the Mustangs and each was to be "attacked" by a pair of aircraft. The furthest target was between the Mitla Pass and Suez, and the other target was about 60 miles (100km) to the east, just west of Thamed. The first pair took-off at 1400, led by Capt Dan *Harry* Barak with Capt Aryeh *Tsiti* Tse'elon as his wingman; both were the Squadron's deputy commanders. The second pair was led by Maj Yavneh, with Lt Hason as his wingman.

'Of the four pilots only Lt Hason was a cable-cutting specialist, having flown the trials. Maj Yavneh and Capt Barak each flew just one training cable-cutting mission whilst Capt Tse'elon had not flown a single cable-cutting training mission!

'The main lesson that Maj Yavneh had learnt from his training was that the whole scheme was suspect! In this training flight he was able to cut the telephone lines successfully but the terrain was flat and his altitude was monitored from the ground. He knew that in the real mission there would not be a ground controller to aid the Mustangs and that the terrain in Sinai, especially the sand dunes, might cause problems.

'On the other hand, Maj Yavneh knew that he and his pilots must cut the telephone lines: there would be no compromise about this specific mission – success was vital. As a veteran Qualified Flying Instructor (QFI), Major Yavneh remembered an incident in which a QFI flying a Stearman inadvertently flew into electrical high tension cables. The Stearman was hardly damaged but it cut the cables and caused a major electrical supply failure. Hence Maj Yavneh thought that if a Stearman could cut electrical cables it should not be difficult for the faster and heavier Mustang to cut the lighter telephone lines. Maj Yavneh instructed his

[1] 'Mustang: The P-51 at War and Peace', *FlyPast*, November 1997.

170

pilots to cut the telephone lines with their propellers if the special cutting device failed. It was an instruction that saved the day.

'At 1400 the first pair took-off and almost immediately Capt Barak's cable detached itself; he recalls: "On October 29, 1956, in P-51 s/n 06 I flew with *Tsiti* on a mission to cut the [telephone] lines at two places near the [Suez] Canal. I allowed enough time for malfunctions and indeed on take-off my cable detached and I had to land and install a new cable. We departed at 1400 and the flight lasted two hours and 15 minutes. In the test flight there were two poles and a single telephone line and I did not know the purpose; it was top secret. I cut it without a problem, like butter, a flat terrain, no hills.

"'But now suddenly there were 30–40 lines and sand dunes. It was obvious that my cable was torn. *Tsiti*'s cable was torn en route so I decided to cut with the propeller. I turned and I signalled him to follow me line astern and I came in low, but at the very last second I pulled-up instinctively. I tried once again, fully fine on the prop to achieve a lot of rpm, 2,000rpm or so, about 400mph, and I felt like a black shadow for a split second. I turned to evaluate the damage but I could not locate the place, so I did it once again and then flew to the next place.

"'I signalled *Tsiti* to lead this time but he signalled me in return that he would not, so I did it again. After the war we went to look at the area and not only had I cut the lines but I had also pulled out the poles!"

'Capt Barak's wingman was Capt Tse'elon in Mustang "29", and his logbook records the flying time as two hours and 25 minutes:

"'I was No 2 and I followed him, I flew a bit too low and my cable was torn off. I felt some sort of a hit and he signalled me that I no longer had the cable. At first he cut with his cable but after the first pass his cable was also torn off, so in the second pass he came in with his propeller and

I did the same, we discussed such an option earlier. If [we lost the cables] then we would try to cut with the propeller."

'On their way back both Capt Barak and Capt Tse'elon saw the IDF/AF C-47s parachuting the Israeli paratroopers into the Mitla Pass. The war had begun.

'The second pair of Mustangs took-off about half an hour after the first and faced the same problems. Maj Yavneh led in Mustang "73" and the mission lasted two and a half hours. *Tsahik* Yavneh recollects that they cruised at about 220mph at a very low altitude – the exact performance of the Egyptian early warning system was not known and the Mustangs did not want to be detected. The cables caused a great deal of drag and, as in the case of the first pair, they were torn off, so Maj Yavneh and Lt Hason used the Mustang's half-ton metal propeller, at 2,500rpm, as the cutting device. In one of the passes, Lt Hason tried to cut the telephone lines with his wingtip and although successful he did not repeat this manoeuvre, flying as he was with his wing dipped at an altitude of only 20ft (6m)!

'The second pair flew a similar profile and when ground forces later inspected the damage they confirmed that the lines had been cut in a number of places. A second mission was mounted by 116 Squadron the following day, to cut lines in the El-Arsih area. The first pair, Capt Tse'elon and Lt Fredlis, used wingtips and props to cut the wires as there seemed to be a problem with the cutting device; the follow-up pair also completed the mission successfully – ending what had been a short, but successful, venture by the Mustangs into this type of mission. Post-war, trials were flown with a modified cutting device but the system was never again called in to operational use.'

Offensive sorties were also being flown. On 31 October Eliezer Cohen was one of six P-51 pilots on such a mission:

'The Mustangs were already fuelled and armed to their wings' capacity with napalm bombs, rockets and ammo for the machine guns. Take-off would be to the tree level, at top speed and with radio silence. Avram [Yaffe] led us . . . if the tank convoy had already passed, we would approach from behind . . . from this point on, we knew that every vehicle before us was enemy . . . "Grasshopper formation transfer fuel selector over to a full tank, arm bombs, activate weapons systems. I want good hits, and watch your partners' tails." Avram's voice was quiet and confident. I checked my fuel gauge; my right tank was almost empty. I switched the fuel lever to my left tank, armed by bomb fuses and unlocked the safeties on my rockets and guns . . . The convoy comprised new Soviet T-34 tanks, along with munitions and supply trucks . . . in training we had learned to release the burning napalm ahead of the target and immediately pull on the stick. I released and pulled . . . hearing the explosion, I could see flames on the tank below, in the centre of the fire . . . [the] second bomb run took out another six tanks . . . I swallowed my saliva, and readied myself for the strafing runs using rockets and my six .50-calibre machine guns.'[1]

One aircraft was damaged in the attack and failed to return to base; it was later found crashed in the desert, the pilot, Uri Schlessinger, having been killed.

The Mustang period was short-lived in Israel as jet fighters soon became available. One aircraft has been preserved at the IAF Museum at Hatzerim.

Italy
Italy received 48 ex-USAAF P-51Ds, and these remained in use from 1948 to 1953.

The Netherlands
In common with all the colonial powers, the Netherlands sought to re-establish her authority over her colonial territories. The Netherlands East Indies had been under Japanese control in the Second World War, during which period an armed resistance had grown up; the situation was further complicated by the Indonesian desire to increase its influence in the region. Thus the Dutch became involved in military action over the Netherlands East Indies, the air element of which included two squadrons operating P-51s, some 40 aircraft having been taken on charge.

New Zealand
One of the minor users of the Mustang, the RNZAF operated some 33 aircraft during 1945–46.

Nicaragua
By far the biggest user of the type in South America, the Nicaraguan Air Force acquired almost 50 Mustangs from 1955 onwards, 'radically altering an already lop-sided balance of power in Central America'.[2] Having signed the Rio Pact in 1947, Nicaragua became eligible for American aid, and military assistance soon followed. The first batch of 26 F-51Ds, deliveries of which commenced in February 1955, were ex-Swedish Air Force, but others were delivered from US stocks, including twelve in 1954, plus two TF-51Ds in February 1957, with a further eight coming from 'miscellaneous sources'. The modernisation of the FAN in the 1960s saw the P-51s disposed of, the aircraft being traded for T-28s and B-26s.

The Philippines
Having been the scene of intensive USAAF P-51 operations during the war and having become reliant and American financial and military aid, it was inevitable that P-51s would find their way into the Philippines Air Force, which operated the type from 1946 to 1960.

South Africa
A number of SAAF units had used Mustangs during the war (see above), and there was even a plan for an SAAF Wing to take a role in the final stages of the war with Japan as part of the expansion and re-equipment of SEAC in mid-1945. How-

Right: N3550 at Stapleton Field, Denver, in 1961. (P. Hildreth)

[1] *Israel's Best Defence*, op. cit.
[2] Dan Hagedorn, *Central American and Caribbean Air Forces*, Air Britain, 1997.

ever, in the post-war period the most notable Mustang employment by the SAAF was that of No 2 Squadron in the Korean War.

Sweden

Sweden received its first P-51s courtesy of forced-landings, USAAF Mustangs arriving in Sweden having been damaged in combat over Germany. At least two of these – 43-6365 (ex-357th FG) and 43-6461 (ex-339th FG) – are known to have been in Swedish Air Force service by April 1945 under the designation J26. With the war over, Sweden placed an order for 157 P-51Ds and this was complete by early 1948, the aircraft serving with F4 at Ostersund and F16 at Uppsala. It was an important but short-lived period, during which Saab was developing a range of new aircraft for the air force, and the P-51s were up for disposal by 1952. The majority of these aircraft went to air arms in Latin America, though some found their way to Israel.

Switzerland

Another air force that in the post-war period took advantage of the availability of ex USAAF P-51s, acquiring 100 of the type. The last of these remained in service to 1956.

Uruguay

A number of P-51s were delivered in late 1950 and equipped Grupo de Aviacion No 2. They served for around ten years, being replaced by F-80Cs. Four surviving aircraft were transferred to Bolivia.

The Civilians

At any air show in the United States, and indeed in Europe, one is almost guaranteed to witness the sight and sound of a P-51 Mustang. At many of the larger warbird shows in the USA it is quite common for Mustangs to be present in squadron strength. One recent Experimental Aircraft Establishment (EAA) show at Oshkosh in Wisconsin attracted over 30 Mustangs, and there are plans afoot to hold a P-51 gathering with the hope of attracting over 50 aircraft. At the last count there were around 300 surviving P-51 Mustangs, of various marks, of which something approaching half are airworthy (see Appendix H for listing) but with many more of this total being stored for restoration or already under restoration.

At the end of the Second World War the USAAF had vast numbers of aircraft that, almost overnight, became surplus to requirements. A great many were destroyed, whilst others went into storage, were used to build up reserve forces such as the Air

National Guard or were sold or otherwise transferred to overseas air forces – especially those in Latin America.

Racers

One of the earliest civilian uses of the Mustang was as an air racer. Air racing had been a popular pre-war sport in the United States, and with the availability of high-performance fighter types after the war – and a desire amongst ex-fighter pilots to fly them – the stage was set for a the P-51 to open the first peaceful chapter in its career. Before long the basic airframes and engines were being modified to squeeze more performance out of them. Mustangs are still regular participants at the annual Reno air races in America, although in many cases they are heavily modified and some are barely recognisable as P-51s.

Warbirds

It was not until the mid-1960s that the warbird market became significant in the United States, and at that point a number of aircraft brokers took an interest. One of these was Courtesy Aircraft, founded by 'Swede' Clark. His son Mark Clark, the present Managing Director, explained the Company's involvement:

'I guess that my interest in these aircraft was really generated by the EAA fly-ins that were held at Rockford. I grew up around these aircraft, but not so much with thoughts of World War Two history but rather the post-war civilian use, such as air racing, and even the use in the so-called "banana republic" wars in South America. It was only as I learned more about the aircraft and met more of the people that my interest began to stretch back into World War Two itself.'

Over the 30 years or so that the company has been in the warbird business it has certainly seen a huge number of changes in the market. In the late 1960s a P-51 could be acquired for around $20,000, but now one thinks in terms of a major six-figure sum (around $750,000 for a really good specimen). Indeed, as Clark points out, it is the current high value of the Mustang that has led to an increase in the number of restoration projects:

'A project that a few years ago would not have looked like a viable proposition has now become a player. The P-51 market in the last two years has really picked up again and prices are continuing to creep up. Owners now demand a very much higher standard of restoration than they did 20, or even ten, years ago, and

175

there are now a number of restoration facilities that turn out really fantastic work.'

With over 130 airworthy examples and an estimated 50 or so restoration projects under way, the P-51 market looks set to remain vibrant.

To most Americans the P-51 is the ultimate piston-engine fighter, with its distinctive look and sound and very distinct character. As a type it certainly had a long and varied career, remaining in operational service in South America into the 1980s. This latter fact helped with the supply of airframes for the private warbird market and the vast majority of such aircraft have been snapped up. Mark Clark continues:

'There are really no new aircraft to find in any quantity. There may be a few more out there – stories of aircraft in China, for example – but the P-51 is now pretty much established and much of the business con-

sists of selling aircraft that are already in the warbird sphere of activity. The major considerations that a potential customer has relate to the overall condition of the aircraft – who restored it, and when, what time is there on the engine and who restored the engine – real practical considerations, rather than the operational history of the aircraft itself. If I had two P-51s on the ramp here that were pretty much equal in condition and one aircraft was a known combat veteran it would not sell for any significant amount extra. There are of course exceptions, as some owners place somewhat more of a premium on such historic considerations.'

This leads to the inevitable question: Who buys a P-51 – apart from the obvious consideration of being able to afford it – and are they really looked on as an investment or as something more than that?

'Although it is true that the P-51s have proved to be a great investment – you

Above: Restoration in progress on Rob Lamplough's Mustang 44-72216/G-BIXL, Duxford, November 1983. (*FlyPast* Collection)

Right, upper: *Precious Metal* (Race 09). (*FlyPast* Collection)

Right, lower: P-51D 67-22580 (N2580) '*Six Shooter*', owned by Chuck Hall. (*FlyPast* Collection)

could keep one a couple of years, look after it reasonably well, and then sell it on to recoup your outlay, plus a bit, this is really just one of the "justifications" that might be used. The real reason that most buyers go for a P-51 is that they want to fly this fantastic fighter – and have fun. The warbird community is a great one and to pitch in to fly-ins and air shows and meet like-minded individuals, as well as veterans, is a great experience. And of course these comments apply to any of the warbird types, not just the P-51 – although many still consider it to be the ultimate. Potential Mustang buyers come from many walks of life, from those who have been involved with the P-51 in the past – a number of veterans fly these aircraft, for example – to lawyers, doctors and businessmen in their forties who have no prior connection at all.'

Whereas in the early days of the warbird scene many aircraft appeared in somewhat fanciful paint schemes and markings, great attention is now paid to achieving an authentic finish, often reflecting the markings of one of the P-51 aces. This can lead to more than one aircraft appearing in the same scheme: there have been two P-51s in the *Big Beautiful*

Doll scheme in recent years. In almost all cases where such authentic schemes are applied, these are the original aircraft that bore the markings and so the observer has always to be wary of the number carried by any warbird: Does it reflect the number of the aircraft in whose scheme it is finished or is it the real number for that airframe? Authenticity is very much a watchword with certain warbird owners in America, to the extent that they want their aircraft to be as 'stock' as possible – i.e. to have original parts, including instruments and equipment – and many restoration workshops have established sources of supply for such original equipment (at a price).

There are no doubt more aircraft still to be found in some parts of the world, or wrecks to be recovered, although in most cases all that can be saved from such wrecks is the maker's plate and the history of the aircraft – which is then transferred to what in effect becomes a 'new-build' Mustang. Others have gone down the road of scale replicas, and a number of these are now on the market. One thing is certain: the P-51 Mustang looks set to be in the air for many years to come

Below: The Fighter Collection's P-51 *Moose* (44-63221). (Ken Delve Collection)

APPENDICES

Appendix A: Mustang Production (all variants)[1]

Model	NA desig.	Serial numbers	Constructor numbers	Qty
NA-73X	73X		73-3097	1
Mustang I	73	AG345/664 (for RAF)	73-3098/3100, 73-3102/3106, 73-3108/3416, 73-4767/4768 73-7812	320
XP-51	73	41-038/039	73-3101 & 3107	2
Mustang I	83	AL958/999, AM100/257, AP164/263 (for RAF)	83-4769/5068	300
P-51-NA	91	41-37320/37351, 41-37353/ 37420, 11981/12130 41-37422/37469		148
P-51A-1NA	99	43-6003/6102	99-22400/22415	100
P-51A-5NA	99	43-6103/6157	?	55
P-51C-1NA	99	43-6158/6312	?	155
XP-51B	101	41-37352, 41-37421 (from P-51-NA order)	91-12013 & 12082	2
P-51B-1NA	102	43-12093/12492	102-24541/24940	400
P-51B-5NA	104	43-6313/6802 43-6803/6912 43-6913/7112	? 104-24431/24540 104-24941/25140	800
P-51B-10NA	104	43-7113/7202 42-160429/106538 42-106541/106738	104-25141/25230 104-25231/25340 104-25343/25540	398
P-51B-15NA	104	42-106739/106978 43-24752/24901	104-25541/25780 104-25781/25930	390
P-51C-1NT	103	42-102979/103328	103-22416/22765	350
P-51C-5NT	103	42-103329/103378	103-22766/22815	50
P-51C-10NT	103	42-103379/103978	103-25933/26332	600
P-51C-10NT	103	43-24902/25251	103-26533/26882	350
P-51D	106	42-106539/106540	106-25341/25342	2
P-51D-5NA	109	44-13253/14052	109-26886/27685	800
P-51D-10NA	109	44-14053/14852	109-27686/28485	800
P-51D-15NA	109	44-14853/15252	109-28486/28885	900
P-51D-1NA	110	To Australia unassembled	110-34386/34485	100
P-51C-10NT	111	44-10753/11152	111-23886/29285	400
P-51D-5NT	111	44-11153/11352	111-29286/29485	200
P-51K-1NT	111	44-11353/11552	111-29486/29685	200
P-51K-5NT	111	44-11553/11952	111-29686/30085	400
P-51K-10NT	111	44-11953/12552	111-30086/30685	600
P-51K-15NT	111	44-12553/12752	111-30686/30885	300
P-51D-20NT	111	44-12853/13252	111-36136/36535	400

[1] Data provided by Mark Nicholls.

P-51D-20NA	122	44-63160/64159	122-30886/31885	1,000
P-51D-20NA	122	44-72027/72126	122-31886/31985	100
P-51D-20NA	122	44-72127/72626	122-38586/39085	500
P-51D-25NA	122	44-73627/74226	122-40167/40766	600
P-51D-30NA	122	44-74227/75026	122-40767/41566	800
P-51D-25NT	124	44-84390/84989 (44-84610/84611 built as TP-51D)	124-44246/44845	600
		45-11343/11742 (45-11443/11450 built as TP-51D)	124-48096/48495	400
XP-51F	105	43-43332/43334	105-26883/26885	3
XP-51G	105	43-43335/43336	105-25931/25932	2
XP-51J	105	44-76027/76028	105-47446/47447	2
P-51H-10NA	126	44-64460/64714	126-37886/38140	255
P-51M-1NT	124	45-11743	124-48496	1
A-36A-NA	97	42-83663/84162	97-15581/16380	500
XP-82-NA	120	44-83886/83887		2
XP-82A-NA		44-83888		1
P-82B-NA	123	44-65160/65168, 44-65171/65179		18
P-82C-NA	123	44-65169		1
P-82D-NA	123	44-65170		1
P-82E-NA	144	46-0255/0354	144-38141/38240	100
P-82G-NA	150	46-0355/0404 (0384-0388 built as P-82H)	150-38241/38290	50
P-82F-NA	149	46-0405/0504 (0469/0504 built as P-82H then converted to G)	149-38291/38390	100
F-51D Cavalier		67-14862/14864 (sold to Bolivia)		3
TF-51D Cavalier		67-14865/14866 (sold to Bolivia)		2
F-51D Cavalier		67-22579/22582 (sold to Bolivia, 22582 as TF-51D)		4
F-51D Cavalier		68-15795/15796		2

Note: The F-6 designation was given to photo-reconnaissance Mustangs that were built as such among the P-51 production runs. Approximately 126 early Mustangs were converted to F-6B and F-6C, while F-6D and F-6K conversions were: F-6D-20NT 44-13020/13039, 44-13131/13140, 44-13181; F-6D-25NT 44-84509/84540, 44-84566, 44-84773/84778, 44-84835/84855; F-6K-5NT 44-11554, 44-11897/11952; F-6K-10NT 44-11993/12008, 44-12216/12237, 44-12459/12471, 44-12523/12534; F-6K-15NT 44-12810/12852. The A-36A designation applied to aircraft that were designed purely for ground attack duties. As well as those built as TP-51Ds, the following were also modified to TF-51Ds: 44-84654/84658, 44-84660, 44-84662/84663, 44-84665/84670, 44-84676. The F-51 Cavalier Mustangs were produced from re-worked P-51D airframes.

Commonwealth Aircraft Corporation Pty Ltd production

Model	Desig.	Serial numbers	Constructor numbers	Qty
Mk 20	CA-17	A68-1/80 (North American P-51D-1NA order)	1326/1405	80
Mk 21	CA-18	A68-81/106	1406/1431	26
Mk 22	CA-18	A68-107/120	1432/1445	14
Mk 22	CA-18	A68-187/200	1512/1525	14
Mk 23	CA-18	A68-121/186	1446/1511	66

Aircraft for the initial batch were supplied by North American (see above) although 20 airframes were used to establish production tooling and as a spares source.

RAF Serial Batches

Mustang	I	AG345–AG664		III	HB821–HB961
	I	AL958–AM257		III	KH421–KH640
	I	AP164–AP263		IV	KH641–KH670
	IA	FD418–FD567		IV	KM493–KM743
	II	FR890–FR939		IVA	KH671–KH870
	III	FB100–FB399		IVA	KM100–KM492
	III	FR411 (ex-USAAF)		III	SR406–SR440 (ex-USAAF)
	IV	FR410			
	V	FR409		F.IV	TK586/589
	III	FX848–FZ919			

Appendix B: Aircraft Specifications

P-51/Mustang I and IA
First flight NA-73X 26 October 1940
First production aircraft AG345
Allison V-1710-39
Max 382mph at 14,000ft
Four .50 cal

P-51A/Mustang II
Allison V-1710-81
Four .50 cal

P-51B/Mustang III
First flight XP-51B 30 November 1942
Packard Merlin V-1650-3 (Merlin 28)
Span 37ft 0in
Length 32ft 3in
Height 8ft 8in
Take-off weight 9,000lb clean
Max speed 440mph at 25,500ft
Combat range 900 miles (with two 75gal tanks)
Service ceiling 42,000ft
Four .50 cal

P-51D and K/Mustang IV
Packard Merlin V-1650-7
Span/length/height as P-51A
Take-off weight 8450lb clean
Max speed 437mph at 25,500ft
Combat range 1,000 miles (with two 100gal tanks)
Service ceiling 42,000ft
Six .50 cal

P-51H
Packard Merlin V-1650-9
Length 33ft 2in
Max speed 495mph
Service ceiling 46,000ft

F-82F Twin Mustang
Two Allison V-1710-143/145
Span 51ft 7in
Length 29ft 2in
Height 13ft 9°in
Max speed 460mph at 21,000ft
Combat range 2,174 miles
Service ceiling 38,400ft
Six .50 cal

Appendix C: Army Air Forces Statistical Digest

The following tables relating to the P-51 (which include A-36 and F-6 aircraft) are taken from the AAF Statistical Digest produced by the Office of Statistical Control in December 1945.

Table 76 – factory acceptances of aircraft by month

	1941	1942	1943	1944	1945
Jan		84		370	857
Feb		84		380	721
Mar		52	70	482	803
Apr		86	121	407	694
May		84	121	580	710

Jun		84	20	581	738
Jul		76	91	569	603
Aug	2	24	175	700	210
Sep	6	60	201	665	
Oct	25		284	763	
Nov	37		295	765	
Dec	68		332	720	

Table 82 – average cost of aircraft

1942	$58,698
1943	$58,824
1944	$51,572
1945	$50,985

Tables 89–93 – airplanes on hand in various theatres

ETO – European Theatre of Operations
PAC – Pacific
FE - Far East Air Forces
JAP – Theatres v Japan
(Figures include P-51, A-36 and F-6.)

1943

Month	ETO	PAC	FE	JAP
Jan	12			
Feb	37			
Mar	70			
Apr	305			
May	302			
Jun	295			
Jul	308			
Aug	288			70
Sep	288			77
Oct	370			82
Nov	220			95
Dec	468			100

1944

Month	ETO	PAC	FE	JAP
Jan	744			112
Feb	878			129
Mar	978			189
Apr	1139			193
May	1052			203
Jun	1116			212
Jul	1895			218
Aug	1934			226
Sep	2030			344
Oct	2128		41	366
Nov	2083	16	75	510
Dec	1914	203	95	736

1945

Month	ETO	PAC	FE	JAP
Jan	1926	254	94	945
Feb	2142	247	216	1114
Mar	2125	327	357	1266
Apr	2245	388	373	1338
May	2179	424	366	1329
Jun	2095	379	465	1432

Jul	1933	10	542	1675
Aug	1884	34	502	1638

Appendix D: Mustang Orders of Battle

RAF
Data based on SD161 plus Command ORBAT returns

APRIL 1943

Army Co-operation Command (ACC)
No 70 Gp
  41 OTU   Hawarden

No 72 Gp
No 32 Wing
  309 Sqn   Kirknewton
  63 Sqn   Macmerry

No 33 Wing
  169 Sqn   Duxford
  613 Sqn   Ouston

No 34 Wing
  2 Sqn   Bottisham
  268 Sqn   Snailwell
  170 Sqn   Snailwell

No 35 Wing
  26 Sqn   Gatwick
  168 Sqn   Odiham

No 36 Wing
  16 Sqn   Andover
  239 Sqn   Stoney Cross

No 39 (RCAF) Wing
  400 Sqn   Dunsfold

  414 Sqn   Dunsfold

JULY 1944

No 83 Gp
  19 Sqn   B-12/Ellon
  65 Sqn   B-12/Ellon
  122 Sqn   B-12/Ellon
  168 Sqn   B-8/Sommerview

No 84 Gp
  2 Sqn   B-10/Plumentot
  129 Sqn   Brenzett
  306 Sqn   Brenzett
  315 Sqn   Brenzett

No 9 Gp
  41 OTU   Hawarden

No 12 Gp
  316 Sqn   Coltishall

MAAF (Mediterranean Allied Air Force)
233 Wing
  260 Sqn   Crete

USAAF – North Africa/Italy
Data based upon official location statements

12 DECEMBER 1943

Twelfth Air Force/NWATAF
XII ASC
  68th TRG   111th TRS
  27th FBG   522nd, 523rd,
  (A-36)   524th
  86th FBG   525th, 526th,
  (A-36)   527th

30 APRIL 1944

Twelfth Air Force
XII TAC
  68th TRG   111th   Pomigliano

  86th FBG   525th, 526th,   Marcianise
  (A-36)   527th

Fifteenth Air Force
306th FW
  31st FG   307th, 308th,   San Severo
              309th
  52nd FG   2nd, 4th, 5th

USAAF – United Kingdom/France

6 MARCH 1944

VIII Fighter Command

4th FG	Debden	86 ac
355th FG	Steeple Morden	52 (+ 66 P-47s)
357th FG	Leiston	77

IX Air Support Command

67th RG	Chilbolton + Middle Wallop	39 (+27 Spitfire VB)
354th FG	Boxted	68
363rd FG	Rivenhall	55

30 MAY 1944

VIII Fighter Command

4th FG	Debden	71
355th FG	Steeple Morden	77
339th FG	Fowlmere	68
57th FG	Leiston	68
352nd FG	Bodney	74
359th FG	East Wretham	69
361st FG	Bottisham	74

IX Tactical Air Command

67th RG	Middle Wallop	107

XIX Tactical Air Command

354th FG	Lashenden	71
363rd FG	Staplehurst	59

8 AUGUST 1944

VIII Fighter Command

4th FG	Debden	71
355th FG	Steeple Morden	79
479th FG	Wattisham	6 (+ 77 P-38s)
55th FG	Wormingford	70
339th FG	Fowlmere	68
357th FG	Leiston	24
20th FG	Kingscliffe + Wittering	73
352nd FG	Bodney	71
361st FG	Bottisham	73 (+ 6 P-38s)

IX Tactical Air Command

67th TRG	Le Molay + Chalgrove	64 (+ 23 23 P-38s)

XIX Tactical Air Command

10th PRG	Chalgrove	41 (+ P-38 and Boston)
354th FG	Criqueville	67
363rd FG	Maupertus	67

Total strength 884 ac

1 JANUARY 1945

VIII Air Force
1st Bombardment Division

20th FG	Kingscliffe	82
352nd FG	Bodney	20
356th FG	Martlesham	89
359th FG	East Wretham	82
364th FG	Honington	103

2nd Bombardment Division

4th FG	Debden	85
355th FG	Steeple Morden	105
361st FG	Little Walden	33
479th FG	Wattisham	84

3rd Bombardment Division

55th FG	Wormingford	91
78th FG	Duxford	85 (+ 7 P-47)
339th FG	Fowlmere	85
353rd FG	Raydon	80
357th FG	Leiston	84

IX Fighter Command

363rd TRG	Le Culot	48 (F-6)

IX Tactical Air Command

67th TRG	Charleroi	40 (F-6 + 17 F-5)

XIX Tactical Air Command

10th PRG	Conflans	46 (F-6 + F-3 and F-5)

Total strength 1,231 ac

Appendix E: Mustang Units

RAF Mustang Squadrons
* Not a major type within squadron UE (Unit Establishment)

Unit	Mark	Dates	Code
2 Sqn	I, IA	4.42–5.44	XV
	II	5.44–1.45	
3 Sqn*			DV
4 Sqn	I	4.42–1.44	TV
16 Sqn	I	4.42–11.43	UG
19 Sqn	III, IV	2.44–3.46	QV
26 Sqn	I	1.42–3.44, 12.44–6.45	XC
34 Sqn*			6J
63 Sqn	I, IA	6.42–5.44	
64 Sqn	III	11.44–5.46	SH
	IV	8.45–6.46	
65 Sqn	III	12.43–3.45	YT
	IV	3.45–5.46	
93 Sqn	III, IV	1.46–12.46	
112 Sqn	III	6.44–5.45	GA
	IV	2.45–12.46	
118 Sqn	III	1.45–3.46	NK
	IV	3.46	
122 Sqn	III	2.44–5.45	MT
	IV	5.45–8.45	
126 Sqn	III	12.44–3.46	SJ
	IV	8.45–3.46	
129 Sqn	III	4.44–5.45	DV
154 Sqn	IV	2.45–3.45	
165 Sqn	III	2.45–6.45	SK
168 Sqn	I	11.42–8.43, 2.44–10.44	OE
	IA	8.43–2.44	
169 Sqn	I	1.42–9.43	
170 Sqn	I	6.42–8.43	BN
	IA	8.43–1.44	
171 Sqn	IA	9.42–12.42	
213 Sqn	III	5.44–2.47	AK
	IV	2.45–2.47	
225 Sqn	I, II	5.42–8.43	
231 Sqn	I	4.43–1.44	
234 Sqn	III	9.44–8.45	AZ
	IV	3.45–8.45	
239 Sqn	I	5.42–9.43	HB
241 Sqn	I	3.42–11.42	RZ
249 Sqn	III	9.44–6.45	GN
	IV	6.45–8.45	
250 Sqn	III, IV	8.45–1.47	LD
260 Sqn	III	4.44–8.45	HS
	IV	6.45–8.45	
268 Sqn	I, IA	3.42–4.45	NM
	II	11.44–8.45	
285 Sqn	I	3.45–6.45	
303 Sqn	IV	4.45–12.46	RF
306 Sqn	III	3.44–1.47	UZ
309 Sqn	III, IV	10.44–1.47	WC
315 Sqn	III	3.44–12.46	PK
316 Sqn	III	4.44–11.46	SZ
516 Sqn	I	4.43–2.44	
541 Sqn	III	6.44–4.45	
611 Sqn	IV	1.45–8.45	FY
613 Sqn	I	4.42–10.43	SY
617 Sqn*			

(Wg Cdr Cheshire pioneered the use of the Mustang as a target-marking aircraft and 617 had a small number on charge in late 1944–45).

A wide range of other RAF units had Mustangs on charge including:

61 OTU (Operational Training Unit) – became 236 OCU
71 OTU
1 APS (Armament Practice School)
1 TEU (Tactical Exercise Unit)
3 TEU
5 RFU (Refresher Flying Unit)
A&AEE (Aeroplane & Armament Experimental Establishment)
CFE (Central Fighter Establishment)
CGS (Central Gunnery School)
FIU (Fighter Interception Unit)
FIDS (Fighter Interception Development Unit)
RAE (Royal Aircraft Establishment)

RCAF Mustang Squadrons

400 Sqn	I	4.42–2.44	SP
414 Sqn	I	6.42–8.44	RU
430 Sqn	I	1.43–1.45	
441 Sqn	III, IV	5.45–8.45	GG
442 Sqn	IV	3.45–8.45	Y2

RAAF Mustang Squadrons

450 Sqn	III	5.45–8.45	
3 RAAF	III	11.44–8.45	

SAAF Mustang Squadrons

1 SAAF	III, IV	6.45–7.45	
2 SAAF	IV	6.45–7.45	
5 SAAF	III	9.44–10.45	
	IV	3.45–10.45	

USAAF P-51 Groups

Gp	First ac	Sqns	Code
4th FG	2.44	334th FS	QP

Group	Date	Squadron	Code	Group	Date	Squadron	Code
		335th FS	WD			318th FS	
		336th FS				319th FS	
3rd FG*		78th FS		332nd FG	6.44	99th FS	
		28th FS				100th FS	
		32nd FS				301st FS	
5th FG		17th FS				302nd FS	
		26th FS		339th FG	3.44	503rd FS	D7
		27th FS				504th FS	5Q
		29th FS				505th FS	6N
10th PRG	9.41	10th TRS		348th FG		340th FS	
		12th TRS	ZM			341st FS	
		15th TRS	5M			342nd FS	
		162nd TRS	IX			460th FS	
15th FG	Late 44	45th FS		352nd FG		328th FS	PE
		47th FS				486th FS	PZ
		78th FS				487th FS	HO
18th FBW		12th FBS		353rd FG	10.44	350th FS	LH
		67th FBS				351st FS	YJ
		80th FBS				352nd FS	SX
20th FG	7.44	55th FS	KI	354th FG	11.43	353rd FS	FT
		77th FS	LC			355th FS	GQ
		79th FS	MC			356th FS	AJ
21st FG	1.45	46th FS		355th FG	3.44	354th FS	WR
		72nd FS				357th FS	OS
		31st FS				358th FS	YF
23rd FG	9.43	74th FS		356th FG	11.44	359th FS	OC
		75th FS				360th FS	PI
		76th FS				361st FS	QI
		118th TRS		357th FG	11.43	362nd FS	G4
31st FG	Spring 44	307th FS				363rd FS	B6
		308th FS	HL			364th FS	C5
		309th FS	WZ	359th FG	4.44	368th FS	CV
35th FG	3.45	39th FS				369th FS	IV
		40th FS				370th FS	C5
		41st FS		361st FG	5.44	374th FS	B7
51st FBG	Mid 44	16th FS				375th FS	E2
		25th FS				376th FS	E9
		26th FS		363rd TRG	8.44	160th TRS	A9
52nd FG	4.44	2nd FS	QP			161st TRS	B3
		4th FS	WD			162nd TRS	
		5th FS	VF	362rd FG		380th FS	A9
55th FG	7.44	38th FS	CG			381st FS	B3
		338th FS	CL			382nd FS	C3
		343rd FS	CY	364th FG	7.44	383rd FS	N2
67th TRG	11.43	107th TRS	AX			384th FS	5Y
		109th TRS	VX			385th FS	5E
68th TRG		111th TRS		370th FG	2.45	401st FS	9D
		154th TRS				402nd FS	E6
69th TRG		10th TRS	YC			485th FS	7F
		22nd TRS	QL	479th FG		434th FS	L2
		111th TRS	N5			435th FS	J2
71st TRG		82nd TRS				436th FS	9B
		110th ?		496th FTG	Mid 44	555th FTS	C7
78th FG	12.44	82nd FS	MX	506th FG	10.44	457th FS	
		83rd FS	HL			458th FS	
		84th FS	WZ			462nd FS	
311th FG		528th FS					
		529th FS		2nd Air Cdo	4.44		
		530th FS		3rd Air Cdo	5.44		
325th FG	5.44	317th FS					

Other units included:			857th BS	9H
8th ATS		VQ		
36th BS		R4	* 3rd FG (Provisional) Chinese-American Composite Wing.	
65th FW		JA		

Appendix F: Mustang Aces

The scores given below are *only* for victories scored whilst flying a P-51; many of the pilots listed had higher overall scores when victories achieved with other aircraft types are taken into consideration. Scores include ground strafe claims. Those with greater than 10 confirmed victories in a P-51 are shown in bold type. The leading scorer was George Preddy, with 23.83 confirmed. Conf. = confirmed; Prob. = probable; Dam. = damaged; Unit = the squadron/group with which the pilot was serving at the time; Aircraft = personal aircraft if appropriate.

Note: For further details concerning Second World War Allied aces, *Aces High* by Chris Shores and Clive Williams and *Stars & Bars* by Frank Olynk (both published by Grub Street) are highly recommended.

	Conf.	Prob.	Dam.	Unit	Aircraft
RAF/Allied					
Bargielowski, J.	6	0	3	315 Sqn	
Burra-Robinson, L.	5.5	0	3	122/65 Sqns	
Collyns, B. G.	5	1	3	65 Sqn	
Hearne, P. J.	5	1	1	65/19 Sqns	
Johnston, G. R. McG.	5.83	0	2	122 Wing	
Lamb, D. P.	5	0	3	19/65 Sqns	
Pavey, A. F.	5	1	5	122 Wing	
Pietrzak, H. J.	5	0	1	306/315 Sqns	
Pinches, M. H.	6.5	0	7	122 Sqn?	
Potocki, W.	5	0	0	306 Sqn	
Vassiliades, B. M.	5.83	1	0	19 Sqn	
USAAF					
Abernathy, R. S.	5	0	1	350FS	P51D 44-15589 LH-Q *Lady Gwen II*
Adams, F. E.	9	0	0	362FS	P-51B 43-12468 G4-L *Southern Belle*
Ainlay, J. M.	6	2	2	309FS	
Allen, C. D.	7	0	1	5FS	
Ammon, R. H.	5	0	2	503FS	P-51D 44-14004 D7-A *Annie Mae*
Amoss, D. M.	5.5	0	0	38FS	P-51D 44-13818 CG-B
Anderson, C. F.	9	0	1	335FS	P-51B 43-6972 VF-N *Paul* P-51B 43-7181 WD-L
Anderson, C. E.	16.25	2	2	363FS	P-51B 43-24823 B6-5 *Old Crow* P-51D 44-14450 B6-5 *Old Crow*
Anderson, W. Y.	7	0	0	353FS	P-51B 43-12172 FT-T *Swedes Steed* P-51D 44-13383 FT-T *SwedesSteed III*
Andrew, S. W.	7	0	0	486FS	P-51B 42-106467 PZ-A
Arasmith, L. L.	6	0	1	530FS	P-51 *Penny*
Aron, W. E.	5	0	1	318FS	P-51D 44-15128 #46 *Big Mike/ Texas Jesse*
Asbury, R. W.	5	0	3	382/356FS	P-51B 42-106519 C3-R *Queenie* P-51D 44-63782 AJ-S *Queenie II*
Aust, A. M.	5	0	3	457FS	

Name				Unit	Aircraft
Bankey, E. E.	8.5	1	0	385FS/364FG	P-51D 44-15019 5E-B
					P-51D 44-73045 5E-B *Lucky Lady VII*
Beavers, E. H.	5	0	0	563FS	P-51D 44-13980 D7-Z
					P-51D 44-14525 D7-Z
Becker, R. H.	7	0	0	362FS	P-51B 42-106783 G4-O *Sebastian*
					P-51B 44-14231 G4-O *Sebastian Jr*
Beerbower, D. M.	15.5	.5	11.33	353FS	P-51B 43-12373 FT-E *Bonnie B*
					P-51B 43-12375 FT-E *Bonnie B II*
Beeson, D. W.	5.33	0	0	334FS	P-51B 43-6819 QP-B *Bee*
Beyer, W. R.	9	0	0	376FS	P-51D 44-14144 E9-N
Bickel, C. G.	5.5	2	1	353FS	P-51B 43-6453 FT-2 *Rhub*
					P-51D 44-13628 FT-U (became FT-U *Bonnie B III ?*)
Bickford, E. F.	5.5	0	0	356FS	P-51D 44-73137 AJ-V *Alice Marie*
Billie, H. S.	6	1	4	357FS	P-51D 44-14314 OS-K *Prune Face*
Blakeslee, D. .J	9.5	0	4	4FG	
Blickenstaff, W. K.	10	0	0	350FS	P-51D 44-72374 LH-U *Betty E*
Buchkay, D. H.	13.83	0	1	363FS	P-51B 43-6933 B6-F *Alice In Wonder Land*
					P-51C 42-103041 B6-F *Speedball Alice*
					P-51D 44-13681 B6-F
					P-51D 44-15422 B6-F
					P-51D 44-72244 B6-F
Bolyard, J. W.	5	0	1	74FS	
Bostrom, E. O.	5	0	0	486 FS	P-51D 44-13929 P2-O *Little Marjie*
Bradley, J. T.	15	3	12.66	353FS	P-51B 43-12102 FT-B *Marjie Maru*
Broadhead, J. E.	8	0	2	362FS	P-51B 43-12227 G4-V *Baby Mike*
					P-51D 44-14798 G4-V *Master Mike*
Brooks, J. L.	13	1	2	307FS	P-51D 44-13382 MX-1
Brown, H. L.	6	0	1	55FS	P-51D 44-13779 K1-N
					P-51D 44-11250 K1-A *Be Good/ Brownies Ballroom*
Brown, H. W.	14.2	0	3	354FS	P-51B 42-106448 WR-Z *Hun Hunter*
					P-51D 44-13305 WR-Z
Brown, R. H.	7	1	1	318FS	
Brown, S. J.	15.5	1	7	309/307FS	P-51D 44-13464 MX-A
Browning, J. W.	7	2	1	363FS	P-51B 43-6563 B6-P *Gentleman Jim*
					P-51D 44-13712 B6-P *Gentleman Jim*
Brueland, L. K.	12.5	3	6	355FS	P-51D 44-63702 GQ-U *Grim Reaper/Weespeck*
Bryan, D. S.	9	0	4	328FS	P-51B 43-6894 PE-B *Little One II*
					P-51D 44-14061 PE-B *Little One III*
Bryan, W. E.	7.5	.5	1	503FS	P-51D 44-130601 D7-J
					P-51D 44-15074 D7-J *Big Noise*
Buck, G. T.	6	0	0	307FS	
Burdick, C. de W.	5.5	0	3	361FS	P-51D 44-15310 Q1-B *DoDo*
Candelaria, R. G.	6	1	0	435FS	P-51K 44-11755 J2-K *My Pride and Joy*
Carder, J. B.	7	0	1	364FS	P-51B 42-106777 CS-3 *Taxpayer's Delight*
Carlson, K. E.	6	0	2	336FS	
Carpenter, G.	12.83	1	3	335FS	P-51B 43-6575 *Virginia*
					P-51B 42-106675 WD-1

Carr, B. W.	15	1	2	353FS	P-51D 44-13693 FT-1 *Angel's Playmate* P-51D 44-63497 FT-1 *Angel's Playmate*
Carson, L. K.	18.5	0	3	362FS	P-51B 43-6634 G4-C *Nooky Booky* P-51D 44-13316 G4-C *Nooky Booky II* P-51D 44-14896 G4-C *Nooky Booky III* P-51K 44-11622 G4-C *Nooky Booky IV*
Cesky, C. J.	8.5	0	0	328FS	P-51D 44-13927 PE-L *Diann Ruth* P-51D 44-13401 PE-L *Diann Ruth II*
Ceullers, G. F.	9.5	0	2	383FS	P-51DD 44-13971 N2-D P-51D 44-15020 N2-<u>D</u> P-51D 44-72719 N2-<u>D</u>
Chandler, V. E.	5	0	1	336FS	P-51D 44-14388 VF-U *Wheezy*
Chapman, P. G.	5	0	0	74FS	
Clark, J. A.	6	0	0	4FG	P-51B 42-106650 QP-W P-51B 43-6726 QP-W P-51B 43-6560 QP-W P-51D 44-13372 QP-W
Cole, C. H.	5	0	0	77/55FS	P-51D 44-11324 LC-U P-51D 44-72160 K1-K
Coons, M. M.	5	1	0	38FS	P-51D 44-14608 CG-C *The Worry Bird*
Cox, R. L.	5	0	0	370/369FS	P-51D 44-14979 CS-H P-51D 44-72154 IV-N
Cramer, D. S.	6	0	1	338FS	P-51D 44-14121 CL-2 *Mick #5*
Cranfill, N. K.	5	.5	1	368FS	P-51B 42-106848 IV-N *Deviless 2nd* P-51D 44-13390 IV-N *Deviless 3rd* P-51D 44-15100 CV-Q P-51D 44-1517 CV-Q
Crenshaw, C. J.	7	1	0	369FS	P-51B 42-106689 IV-S P-51D 44-13306 IV-1 *Louisiana Heatwave* P-51D 44-15016 IV-1 *Heatwave*
Crim, H. C.	6	0	5.25	531FS	
Cullerton, W. J.	5	0	0	357FS	P-51D 44-13677 OS-X *Miss Steve*
Cummings, D. M.	5.5	0	0	38FS	P-51D 44-15192 CG-U
Cundy, A. C.	6	0	0	352FS	P-51D 44-15092 SX-B *Alabama Rammer Jammer*
Curtis, R. C.	13	1	5	2FS	P-51 *Julie*
Dahlberg, K. H.	11	0	1	353FS	P-51B 43-7163 FT-0 *Dahlberg's Dilemma*
Dalglish, J. B.	7	0	5	355FS	P-51B 42-106834 B3-X P-51D 44-63732 FT-P P-51D 44-72774 GQ-K *Put. Betty Mae*
Daniel, W. A.	5	0	0	307/308FS	P-51D HL-H *Tempus Fugit*
Davis, B. S.	6	0	0	317FS	P-51B 42-103519 #24 P-51D #24 *Bee* (later *Honey Bee*)
Davis, G. V.	7.5	0	0	364FS	P-51B 43-6878 C5-0 *Pregnant Polecat*
Dillard, W. J.	6	3	2	307FS	
Doersch, G. A.	8.5	0	2	370FS	P-51B 43-24810 CS-J P-51D 44-72067 CV-R *Ole' Goat*
Dorris, H. W.	5	0	4	308FS	
Dorsch, F. J.	8.5	0	2	309FS	

Dregne, I. H.	5	0	3	357FG	P-51D 44-13408 C5-Q *Ah Fung Goo II/Bobby Jeanne* P-51K 44-11678 C5-Q *Ah Fung Goo/Bobby Jeanne*
Drew, U. L.	6	0	1	375FS	P-51D 44-14164 E2-D *Detroit Miss*
Dunkin, R. W.	5	0	1	317 FS	P-51D 44-13336 #7 *This izit*
Eagleston, G. T.	18.5	2	9	353FS	P-51B 43-12308 FT-U P-51D 44-63607 FT-L
Elder, J. L.	7	0	1	357FS	P-51B 42-106732 OS-R *Moon* P-51D 44-63633 OS-R
Elder, R. A.	5	0	0	353FS	P-51D 44-72736 LH-S *Miss Gamble*
Emmerson, W. S.	6	1	3	355FS	P-51B 42-166445 GQ-Q
Emmer, W. N.	14	1	2	353FS	P-51D 44-13948 FT-G *Arson's Reward*
Emmert, B. H.	5	0	5	318FS	P-51V 42-106943 #47
Empey, J. W.	5	0	0	5FS	P-51B *Little Ambassador*
England, J. J.	10	1	3	530FS	P-51A 43-6077 #75 *Jackie*
England, J. B.	17.5	0	1	362FS	P-51B 42-106462 G4-H *U've Had It* P-51D 44-13735 G4-H *U've Had It* P-51D 44-14709 G4-E *Missouri Armada*
Evans, A J	6	0	0	357FG	P-51D 44-64051 G4-B *Little Sweetie 4*
Fiebelkorn, E. C.	8.5	0	1	77FS	P-51D 44-11161 LC-N *June Nite*
Fiedler, A. C.	8	1	0	317FS	P-51D #35 *Helen*
Fisk, H. E.	5	1	1	356FS	P-51B 43-6621 AJ-F *Duration Plus*
Fortier, N. J.	5.5	0	2	354FS	P-51B 42-106870 WR-N P-51D 44-15373 WR-N P-51D 44-72361 WR-N
Fowle, J. M.	8	0	1	384FS	P-51D 44-13829 SY-J *Terry Claire* P-51D 44-14184 SY-Q *Terry Claire III*
Foy, R. W.	15	0	2	363FS/ 357FG	P-51D 44-1371? B6-V *Reluctant Rebel* P-51D 44-63621 B6-V *Little Shrimp*
Frantz, C. M.	7	0	3	353FS	P-51B 42-106701 FT-Q *Joy*
Gailer, F. L.	5.5	0	0	363FS	P-51D 44-11331 B6-A *Expectant*
Gentile, D. S.	16.5	0	1	336FS	P-51B 43-6913 VF-T *Shangri-La*
Gleason, G. W.	9	0	1	434FS	P-51D 44-14740 L2-H *Hot Toddy*
Glover, F. W.	10.33	1	0	336FS	P-51B 43-12214 VF-C *Rebel Queen* P-51D 4-14787 VF-B P-51D 44-64153 VF-B
Godfrey, J. T.	13.83	2	3	336FS	P-51B 43-6765 VF-P P-51B 42-106730 VF-P *Reggie's Reply* P-51D 44-13412 VF-F
Goebel, R. J.	11	1	0	308FS	P-51D 44-13300 HL-D *Flying Dutchman*
Goodnight, R.	7.25	1	2	356FS	P-51B 43-12206 AJ-G P-51B 43-12213 AJ-G *Mary Anne*
Goodson, J. A.	9	0	0	336FS	P-51B 43-24848 VF-B P-51B 43-6895 VF-B P-51D 44-13303 VF-B
Graham, G. M.	7	1	1	354FS	P-51D 44-14276 WR-F *Down for Trouble* P-51D 44-15255 WR-F
Green, H. H.	5	0	5	317FS	P-51C 42-103324 #11 P-51D 44-13498
Gross, C. K.	6	.5	3	355FS	P-51B 43-12451 GQ-1 *Live Bait/ Peggy*

					P-51D 44-63668 GQ-1 *Live Bait*
Gumm, C. F.	6	2.5	8	355FS	P-51B 43-6320 GQ-V *Toni*
					P-51B 42-166749 GQ-V
Halton, W. T.	9.5	0	0	487FS	P-51B 42-106717 PE-T *Slender, Tender and Tall*
					P-51D 44-13966 PE-T *Slender, Tender & Tall*
					P-51D 44-14812 HO-T *Slender, Tender & Tall*
Hanes, W. F.	6	0	1	4FS	
Hanseman, C. J.	5	0	0	505FS	P-51D 44-13556 6N-H *Eleanore IV*
Harris, T. L.	5	1	0	364FS	P-51B 43-6653 C5-5 *Lil' Red's Rocket*
Hatala, P. R.	5.5	0	0	364FS	P-51B C5-B *Jeanne*
Hauver, C. D.	5	0	1	354FS	P-51B 43-6917 WR-K *Patrica*
					P-51D 44-14704 WR-R *Princess Pat*
Haviland, F. R.	6	0	2	357FS	P-51D 44-14403 HS-H *Barbara*
Haworth, R. C.	5	0	1	338FS	P-51D 44-13642 CL-K *Krazy Kid*
Hayes, T. L.	8 5	1	0	364FS/ 357FG	P-51D 44-13318 C5-N *Frenesi*
Heller, E. L.	5.5	0	1	486FS	P-51B 43-6704 P2-H *Hell-er Bust*
					P-51D 44-1496 P2-H *Hell-er Bust*
Herbst, J. C.	14	1	2	74FS	P-51B 43-7060 40 *Tommy's Dad*
Hiro, E. W.	5	2	2	363FS	P-51B *Horse's Hitch*
					P-51D 44-13518 B6-D *Horse's Hitch*
Hively, H. D.	5	2	2	334FS	P-51B 43-6898 QP-I *Deacon*
					P-51D 44-15347 QP-I *Deacon*
Hofer, R.	13	0	2	334FS	P-51B 42-106924 QP-L *Salem Representative*
Hoffman, J. F.	6.5	2	1	2FS	
Hovde, W. J.	9.5	0	1	358FS	P-51B 43-6928 YF-1 *Ole II*

Below: Don Gentile poses with his P-51 *Shangri-La*. (Robert F. Dorr)

					P-51D 44-13531 YF-1 *Ole III*
					P-51D YF-1 *Ole IV*
					P-51D YF-1 *Ole V*
Howard, J. H.	6	1	2	356FS/	P-51B 43-6375 AJ-A *Ding Hao!*
				354FG	P-51B 43-6515 AJ-A *Ding Hao!*
Howe, D. W.	5	0	0	334FS	P-51D 44-13884 QP-G
Howes, B. H.	6	0	0	343FS	P-51K 44-11370 CY-E *My Lil Honey*
					P-51D 44-63567 CY-E *My Lil Honey*
					P-51D 44-63745 CY-C *My Lil Honey*
Hunt, E. E.	6.5	2	3	353FS	P-51B 42-106597 FT-S *Smoklering Boulder*
					P-51D 44-13559 FT-5 *Ready Eddy*
Jackson, W. O.	6	0	2	486FS	P-51B 42-106661 P2-J *Hot stuff*
					P-51D 44-13398 P2-J
					P-51D 44-14709 P2-J
Jamison, G. L.	7	0	1	385FS	P-51D 44-14035 5E-A *Etta Jane*
Jeffrey, A. F.	10	0	2	434FS	P-51D 44-14423 L2-0 *Boomerang*
					P-51K 44-11674 L2-0 *Boomerang Jr*
Jenkins, O. D.	8.5	0	0	362FS	P-51B 42-106829 G4-P *Floogie/Joan*
					P-51D 44-14245 G4-P *Floogie II*
					P-51D 44-63189 G4-X *Toolin Fool's Revenge*
Johnson, A. G.	6.5	0	0	2FS	
Johnson, E. M.	5	0	1	505FS	P-510 44-13471 6N-J *The Comet*
Jones, C. W.	6	0	1	370FS	P-510 44-14071 CS-W *Dora Dee*
Jones, F. G.	5	1	3	335FS	P-51B 43-6897 WD-P
					P-51D 44-13389 WD-P
Karr, R. A.	6	0	2	5FS	
Kemp, W. T.	6	0	1	375FS	P-51C 42-103749 E2-X *Betty Lee*
					P-51D 44-14270 E2-X *Betty Lee II*
					P-51D 44-15076 E2-X *Betty Lee III*
King, W. B.	5.5	0	2	355FS	42-106424 GQ-B *Atlanta Peach*
					P-51B 43-6724 GQ-D *Atlanta Peach?*
Kinnard, C. H.	8	0	1	354FS/	P-51B 43-6431 WR-A *Man O war*
				355FG	
					P-51D 44-15625 WR-A
					P-51D 44-73144 *Man O war*
					P-51D 44-14292 QP-A *Man O war*
Kirla, J. A.	11.5	0	0	362FS	P-51D 44-14624 G4-H *Spook*
					P-51D 44-14624-72180 G4-H *Spook*
Koenig, C. W.	6.5	1	2	353FS	P-51D FT-K *Little Horse*
Lamb, G. M.	7.5	1	1.5	356FS	P-51D 44-132882 AJ-I *Uno Who II*
					P-51D 44-72513 AJ-I *Uno Who III*
Lampe, R. C.	5.5	0	1	2FS	
Lang, J. L.	7.83	0	1	334FS	P-51D 44-14123 QP-2
Larson, D. A.	6	1	1	505FS	P-51B 6N-B *Mary Queen of Scots*
					P-51D 44-13609 6N-B *Mary Queen of Scots*
Lasko, C. W.	7.5	0	5.5	355FS	P-51B 43-6451 GQ-L
					P-51B 43-6764 GQ-E *Suga*
					P-51B 42-106935 GQ-E *Suga*
					P-51D 44-13622 B3-
Lawler, J. B.	7.5	2	3	2FS	P-51D *Cathy*
Lazear, E. R.	5	1	0	486FS	P-51D 44-14877 P2-L *Pennie's Ear I*
Lenfest, C. W.	5.5	0	2	354FS	P-51B 43-6948 WR-F *Lorie II*
					P-51B 42-106874 WR-F *Lorie III*

					P-51D 44-14409 WR-F *Lorie IV*
					P-51D 44-14274 WR-F *Lorie V*
Lewis, W. H.	7	0	1	343FS	P-51D 44-13907 CY-S
					P-51D 44-14907 CY-S –?
Lines, T. E.	10	0	0	335FS	P-51B 43-7172 WD-H
					P-51D 44-13555 WD-D *Thunderbird*
Littge, R. H.	10.5	0	0	487FS	P-51D 44-13320 HO-M *Silver Dollar*
					P-51D 44-72216 HO-M *Helen*
Long, M. G.	5.5	0	0	355FS	P-51D 44-13328 GQ-L *Mary Pat III*
					P-51D 44-63815 GQ-L *Mary Pat*
Loving, G. G.	5	0	2	309FS	P-51B 42-106538 WZ-D
Lowry, W. L.	11	1	0	317FS	P-51C 42-103501 13
					P-51D 13 *My Gal Sal*
Luksic, C. J.	8.5	0	0	487FS	P-51B 43-7145 HO-Z *Elly's Lucky Boy*
					P-51B 43-7588 HO-Z
Markham, G. E.	5	0	2.5	351FS	P-51D 44-14929 YJ-Q *Mr Gray*
					P-51D 44-14949 YJ-Q *Mr Gray*
					P-51D 44-72171 YJ-Q *Mr Gray*
Marsh, L. C.	5	1	1	503FS	P-51D 44-14947 D7-P
Marshall, B. W.	7	0	1	354FS	P-51D 44-14440 WR-B *Jane III*
					P-51D 44-14409 WR-F
					P-51D 44-14276 WR-F *Down fer Double*
					P-51D 44-72253 WR-B *Jane VI*
					P-51D 44-72953 WR-B *Jane VII*
Martin, K. R.	5	0	1	354FG	P-51B 43-6359 GQ-E
Maxwell, C. K.	5	0	0	364FS	P-51D 44-63861 C5-H
McComas, E. D.	14	1	1	118TRS	P-51 *Kansas Reaper*
					P-51 600
McCorkle, C. M.	6	0	1	31FG	P-51B 42-1065?1 CM-M *Betty Jone*
McDaniel, G. H.	6	0	0	318FS	P-51D 44-14467 40 *Mary Mac*
McDowell, D.	8.5	0	.5	353FS	P-51B 43-7136 FT-l *Ho Tel*
					P-51B 42-106712 FT-l *Ho Tel II*
McElroy, J. N.	5	0	6	358FS	P-51 YF-5 *Big Stoop III*
McGrattan, B. L.	7.5	0	0	335FS	P-51B 43-6767 WD-D
McKennon, P. W.	7.5	0	1	335FS	P-51B 42-106911 WD-A *Yippi Joe*
					P-51B 43-6896 WD-A
					P-51D 44-13883 WD-A
					P-51D 44-14221 WD-A *Ridge Runner*
					P-51D 44-14570 WD-A *Ridge Runner*
					P-51D 44-63166 WD-A
					P-51D 44-72308 WD-A *Ridge Runner III*
McLaughlin, M. D.	7	1	5	309FS	
Megura, N.	11.83	0	6	334FS	P-51B 43-6636 QP-N III *Wind*
					P-51B 43-7158 QP-F
Meyer, J. C.	21	0	2	487FS	P-51B 42-106471 HO-M *Lambie II*
					P-51D 44-14151 HO-M *Petie 2nd*
					P-51D 44-15041 HO-M *Petie 3rd*
Miklajcyk, H. J.	7.5	0	0	486FS	P-51B 42-106430 P2-K *The Syracusan*
					P-51D 44-13690 P2-K *Syracusan The 3rd*
Miller, T. F.	5.25	1	1	356FS	P-51B 42-106716 AJ-Z *Gnomee*

Minchew, L. D.	5.5	0	5	354/357FS	P-51D 44-14753 05-O
Moats, S. K.	8.5	0	1	487FS	P-51B 42-106751 HO-U *Kay*
					P-51D 44-14848 HO-K *Kay III*
Molland, L. P.	6	0	0	308FS	P-51D 44-13311 HL-C
Moore, R. W.	11	1	3	78/45FS	P-51D 119 *Stinger VI*
					P-51D 44-63483 67 *Stinger VII*
Moran, G. T.	12	0	2	487FS	P-51C 42-103320 HO-M *Little Ann*
					P-51D 44-13320 HO-M
Mulhollem, R. F.	5	2	2	530FS	
Murphy, A. C.	6	0	0	362/364FS	P-51D 44-13334 44-U *Bite Me*
Norley, L. H.	9	0	0	336/335/	P-51B 43-12416 UF-O
				334FS	P-51B 43-6666 UF-O
					P-51B 43-6802 UF-0
					P-51D 44-15028 WD-O
					P-51D 44-15350 UF-?
					P-51D 44-72196 QP-O
					P-51D 44-73108 QP-O *Red Dog XII*
O'Brien, G. M.	7	0	2.5	362FS	P-51B 43-6787 G4-Q *Shanty Injh*
O'Brien, W. R.	5.5	2	1	363FS	P-51D 44-13622? B6-G *Billy's Bitch*
O'Connor, F. Q.	10.75	2	3	356FS	P-51B 43-6322 AJ-Q *The Verna Q/ Stinky*
					P-51D 44-14016 AJ-Q *The Verna Q*
					P-51D 44-63729 AJ-Q *The Verna Q*
Ohr, F.	5	0	0	2FS	P-51D 44-13298 Q *"Marie"*
Older, C. H.	8	0	0	23FG	P-51D 44-11278
Olds, R.	8	0	1	434FS	P-51D L2-W *Scat IV*
					P-51D 44-14426 L2-W *Scat 5*
					P-51D L2-W *Scat VI*
					P-51D 44-72922 L2-W *Scat VII*
Overfield, L. J.	9	0	0	353FS	P-51C 42-103683 FT-A
Parker, H. A.	13	0	7	318FS	P-51D 57
Paswe, J. J.	5	0	1	385FS	P-51D 44-13890 5E-W *Green Eyes*
					P-51D 44-???? *Desert Rat*
Peterson, R. A.	15.5	1	2	364FS	P-51B 43-6935 C5-T *Hurry Home Honey*
					P-51D 44-13386 C5-T *Hurry Home Honey*
					P-51D 44-14868 C5-T *Hurry Home Honey*
Pierce, J. F.	7	0	1	363FS	P-51B 43-6644 B6-N
Preddy, G. E.	23.83	3	4	487/328FS	P-51B 42-106451 HO-P *Cripes A'mighty 2nd*
					P-51D 44-13321 HO-P *Cripes A'mighty 3rd*
					P-51D 44-14906 PE-P *Cripes A'mighty*
Priest, R. W.	5	0	0	354FS	P-51D WR-E *Eaglebreak*
Pugh, J. F.	6	0	0	362FS	P-51B 42-106473 G4-N *Geronimo*
Reese, W. C.	5	0	0	364FS	P-51B 43-12313 C5-F *Bear River Betsy*
Reeves, L. R.	6	0	2	530FS	P-51C *My Dallas Darlin*
Reynolds, R.	7	0	1	353FS	P-51B 43-6517 FT-U 50 *Calibre Concerto*
Riddle, R. E.	11	1	2	307FS	P-51D MX-N *Angel 3*
Righetti, E. G.	7.5	1	2	338FS/55FS	P-51D 44-14223 CL-M *Katydid*
					P-51D 44-72227 CL-M *Katydid*
Riley, P. S.	6	2	2	353FS	P-51B 43-6922 WD-Y
Ritchey, A. J.	5	0	2	353FS	P-51D FT-E
Roberson, A. J.	6	1	0	362FS	P-51B 43-6688 G4-A *Passion Wagon*

					P-51D 44-13691 G4-A *Passion Wagon*
Rogers, F. S.	7	0	2	353FS	P-51B 43-12161 FT-C *Beantown Banshee*
					P-51B 43-6833 FT-O *Beantown Banshee*
Rose, F.	5	0	1	353FS	P-51B 42-106897 FT-U
					P-51D 44-63584 FT-U
					P-51D 44-63624 FT-U
Ruder, L. A.	5.5	0	0	364FS	P-51B 43-6872 C5-X *Lindu Lu*
					P-51B 42-106768 *Lindu Lu*
Rudolph, H. S.	5	1	0	353FS	P-51D 44-63685 FT-J
Sangermano, P.	8	0	1	318FS	P-51C 42-103581 63 *Mary Norris*
Scheible, W. R.	5	0	2	356FG	p-51D 44-15083 Q1-2
Schimanski, R. G.	6	0	1	364FS	P-51D 44-14334 C5-O
Schlegel, A. L.	7.5	1	0.5	335FS	P-51B 42-106464 WD-O
					P-51D 44-14066 WD-O
Schuh, D.	5	0	0	487FS	P-51D 44-13530 HO-A *Dutchess*
Sears, A. F.	5	0	0	487FS	P-51B 43-6454 HO-O
Shaw, R. M.	8	1	3	364FS	P-51D 44-1375 C5-H
Shipman, E.	7	1	3	307FS	P-51B 42-106478 MX-B
Shoup, R. L.	5.5	0	0	356FS	P-51C 42-102997 AJ-S *Fer De Lance*
Simmons, J. M.	7	0	0	355FS	P-51B 43-7065 GQ-W
Skogstad, N. C.	12	0	0	307FS	
Smith, J.	5	0	0	308FS	
Spencer, D. F.	9.5	0	1	376FS	P-51B 42-106538 E9-5 *Little Luke*
					P-51B 43-24808 E9-D
					P-51D 44-14217 E9-D
Stangel, W. J.	5	0	0	328FS	P-51D 44-14015 PE-C *Stinky 2*
Stanley, M. A.	5	0	0	364FS	P-51D 44-13678 C5-V
Starck, W. E.	6	1	2	487FS	P-51B 43-24807 HO-X *Starck mad/Even Stevens*
Starnes, J. R.	6	0	0	505FS	P-51B 42-106936 6N-X *Tar Heel*
					P-51D 44-14113 6N-X *Tar Heel*
					P-51D 44-14387 6N-X *Tar Heel*
Stephens, R. W.	13	0	1	355FS/ 354FG	P-51B 43-12152 GQ-B *Killer*
					P-51B 43-12209 GQ-5 *Killer*
					P-51B 43-6382 GQ-5 *Killer*
					P-51B 42-106685 GQ-5 *Killer*
					P-51D GQ-5 *Killer!*
Stewart, E. W.	7.33	1	3	328FS/ 355FG/4FG	P-51B WR-5 *Sunny V*
					P-51D 44-13540 WR-5 *Sunny VI*
					P-51D 44-15255 WR-5 *Sunny VII*
					P-51D 44-72181 UF-5 *Sunny VIII*
Storch, J. A.	10.5	0	1	364FS	P-51D 44-13546 C5-R *The Shillelagh*
					P-51D 44-72164? C5-R *The Shillelagh*
Strait, D. J.	10.5	0	0	361FS	P-51D 44-15152 Q1-T *Jersey Jerk*
Sublett, J.	8	0	1	362FS	P-51D 44-11190 G4-Q *Landy Ovella*
Sykes, W. J.	5	2	0	376FS	P-51D 44-14520 E9-5 *Wilma Lee*
Talbot, G. F.	5	0	2	355FS	P-51B 43-6737 *Peggy*
					P-51D 43-63666 GQ-P *Peggy/ Deacon*
Tapp, J. B.	8	0	2	78FS	
Thompson, R. D.	5	0	3	309FS	
Thornell, J. F.	13	0	1	328FS	P-51B 42-106872 PE-I *Pattie II*
Trafton, F. O.	5	1	1	308FS	

Turner, R. E.	11	0	8	356FS	P-51B 43-12434 AJ-T *Short Fuse Sallee*
					P-51D 44-13561 AJ-T *Short Fuse Sallee*
					P-51D 44-15622 AJ-T *Short Fuse Sallee*
Tyler, G. E.	7	0	0	364FS	P-51B 43-6376 C5-J *Little Duckfoot*
					P-51D 44-14660 C5-J *Little Duckfoot*
Varnell, J. S.	17	0	2	2FS	P-51D 44-13431
Voll, J. J.	21	4	3	308FS	P-51D 44-15459 HL-B *American Beauty*
Waggoner, H. Q.	5	0	0	352FS	P-51D 44-14802 SX-X *Miss Illini III*
Warford, V. E.	8	1	1	309FS	
Warner, J. A.	5	0	1	356FS	P-51B C3-? *Lady Jane*
					P-51D 44-14010 AJ-G *Chicago's Own*
Watts, O. S.	5	0	1	118TFS	P-51C 43-25225
Weaver, C. E.	8	1	1	362FS	P-51D 44-72199 G4-A
Welch, R. E.	6	0	1	343FS	P-51D 44-14140 CY-O *Wing of the Morning*
					P-51D 44-72138 CY-Z
Welden, R. D.	6.25	0	1	356FS	P-51B 43-6687 AJ-W *Maekie*
					P-51B 43-12172 AJ-W *Maekie 2nd*
					P-51B 43-12433 AJ-W *Maekie 3rd*
Wetmore, R. S.	17	0	0	370FS	P-51D 44-14733 *Daddy's Girl*
Whisner, W. T.	13.5	2	0	487FS	P-51B 42-106449 HO-W *Princess Elizabeth*
					P-51D 44-114237 HO-W *Moonbeam McSwine*
Wilhelm, D. C.	6	1	3	309FS	
Williams, R. D.	5	0	1	118TFS	
Wilson, W. F.	5	0	1	385FS	P-51D 44-14258 5E-Y
					P-51D 44-14838 5E-Y
Winks, R. P.	5.5	0	0	364FS	
Wise, K.	5	0	0	353FS	P-51D FT-H 44-64104 *Wano*
Woody, R. E.	7	1	1	354FS	P-51B 43-6520 WR-W *Woody's Maytag*
Yeager, C. E.	11.5	0	3	363FS	P-51D 44-13897 B6-Y *Glamorous Glen II*
					P-51D 44-14888 B6-Y *Glamorous Glen III*
York, R. M.	5	1	0	370FS	P-51D 44-14159 C5-Y *Rudy*
Zoerb, D. J.	7	0	0	2FS	P-51B *Hey Rube! II*

Appendix G: Trials Reports

An extensive selection of RAF and USAAF trials and evaluation reports were referenced during the research for this book; *extracts* from various reports have been quoted throughout the book, but it seems appropriate to publish a selection of the more relevant reports in more detail as an appendix. The following reports are included:

1. Tactical Suitability of P-51 Type Aircraft. (USAAF, December 1942)
2. Comparative trials of new low altitude fighters Spitfire IX and Mustang X. (RAF, February 1943)
3. Climb and Level Speed performance, Mustang X AM208. (RAF)
4. Tactical employment trials P-51B-1. (USAAF, February 1944)
5. Tactical trials Mustang III. (RAF, March 1945)

1. Tactical Suitability of P-51 Type Aircraft, dated December 1942.

1. Object
   To determine the relative tactical value of the P-51 type fighter aircraft for combat service.

2. Introduction
   This test was authorised by letter from HQ Army Air Forces, Director of Air Defense, dated July 13, 1942, to Commanding General, Air Forces Proving Ground, Eglin Field, subject: 'Test of P-51 Airplanes.' This test was started August 7, 1942 and was finished on November 1, 1942.

   The articles tested are P-51 type airplanes, Air Corps Serials 41-37323, 41-37324 and 41-37325.

3. Conclusions

   It is concluded that:

   a. The subject aircraft is the best low altitude American fighter aircraft yet developed, and should be used as the criterion for comparison of subsequent types.

   b. If possible, the power loadings of this fighter aircraft should be materially reduced, without increasing the wing loading.

   c. To reduce the power loadings of the aircraft, excess weight in the structure, and accessories not vital to operational use should be eliminated, and engine performance increased.

   d. Pilots become completely at home in this aircraft immediately after the first take-off due to the remarkable sensitivity of control, simplicity of cockpit, and excellent flying characteristics.

   e. The rate of roll is not as rapid as is desired for combat operations.

   f. The view downward over the nose is not sufficient to allow full deflection shooting in a turn.

   g. The automatic manifold pressure regulator is completely satisfactory.

   h. With the exception of the radiators, the airplane is satisfactory from a maintenance standpoint.

   i. The range of speeds obtainable in the throttle limits in level [flight] is excellent.

   j. Up to 15,000ft this is faster than all American fighters with the exception of the P-47C-1.

4. Recommendations:

   It is recommended that:

   a. The subject aircraft be equipped with an engine which will permit satisfactory tactical combat maneuvering between 25,000ft and 30,000ft.

   b. The present armament in the subject aircraft be changed from four 20mm cannon to four .50 caliber machine guns, wing mounted, and that these be high cyclic rate of fire guns and standardisation is affected.

   c. Provisions be provided for carrying external combat and ferrying fuel tanks.

   d. The subject aircraft be equipped with the modified N-7 type gun sight to allow changing of bulb while in flight and to set dropping single for low level bombing.

   e. The subject aircraft be equipped with the Stoddard radio (Model MRT-3A) for test at this station. This radio weighs forty-six (46) pounds installed.

   f. The brakes of the subject aircraft be redesigned for more satisfactory operations.

   g. The throttle and propeller controls be hooked together to operate as a unit, if the pilot so desires.

   h. The coolant and oil radiators be redesigned for more satisfactory service, and the mountings be modified to permit much faster installation and removal.

   i. Study be made of canopy structure to determine the weakness which allows the canopy to bulge at high speed, and steps be taken to correct this condition.

   j. The subject aircraft be equipped with an automatic shutter control (factory has installation).

   k. It be equipped with a stick locking tail wheel (factory has installation).

   l. It be equipped with more effective aileron

control to produce higher rate of roll at all speeds (factory has installations).

m. It be equipped with left wing landing light only.

n. It be equipped with a 'demand' oxygen system (now standard equipment).

o. The electrical compass indicator magnesyn remote indicating compass be installed.

p. The automatic manifold pressure regulator be incorporated on all subsequent models of this airplane.

6. Discussion

b. Maneuverability. The subject aircraft was flown in mock combat against the P-38F, P-39D, P-40F, P-47B and the Mitsubishi '00' type of aircraft. The following results were obtained:

1. The subject aircraft was found to be superior in speed of the Mitsubishi '00', P-39D, P-40F at all altitudes and the P-47B and P-38F up to 15,000ft.

2. The subject aircraft was found to be superior in rate of climb to the P-39D, P-40F and the P-47B up to 15,000ft.

3. The acceleration in dives and max permissible diving speed of the subject aircraft is superior to all types tested.

4. The turning characteristics of the subject aircraft are substantially the same as the P-40F and the P-39D. None of these appears to have any definite superior turning characteristics.

5. In close 'dog fighting' the subject aircraft has the very decided advantage of being able to engage or break combat at will. However, if neither airplane attempts to leave the combat, the P-40F is considered to have a slight advantage.

c. Ceiling. The absolute ceiling of the subject aircraft at the date of this report was found to be approx 31,000ft. It is believed that the fighting ceiling of this aircraft is 20,000ft as the engine loses power very rapidly above 18,000ft. This limited ceiling is the most serious handicap to this aircraft, and every effort should be made to increase the power and critical altitude of the engine.

f. Flying characteristics – General

1. The flying characteristics of the P-51 are exceptionally good and the aircraft is very pleasant and easy to fly. Its taxiing visibility is limited in view over the nose as are all standard gear fighters having engine in front of pilot. There is no objectional amount of torque on take-off and the ship becomes airborne very nicely. A pilot flying this plane for the first time feels immediately at home when his ship leaves the ground, and he has a feeling that he has flown this ship for a very large number of hours. The plane picks up speed very rapidly after leaving the ground and will climb equally well between 165 mph and 205 mph IAS. This ability to climb well at a high indicated speed should be a great aid in helping catch targets having altitude and attempting to escape. In level flight trimmed up, the aircraft will fly practically hands off. There is a speed range of about 200 miles difference in which it is possible for the pilot to control the plane without aid of trim. The plane handles nicely in a dive, using a very small amount of trim, and accelerates faster than any other American fighter. At 500 miles indicated with small aid from the trim tabs, the plane still maintains its stability. In normal flight the plane responds quickly to the controls, however, the aileron roll is slower than desired and tightens at very high speeds. It is very easy to put through all normal aerobatics, and it has sufficient speed to perform all these aerobatics from level flight without diving to pick up speed. At slow speeds when approaching the field for a landing, there is a mushy feeling in the ailerons but the control is still there. The plane lands nicely, has a tendency to skip several times if landed fast, and it rolls in a straight line without attempting to swing or break noticeably in either direction.

h. Armament
The present armament is considered adequate, but it is functionally unsatisfactory. It is believed that four caliber .50 (high rate of fire) guns would furnish ideal fire power for the P-51 airplane. The present N-3A gun sight should be replaced with the N-7 type sight in order to permit changing of the bulb while in flight.

i. Armor
The pilot is covered from behind by armor plate 1/4th inch thickness and in front by the engine and a bulletproof glass panel. All fuel tanks are self-sealing.

j. Vulnerability of vital installations

1. The engine and oil tank are mounted in the nose of the subject aircraft and are not considered as vulnerable as those mounted to the rear of the cockpit.

2. The coolant and oil radiators are combined into one assembled unit and are located in the belly of the aircraft just behind the cockpit. For the reason that most hits on an airplane in combat are to the rear of the cockpit, it is believed that this radiator installation may prove to be quite vulnerable. It is recommended that the designer of the subject aircraft make a study of the possibilities of incorporating a sheet of armor plate to protect the radiator from fire from the rear.

k. Visibility

1. The pilot's visibility is in general very similar to that afforded him in the P-40 type aircraft. The view to the rear is somewhat restricted but not dangerously so.

2. The visibility forward in flight attitude is good except over the nose, but on the ground is extremely poor.

3. Every effort must be made to increase the angle of view over the nose. At present the view over the nose is restricted to 3 deg 4 min below the sight line. A mirror arrangement to increase angle of view should be developed.

l. Night Flying. The subject aircraft is suitable for night flying, but because of the very restricted view forward, it is a bit difficult on the run after landing.

m. Instrument Flying. The subject airplane due to its excellent stability is easily flown by the use of instruments.

n. Speed of Servicing. The subject aircraft can be completely serviced (fuel, oil, coolant, oxygen, ammunition and radio check) in 5 minutes by a crew consisting of four armorers, two mechanics and one radioman.

o. Maintenance. The regular 50 hour inspection can be completed in approx 8 hours by using the optimum crew, or it can be completed in approx 10 hours by a crew of two men. The most common maintenance difficulties were found to be:

1. Radiator leakage and the time required to remove and install the radiator unit is un-satisfactory. It is believed by maintenance crew that most leaks in the radiator are due to poor workmanship rather than faulty design.

2. Considerable trouble was experienced with brake action. It is recommended that both of the above deficiences be corrected.

3. In order to change magneto, retime or change points, carburetor airscoop must be removed. It is recommended that, if possible, the carburetor airscoop be redesigned to give more room for working on the magneto.

4. Cuno strainers are too difficult to remove and install.

5. Larger inspection plates for fuel tank sump drain are desired.

6. Separate drains for supercharger section, distributor section, and coolant pump are desired.

Inclosures

The average trial true speeds of the three subject aircraft are set forth in the table below:

Alt	RPM & HG Max cruise	RPM & HG Max operation	RPM & HG Max power
5,000	284 mph 2280 RPM 30.5 in	319 mph 2600 RPM 37.5 in	343 mph 3000 RPM 44.6 in
10,000	305 mph	343 mph	369 mph
15,000	330 mph	367 mph	385 mph
20,000		356 mph	373 mph
25,000		334 mph	357 mph

Rate of Climb. The average of the best time of the three subject aircraft during the climb trials is set forth in the table below:

Manifold Pressure	RPM	Alt	Time	Rate of climb	IAS
55in	3000	5,000	2'10"	2314 ft/min	170
		10,000	4' 7"	2427 ft/min	170
		15,000	6' 34"	2287 ft/min	170
		20,000	9' 54"	2020 ft/min	160
		25,000	15' 20"	1631 ft/min	135

(The time taken is based on the time from the start of the take-off run to the indicated altitude.)

Long range cruising. Take-off – as low a power setting as possible, climb to 15,000 ft true altitude – 2280 RPM, 30.5in Hg at 200 mph IAS (shutters closed). Cruise at 15,000 ft – 1650 RPM and 22.5in Hg (shutters closed and auto-lean mixture). This procedure will give a range of 1,000 miles with 30 gallon gasoline reserve. No appreciable winds. IAS – 192 mph.

Maximum cruising. Take-off – as low a power setting as possible. Climb to 15,000 ft true altitude at 200 mph. AS and cruise – 2280 RPM and 30.5in Hg (shutters closed and auto-lean mixture). This procedure will give a range of 900 miles (55 to 60 gallons/hour) with no reserve. IAS 265 mph.

Combat Range

Interception at 20,000ft:

Climb 10 min at 3000 RPM using 46in Hg to 20,000ft.

Cruise at 2600 RPM using 28.5in Hg and IAS 255.

Combat 20 min at 3000 RPM using 34in Hg and IAS 273.

Total distance covered – 540 miles.
Total gas at take-off – 180 gal.
Gas remaining after landing – 36 gal.
Time of flight – 1 hr 35 min.

Escort convoy of medium bombers at 14,000ft:

Climb to 14,000ft at 2200 RPM at 150 mph.
Cruise at 1650 RPM using 23.5in Hg and IAS 193.
20 minutes combat at 3000 RPM using 41.5in Hg.

Total distance covered – 650 miles.
Total time in air – 3 hr 26 min.
Fuel used – 159 gal.

2. AFDU report dated February 1943

AFDU Interim Report No 64

Comparative trials of new low altitude fighters Spitfire IX (Merlin 66) and Mustang X (Merlin 65)

INTRODUCTION

In accordance with instruction from Air Ministry (DAT), CS 1800 dated 30th September 1942, tactical trials have now been carried out with the Mustang X. Aircraft No AM203 was delivered to this unit on 23.12.42 and this aircraft has been compared with Spitfire IX No BS552 fitted with a similar engine which was available throughout the trial. A second Spitfire IX with this type of engine, No BS543, had also been flown at this unit. Further flying is to be done by pilots from the USAAF on the Mustang X, when it will be compared with modern American fighters, but the arrangements of the USAAF made it impossible for these pilots to be made available during the early part of the trials and a report will therefore be rendered at the completion of their flying.

DESCRIPTION

General
Both aircraft were fitted with the same type of Merlin engine which is known as the Merlin 65 when fitted to the Mustang, and the 66 when installed in the Spitfire. Both are developments of the Merlin 61, and are specially designed for high performance at low altitude. The engines differ only in that the Mustang has a propeller reduction gear of .42, while that of the Spitfire is .477. A Bendix carburettor which prevents cutting under negative 'G' is fitted in both cases and the full throttle boost allowable for combat has been increased to +18 lb. The supercharger gear ratios are 5.79 and 7.06, but Spitfire BS552 was in fact fitted with an earlier type engine having an MS gear of only 5.52, giving a full throttle height of 7,000 feet. The slightly higher MS gear of 5.79 increases the full throttle height to 11,000 feet and will be the standard gear provided in production. Spitfire IX No BS543 was flown for a short time at this unit having the higher MS supercharger gear.

Spitfire IX
[Omitted]

Mustang X
With completely redesigned nose cowlings the Merlin 65 has fitted very neatly into the Mustang. This engine runs more smoothly than any other that has been flown at this Unit previously as it is mounted on large rubber blocks. The radiator has been retained in the original

position as for the Allison motor and the air intake has been placed underneath the engine along with the intercooler radiator instead of on top as with the Allison, in order to improve the pilot's view. The front scoop of the radiator has been sealed in the fully closed position so that only the rear flap moves. The operation of the radiator flap is automatic, being controlled hydraulically on the earlier models and by compressed air on the later aircraft through a thermostat control. Immersed pumps are fitted to both fuel tanks and are required for all flying above 18,000 feet. No pressuring of the tanks appears necessary and both tanks have had their capacity increased to 75 gallons, thus giving a total capacity of 150 gallons. The full throttle heights for this engine in the Mustang are about 11,000 and 22,000 feet. The automatic supercharger change operates at 12,500 feet on the climb. The aircraft available at this unit had an Hydulignum propeller of 11ft 4in diameter, but it is known that trials are being conducted elsewhere with the standard Spitfire propeller of 10 ft 9ins.

The Model 83 Mustang was used for the Merlin installation as a test bench and so the armament consists only of 2 x .50 and 4 x .30 calibre guns in the wings, there being no room for the installation of .50 guns in the fuselage. It is thought that the 4-cannon wing which is now available of the Model 91 Mustang will provide a quite satisfactory armament if this engine installation is to go into production. The aircraft flown in this Unit weighed 9,065 lb, and is thus about 1,800 lb heavier than the Spitfire; with the cannon wing it would weigh 9,200 lb. Ballast weighing 70 lb was carried in the tail. The aircraft also had a special high polish finish which is particularly easy to keep free from oil and grit, but is thought that owing to the already clean design of the airframe that this special finish has not added noticeably to the aircraft's performance.

The flying trials on this aircraft were delayed partly for the fitting of locks to the leading edges of the wheel fairings which were tending to blow open at high speeds, and also for the removal of the engine which became necessary owing to the destruction of a washer between the supercharger casing and the crankcase.

TACTICAL

Flying Characteristics
(i) Spitfire IX. [Omitted]

(ii) Mustang X. The Mustang X is capable of very high speeds in level flight and dive, the aileron control being particularly good at the higher speeds. The elevators have become a trifle heavier than in the Allison engined version and the longitudinal stability has been increased making steady climbs and instrument flying easy. The rudder requires more trimming than previously with the increased torque from the engine and accurate turns, especially to the right, are difficult to carry out. In particular, changes in engine setting during a turn at once produced a noticeable wander. These are serious disadvantages in a fighter, as no matter how good a marksman the pilot is he will not be able to shoot accurately in a turn which has an element of skid or slip in it. These inaccurate turns were also very noticeable at altitude as they caused temporary misting up of the cockpit on the side towards which the aircraft skidded. Steps are, however, in hand to increase the fin area and improve the rudder control which is at present considered inadequate. Take-off is straightforward with little tendency to swing and the approach and landing easy at an IAS of 110 mph.

Performance
The Spitfire IX being the lighter aircraft has a slightly better acceleration from cruising flight to its maximum speeds. The Mustang varies between 12 and 22 mph faster than the Spitfire up to about 34,000 feet, at which height the Spitfire becomes the faster. Maxima for the Spitfire and Mustang as given by the A&AEE are as follows:

	Spitfire	Mustang
11,000 feet in MS gear	384 mph	404 mph
22,000 feet in FS gear	407 mph	430 mph

Climb
The Spitfire climbs about 800 ft/min faster than the Mustang up to 20,000 feet, after which its superiority drops off slightly. The rates of climb as obtained by the A&AEE were for a Spitfire with a dural propeller and other fittings likely to be removed in operations, which made it about 200 lb heavier than the aircraft will probably be in service, so that better results still can be expected. In the case of the Mustang the figures given are for an aircraft with the smaller propeller, so that a better climb can be anticipated with the larger one as flown by this Unit. The operational ceiling of 1,000 ft/min is reached at 37,500 feet in 13 minutes in the Spitfire and at 34,000 feet in 13∫ minutes in the Mustang. The angle of climb for both aircraft is very steep; in the Spitfire it is

particularly difficult for the pilot to see the horizon in the initial parts of the climb owing to the high angle of the nose. The Mustang climbs at a higher speed (195 mph IAS to 19,000 feet) and is much more stable than the Spitfire, it being possible to trim with hands and feet off. Zoom climbs were carried out to compare the two aircraft in which it was found that from fast cruising conditions the Spitfire was faster from ground level to 10,000 feet by 15 seconds, from 10,000 to 20,000 feet by 17 seconds, and from 20,000 to 30,000 feet by 40 seconds.

Dive

10. The Mustang out-dives the Spitfire very easily, being especially quick to accelerate away at full throttle. In the dive the rudder requires a considerable amount of left trim, but the elevator control is good, there being no tendency to recover fiercely and the amount of trim required from cruising flight is only very little. At the end of a dive the Mustang retains its speed very much longer than the Spitfire.

Manoeuvrability

11. The aircraft were compared at varying heights for their powers of manoeuvrability and it was found throughout that the Mustang, as was expected, did not have so good a turning circle as the Spitfire. By the time they were at 30,000 feet the Mustang's controls were found to be rather mushy, while the Spitfire's were still very crisp and even in turns during which 15 degrees of flap were used on the Mustang, the Spitfire had no difficulty in out-turning it. In rate of roll, however, it found that while the Spitfire is superior in rolling quickly from one turn to another at speeds up to 300 mph, there is very little to chose between the two at 350 mph IAS and at 400 mph the Mustang is definitely superior, its controls remaining far lighter at high speeds than those of the Spitfire. When the Spitfire was flown with wings clipped, the rate of roll improved at 400 mph so as to almost identical with the Mustang. The manoeuvrability of the Mustang, however, is severely limited by the lack of directional stability which necessitates very heavy forces on the rudder to keep the aircraft steady. The trim requires re-setting for almost every alteration of engine setting of increase or decrease of speed. If trimmed for the climb and then suddenly rolled over into a dive, it is difficult to hold the Mustang in the required line of flight and shooting at or even following the curve of another aircraft is a dive is

not easy unless the aircraft is retrimmed as it gather speed.

Sighting view

12. The replacing of the air intake below the engine on the Merlin 65 installation of the Mustang has improved the pilot's sighting view to 120 mph.

Low flying

13. Although the view forwards and downwards from the Mustang is better than from the Spitfire, low flying is extremely uncomfortable with the present difficulty of executing accurate turns. As a result, any flying except straight and level makes the pilot feel that he lacks sufficient control to fly with sufficient precision to evade ground defences or natural obstacles.

Night flying

14. No night flying was carried out as both aircraft were fitted with open exhaust stubs.

OTHER POINTS

Mustang Pilot's Cockpit

15. For a tall pilot the Mustang's cockpit is cramped so that he never gets a chance to sit up straight as in the Spitfire, and even an average pilot with parachute and dinghy has to keep leaning forward to clear the roof. The view compares unfavourably with that from the balloon hood fitted to the Spitfire; in the Mustang the horizontal frames of the hood are level with the eye and are very wide, and the frames of the bullet-proof windscreen cause a fairly serious obstruction.

Mustang Heating

16. The Mustang, now capable of good performance at higher altitude than was possible with the Allison engine, is considered to have inadequate cabin heating for work during winter months. While there is a good flow of warm air through the warm duct, it is impossible for the pilot to close the cold duct completely.

Mustang Maintenance

17. The only trouble encountered during the flight trials was that the wheel fairings were inclined to blow open at high speed. Front locks were fitted by the North American Company and a further modification was added by this Unit in order to prevent hanging up which might happen if the cable used for the emergency gear should break. The modification consisted of stiff-

ening Nos 1 & 2 formers and fitting with dural shear pins on to the front locks.

18. As mentioned above, the special finish on AM203 is very easy to keep clean compared with the standard camouflage, and the adhesion to the skin of the airframe is better than that of British dope.

19. The Mustang has a more robust undercarriage and much wider track which can be used on rough ground with far greater safety than the Spitfire's.

CONCLUSIONS

20. The Development of the Merlin 61 and Merlin 65 and 66 and fitted in the Spitfire IX and Mustang X has made available two high performance low-altitude fighters than can be compared as follows:

In level speed the Mustang is 12–22 mph faster than the Spitfire up to 30,000 ft.

In rate of climb the Spitfire is better than the Mustang by about 800 ft/min up to 20,000 ft, the operational ceiling of 1,000 ft/min being 37,000 ft for the Spitfire and 34,000 for the Mustang.

In the dive the Mustang is able to outpace the Spitfire without difficulty.

In turning and rolling maneuvers the Spitfire is better, save that at 400 mph IAS, with standard wing it was a little inferior to the Mustang in rate of roll. With the Spitfire wing tips clipped their roll is identical at this speed. At altitude the Mustang's aileron control does not appear sufficient.

The Mustang suffers badly from lack of directional stability and adequate rudder control, both of which detract seriously from its fighting capabilities. Modifications are in hand to improve these qualities.

The view for fighting and search generally from the Mustang is inferior to that from the Spitfire.

The Mustang carries 150 gallons as compared with the Spitfire's 85 gallons. The latter can be increased by 30 gallons in a jettison tank.

D O Finlay
Wing Commander
Commanding AFDU
AFDU/3/20/35
9th February 1943

3. A&AEE, Climb and Level Speed performance, Mustang X AM208

Introduction
Climb and level speed performance has been measured on Mustang X AM208. The aircraft was basically an NA-83 version, modified by Messrs. Rolls-Royce to take a Merlin 65, an intercooled, two-stage supercharged engine with a .42 reduction gear and a Stromberg carburettor. A 4-bladed 10ft 9in propeller was fitted for these tests.

Condition of aircraft relevant to tests
General. The aircraft, together with the modifications entailed through fitting the Merlin 65 engine, has been described in the first part of Report No A&AEE/781.a. A brief description of the aircraft as tested is given below:

2.11 Engine and cooling installation
A Merlin 65 engine housed in a modified cowling.
Engine air intake, intake for intercooler radiator duct and intercooler radiator, all housed in a common fairing beneath the engine.
Rectangular louvred exits for intercooler radiator air on either side of the engine cowling.

No air cleaners of ice guard over the engine air intake.
Individual ejector exhaust stubs.
A 10ft 9in diameter, 4-bladed Rotol propeller, type R5/4F5/4.
Coolant radiator and oil cooler installed in the normal NA-83 under-fuselage duct.

2.12 Armament and external fittings
4 x .30" and 2 x .50" guns in the wings with their ejection chutes open and leading edge ports sealed.
No fuselage guns fitted.
Bead sight in front of bullet proof windscreen.
Aerial mast behind pilot's hood with a W/T aerial to the fin tip.
IFF aerials from the tailplane tips to the sides of the fuselage.

Loading. The tests were made at a take-off weight of 9,100 lb.

2.3 Engine numbers and limitations. Two Merlin 65 engines were used for these tests. The first engine, Nos 81953/A331468, failed during the tests and was replaced by another Merlin 65, Nos 82445/A331715.

The operational limitations of the above engines applicable to the tests made are given below:

RPM (lb/sq in)		Boost
Max for all-out level flight and combat (5 min limit)	3000	+18
Max for climb at normal rating (1 hr limit)	2850	+12

Tests Made

As mentioned in para 2.3, the first engine fitted to this aircraft failed during the course of the tests and they were completed with a second engine which was installed by Messrs. Rolls-Royce Ltd. Preliminary results obtained with the second engine made it clear that the speed performance was worse with this engine and accordingly the performance is given for both engines.

Details of the tests made are:

With the first engine fitted.

Partial climbs at combat rating to determine the best climbing speed.
    One climb at combat rating using MS supercharger gear only, and two using FS supercharger gear only to determine the optimum height to change supercharger gear.
    The radiator exit duct was fully open for the above tests. The engine failed before any full climbs could be carried out.
    Measurements of maximum level speeds with radiator exit duct flap closed in MS and FS supercharger gears. Heights from 2,000 to 32,000 ft were covered by these measurements.

With the second engine fitted.

Several climbs at combat rating using the climbing speed obtained with the first engine fitted and changing supercharger gear at the optimum height also obtained with the first engine. All except one of these climbs were terminated at 35,000 ft owing to fuel pressure failure and resultant engine cutting. This was cured by fitting an SPE booster pump, and a climb was made to 38,000 ft to determine the performance near the aircraft's ceiling.
    Two climbs at normal rating (SPE pump fitted) using the same climbing speed as that for combat rating. As explained in the first part of this Report, this speed was used for cooling purposes. A brief partial climb test was made

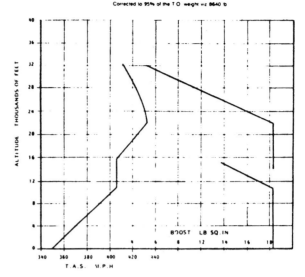

Mustang X AM 208
Level speeds and boosts at heights
Corrected to 95% of the T O weight viz 8640 lb

LEVEL SPEED PERFORMANCE – 3000 RPM

Corrected to 95% of take-off weight – 8650 lb

Merlin 65 No. 81953

HEIGHT Feet	T.A.S. m.p.h	A.S.I. m.p.h	CORRECTIONS m.p.h. P.E.	C.E	STRUT	BOOST lb/Sq.in	S/C GEAR
2000	360	363.5	-14.5	+0.5	+0.1	18.2	MS
4000	370.5	364	-14.5	-0.4	+0.2	18.2	"
6000	381	364.5	-14.6	-1.4	+0.3	18.2	"
8000	391.5	363	-14.5	-2.4	+0.4	18.2	"
*10800	406	362	-14.4	-3.9	+0.6	18.2	"
12000	405.5	355	-13.8	-4.3	+0.7	17.0	"
14000	405	343.5	-13.0	-5.1	+0.7	14.8	"
15500	404.5	335.5	-12.4	-5.6	+0.8	13.6	"
						18.2	FS
16000	407	335.5	-12.4	-6.0	+0.8	18.2	"
18000	416	332	-12.1	-7.0	+1.1	18.2	"
20000	424.5	328.5	-11.8	-8.1	+1.4	18.2	"
*22000	433	325	-11.5	-9.2	+1.8	18.2	"
23000	430.5	312	-10.6	-9.5	+1.8	16.0	"
26000	427	293.5	-9.6	-9.8	+1.7	13.7	"
28000	421	285	-8.6	-10.0	+1.6	11.4	"
30000	417.5	271	-7.5	-10.1	+1.5	9.2	"
32000	411.5	257.5	-6.5	-10.1	+1.4	6.9	"

*Full throttle heights   Supercharger gear change at 15,500 ft.

at normal rating indicating a best climbing speed slightly lower than that used, but it also indicated that the climbing speed was not critical from the point of view of performance. The radiator exit duct flap was fully open during all climbs.
    Measurements of maximum level speeds with the radiator exit duct flap closed, in MS and FS supercharger gears. Heights from 2,000 to 33,000 ft were covered by these measurements.

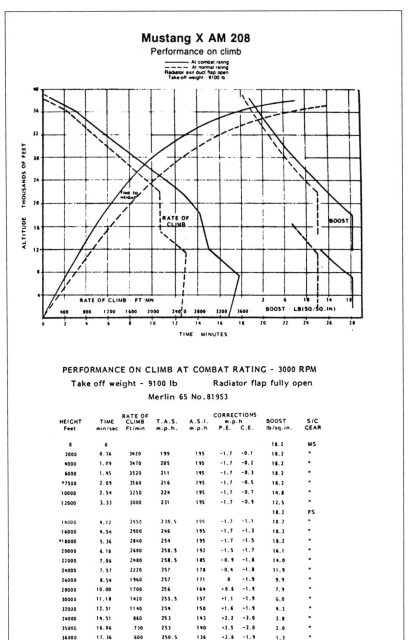

Mustang X AM 208
Performance on climb
— At combat rating
--- At normal rating
Radiator exit duct flap open
Take-off weight - 9100 lb

PERFORMANCE ON CLIMB AT COMBAT RATING - 3000 RPM

Take off weight - 9100 lb   Radiator flap fully open

Merlin 65 No.81953

HEIGHT Feet	TIME min/sec	RATE OF CLIMB Ft/min	T.A.S. m.p.h.	A.S.I. m.p.h	CORRECTIONS m.p.h P.E.	C.E.	BOOST lb/sq.in.	S/C GEAR
0	0						18.2	MS
2000	0.36	3420	199	195	-1.7	-0.1	18.2	"
4000	1.09	3470	205	195	-1.7	-0.2	18.2	"
6000	1.45	3520	211	195	-1.7	-0.3	18.2	"
*7500	2.09	3560	216	195	-1.7	-0.5	18.2	"
10000	2.54	3250	224	195	-1.7	-0.7	14.8	"
12000	3.33	3000	231	195	-1.7	-0.9	12.5	"
							18.2	FS
14000	4.12	2950	238.5	195	-1.7	-1.1	18.2	"
16000	4.54	2900	246	195	-1.7	-1.3	18.2	"
*18000	5.36	2840	254	195	-1.7	-1.5	18.2	"
20000	6.18	2680	258.5	192	-1.5	-1.7	16.1	"
22000	7.06	2480	258.5	185	-0.9	-1.8	14.0	"
24000	7.57	2220	257	178	-0.4	-1.8	11.9	"
26000	8.54	1960	257	171	0	-1.9	9.9	"
28000	10.00	1700	256	164	+0.6	-1.9	7.9	"
30000	11.18	1420	255.5	157	+1.1	-1.9	6.0	"
32000	12.51	1140	254	150	+1.6	-1.9	4.3	"
34000	14.51	860	253	143	+2.2	-2.0	2.8	"
35000	16.06	730	253	140	+2.5	-2.0	2.0	"
36000	17.36	600	250.5	136	+2.8	-1.9	1.3	"
37000	19.39	400	252	133	+3.0	-1.9	0.6	"
38000	23.03	200	250.5	129	+3.4	-1.9	0.2	"

*Full throttle heights   Supercharger gear change at 12,000 ft.

Estimated Service ceiling = 38,500 ft.

Estimated absolute ceiling = 39,000 ft.

The position error the pressure head installation was measured over the aircraft's speed range in level flight, flaps and undercarriage up, by the aneroid method.

Results of tests
The performance results have been corrected to standard atmospheric conditions and the level speeds to 85% of the take-off weight, viz. 8,650 lb by the methods given in Report No A&AEE/Res/170. The compressibility corrections in the level speed results have been calculated using the methods of the Addendum to Report No A&AEE/Res/147. A strut correction has also been applied to the indicated airspeeds in the level speed results. The source of this correction is ARC Report 6420. Insufficient evidence was obtained of the climb performance at combat rating with the first engine fitted to enable two sets of climb results to be given. Hence only that measured with the second engine is given.

The full results of the tests made are to be found in the Tables and Figures at the end of the report. A summary of the performance results is given below:

Climb at combat rating (2nd engine, radiator flap open).

Best climbing speed	= 195 mph ASI to 19,000ft

Decreasing speed by 7 mph per 2,000 ft thereafter.

Rate of climb at FTH, MS gear	= 3560 ft/min at 7,500ft.
Rate of climb at FTH, FS gear	= 2840 ft/min at 18,000ft.
Time to reach 10,000ft	= 2.9 mins.
Time to reach 20,000ft	= 6.3 mins.
Time to reach 30,000ft	= 11.3 mins.
Estimated Service Ceiling	= 38,500ft.
Estimated absolute ceiling	= 39,000ft.
Optimum height to change supercharger gear	= 15,000ft.

Climb at normal rating (2nd engine, radiator flap open).

Climbing speed used	= same as for climb at combat rating.
Rate of climb at FTH, MS gear	= 2600 ft/min at 11,300ft.
Rate of climb at FTH, FS gear	= 2110 ft/min at 22,000ft.
Time to reach 10,000ft	= 3.9 mins.
Time to reach 20,000ft	= 8.3 mins.
Time to reach 30,000ft	= 14.3 mins.
Estimated Service Ceiling	= 37,700ft.
Estimated absolute ceiling	= 38,200ft.
Optimum height to change supercharger gear	= 15,000ft.

All-out level speeds. (Radiator flap closed)

	1st engine	2nd engine
Max true airspeed, 2,000ft/MS gear =	360 mph	356 mph
Max true airspeed, FTH/MS gear =	406/10,800ft	395/9,800ft
Max true airspeed, FTH/FS gear =	433/22,000ft	425/21,400ft
Optimum ht to change supercharger =	15,500ft	14,000ft

Discussion of results

It will be seen from the level speed results that there is an appreciable difference in the performance of the aircraft with the two engines fitted. No changes likely to affect the level speed performance were made between the two sets of tests with the exception of the change of engine. The difference in speed performance, therefore, must be accounted for by differences in the powers of the engines and any small differences in the installation (such as a badly fitted or deformed air intake).

4. Tactical Employment Trials North American P-51B-1 (Army Air Forces Board Report dated 12 February 1944).

INTRODUCTION

1. In accordance with instructions from the Commanding General, Army Air Forces, and the Executive Director, Army Air Forces Board, Orlando, tactical employment trials have been carried out on the North American P-51B-1 airplane by Army Air Forces Proving Ground Command. Three P-51B-1's were used, carrying the normal combat load throughout the trials.

BRIEF DESCRIPTION OF THE AIRPLANE

2. The North American P-51B-1 closely resembles the previous P-51 models. The main visible differences are: the four-blade propeller, the location of the carburetor air intake scoop under the nose, and the larger radiator scoop assembly under the fuselage. However, there is a considerable difference in the over-all handling and performance in that the P-51B-1 is far superior, particularly at high altitude. The P-51B-1 is a single seat, low-wing fighter with conventional landing gear, and laminar-flow wing. The 12 cylinder, liquid cooled, Packard-Merlin V-1650-3 engine has a war emergency output of 1670 hp at 15,500ft in low blower, and 1480 hp at 27,000ft with high blower. The engine drives a four-blade, hydromatic Hamilton-Standard propeller, and includes a two-stage, two-speed, gear-driven, and automatically controlled supercharger. An engine driven pump provides the pressure for the hydraulic system; a hand pump may be used in the event of pump failure. The landing gear, wing flaps, oil and coolant shutters, and brakes are operated hydraulically. The split-type trailing edge flaps may be used as maneuver flaps. The armament consists of four .50 caliber, free firing machine guns, two in each wing. The weight with normal combat load is appox 9,000 lbs, with a wing loading of about 39lbs per square foot.

PILOT'S COCKPIT

3. The cockpit is small but adequate. Entry and exit are a little difficult due to the smooth wing surface. The left side and top of the canopy are hinged for entry and exit, but difficult to close without help from the outside. The entire canopy can be released in an emergency. The sliding windows on both sides should be opened only at moderate speeds. The forward vision has been improved by omitting the clear view panel which was installed in the left windshield on the previous models. The windshield is defrosted from the inside by hot air. The pilot's seat is a little uncomfortable for long flights. Provision is made on the left side of the cockpit for firing the Very Pistol. Warm air for cockpit heating and defrosting is supplied by a duct from the coolant radiator. The heating, however, is inadequate for high altitudes, and is unevenly distributed in the cockpit. Cold air ventilation is provided, but is not satisfactory as the cockpit gets very hot during operations at low altitudes in warm weather.

CONTROLS AND INSTRUMENTS

4. All flight and engine controls are ideally located; however, the rudder pedals have insufficient adjustment for a short pilot to obtain full rudder travel unless he stretches, or uses a cushion behind his back. Standard instruments are installed with standard grouping, but the view of the turn and bank, and rate of climb instruments, is partially obstructed by the control stick and the pilot's hand. Two direct reading gas gauges are located on the cockpit floor on each side of the pilot's seat. The right gas gauge is partially hidden by the oxygen delivery tube and the radio cable.

ARMOR PROTECTION

5. Protection for the pilot from behind is given by a sheet of 5/16 inch armor plate from the bottom of the seat to the top of

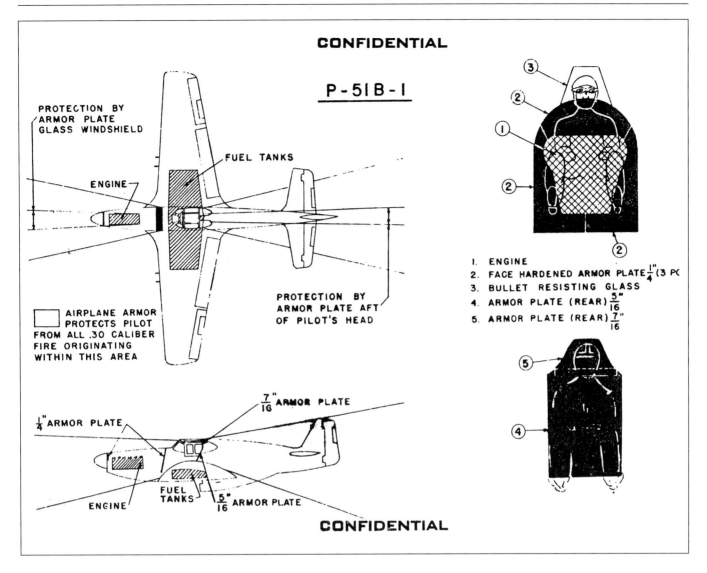

CONFIDENTIAL

P-51B-1

PROTECTION BY ARMOR PLATE GLASS WINDSHIELD

ENGINE

FUEL TANKS

☐ AIRPLANE ARMOR PROTECTS PILOT FROM ALL .30 CALIBER FIRE ORIGINATING WITHIN THIS AREA

PROTECTION BY ARMOR PLATE AFT OF PILOT'S HEAD

1. ENGINE
2. FACE HARDENED ARMOR PLATE $\frac{1}{4}$" (3 PC
3. BULLET RESISTING GLASS
4. ARMOR PLATE (REAR) $\frac{5}{16}$"
5. ARMOR PLATE (REAR) $\frac{7}{16}$"

$\frac{7}{16}$" ARMOR PLATE

$\frac{1}{4}$" ARMOR PLATE

FUEL TANKS

ENGINE

$\frac{5}{16}$" ARMOR PLATE

CONFIDENTIAL

the pilot's shoulders, and by a sheet of 7/16 inch armor plate behind the pilot's head. Protection forward is furnished by a 1 1/2 inch bullet resisting windshield, and a sheet of 1/4 inch armor plate. A 1/4 inch sheet of steel is fitted behind the propeller spinner to protect the engine coolant tank.

RADIO

6. A standard SCR-522 is installed in the fuselage behind the pilot's seat. The radio equipment is readily accessible for maintenance. Two men can change the set in approx 20 minutes, and ground check it in about 7 minutes. The radio operates satisfactorily at all altitudes. The button control box is located on the right side of the cockpit, requiring a crossover by the pilot to select a channel. An SCR-695 is also installed.

OXYGEN SYSTEM

7. The oxygen system is of the demand type and the supply consists of four D-2 type low pressure cylinders which are carried in the fuselage aft of the radio compartment. Oxygen endurance is approx 4 hours at 25,000ft, auto mix, and 2 and 1/2 hours auto mix 'off'.

COMPASS

8. The compass in the P-51B-1 is the standard B-16 liquid, magnetic type. The long range version, type P-51B-5 is equipped with an electric, remote indicating type compass, located in the left wing.

ARMAMENT

9. The total armament installation consists of four fixed, free firing, .50 caliber machine

guns, two inside of each wing. Gun charging is done manually before flight.

10. A selector switch on the left side of the armament switch panel provides three selections: 'guns and camera', 'off', 'camera'. Guns are fired with a trigger mounted on the forward top of the control stick.

11. An 'on–off' switch on the armament panel controls the electric gun heaters which are fitted to each individual gun.

12. The normal combat load is 275 rounds per gun. Each inboard gun can carry a maximum load of 350 rounds, and each outboard gun, 280 rounds.

13. The duration of fire with normal combat load is approx 20 seconds.

14. The gun installation is good, and all guns are easily accessible. However, the rear mounts on the inboard guns become loose in operation, and are not easy to get to for complete tightening. The guns can be removed in about 3 minutes, and installed in about 7 minutes by a crew of four men.

15. Rearming is easily done. All guns can be rearmed with a normal combat load in approx 3 1/2 minutes, and a maximum load in approx 5 1/2 minutes, by a crew of four men.

16. An N-3B optical electrical gun sight with a 70 mil ring and dot reticle is mounted between the pilot and the windshield. The bulb cannot be changed in flight. The sighting view over the nose is approx 5 degrees or 2 1/2 radii with a regular head, and approx 6 1/4 degrees or 3 1/8 radii with a variable reflector head sight. An auxiliary ring and bead sight is also furnished.

17. Total harmonization of guns, sight, and camera requires approx 2 1/2 hours.

18. An N-1 type gun sight aiming-point camera is fitted in the left wheel well. It is adjusted to converge with the line of sight at 900 ft, and can be operated with or without the guns. The camera is heated electrically with compensation for temperature changes when the camera is used. The camera is securely mounted and pictures can be obtained showing little sign of vibration, with or without the guns firing. The camera is not easily accessible, and adjustment in the vertical plane is difficult.

19. The guns were fired under various conditions of flight and functioned satisfactorily except for some stoppages due to links jamming in the link chutes. The rear mounts on the inboard guns must be tightened occasionally.

20. The guns when fired at night, have a temporary blinding effect on the pilot, but not as much as on day fighters equipped with six guns.

21. External bomb racks are designed to carry a maximum load of one 500lb bomb or equivalent external fuel under each wing. Although racks were not designed originally for 1,000lb bombs, two such bombs were carried during tests with 'Towner board' sway braces, and no ill effects were noted.

TACTICAL TRIALS

22. With its direct drive starter, the engine can be started electrically in approx 5 seconds, and manually in 20 seconds. Manual starting is difficult and should be regarded as an emergency procedure only. Care is necessary to avoid over-priming during initial starting. The engine warms up rapidly, but does not overheat with prolonged ground operation. When the airplane is parked on the line, the flaps should be lowered and left down, to prevent ground personnel from inadvertently damaging them while climbing on the wing.

23. Taxiing is not difficult, but is hampered by the weak brakes and the poor view from the cockpit. The canopy must be locked closed, or it will be damaged by the prop wash. With the control stick forward of neutral, the tail wheel is full swiveling. Moving the stick back of neutral, locks the tail wheel so that it is steerable six degrees in either direction. This is an excellent method of locking the tail wheel as it is very handy and easy to operate. The brakes are generally unsatisfactory; they are weak and require continual pumping, and overheat easily.

24. No undue change in rudder force is evident during take-off. Engine torque may be corrected by foot pressure or eliminated entirely by rudder trim. To take advantage of the steerable tail wheel and to minimize torque effect, it is advisable not to raise the tail during the early part of the take-off run. It is impossible to retract the land-

ing gear inadvertently, in the event of engine failure during take-off, if the airplane is still in contact with the ground. The pilot can settle himself in the cockpit, lock the canopy, start the engine, and be ready to taxi, in about one minute, in a scramble take-off. The distance needed for take-off, compares favourably with that of other fighters. The average take-off run, with maximum power and no wind, and carrying a normal combat load, is about 1,000ft, and about 2,000ft to clear a 50 foot obstacle. The shortest take-off run is made with 30 degree flaps, when letting the airplane fly itself off the ground, the average take-off is about 1,400ft flaps down 20 degrees, and about 2,500ft flaps up.

25. No other American fighter airplane of the present types, can equal the excellent overall flying characteristics and performance of the P-51B-1 above 25,000ft. The airplane handles beautifully and feels extremely good in all maneuvers. The sealed gap type ailerons are very satisfactory, affording lighter stick forces and better aileron control. Inverted flight is limited to 10 seconds because of scavenger pump operation and loss of oil pressure.

26. The P-51B-1 at war emergency power (3000 RPM, 67" Hg) has a greater initial climb than any other fighter. It will get to 5,000ft at the same time as the P-39N-0, even though the P-39 gets off the ground sooner. At war emergency power, the initial rate of climb of 3,900 feet per minute falls off slightly, but the average rate of climb is higher than that of any other fighter. At military power, the initial rate of climb of 2,500 feet per minute is sustained all the way up to 25,000ft.

27. The stall characteristics with power on or off are normal, with good warning and recovery. Power spins are prohibited; power off spins are normal, and recovery is easy. The airplane is stable and has only the slightest tendency to drop a wing. The stalling speed is about 95 IAS, wheels and flaps up, and about 85 IAS, wheels and flaps down.

28. The turning circle can be decreased by using the trailing edge wing flaps as maneuvering flaps (30 degrees maximum), but there is a speed loss which leaves the pilot at a disadvantage for breaking off combat. When the maneuvering flaps are dropped in a turn, the airplane becomes nose heavy, and trimming is desirable.

29. The trim characteristics of the airplane are superior. Changes of trim with in speed or power, are very small. ' trols are effective, easy to operat quire little movement. The contrc three axes of rotation operate each about its own axis of correction.

30. Due to its good handling qualities, the airplane performs all normal acrobatic maneuvers beautifully, and the pilot feels very much at ease in all flight positions.

31. With full flaps, the best landing approach speed is about 120 IAS. If trimmed full tail heavy, three-point landings can be accomplished. With full flaps the airplane presents sufficient resistance to make the landing run short without excessive breaking. Brakes should be used sparingly, as they overheat easily. The average landing roll, over a 50 foot obstacle, with full flaps and easy use of the brakes is approx 2,500 ft.

32. The good longitudinal and directional stability of the P-51B makes it excellent to fly on instruments. It is far superior to any other single engine fighter type aircraft. It is equipped with standard blind flying instruments.

33. The poor visibility in the P-51B, in the three-point position, makes it difficult to line up the runway on take-off and landing at night. The landing light does not focus dead ahead, and some reflection from the instruments is noticeable on the windshield. The airplane should be moved to and from the take-off position during daylight hours, if night missions are planned, to minimize taxiing difficulties from dispersal points. The exhaust glow is noticeable from approx 600ft to the side, and from about 100ft above. From the front and rear the glow is almost invisible.

34. Internal fuel is carried in two main 92 gallon self-sealing tanks, one in each wing. The feed lines from these tanks are also self-sealing. Two 75 gallon droppable combat tanks, or two 150 gallon ferry tanks may also be carried, one under each wing. In addition to the regular engine-driven pump, there is an electrically-driven booster pump mounted inside of each tank, and controlled independently by switches on the instrument panel. In an emergency, either booster pump will drain both tanks, and if both booster pumps cease operating,

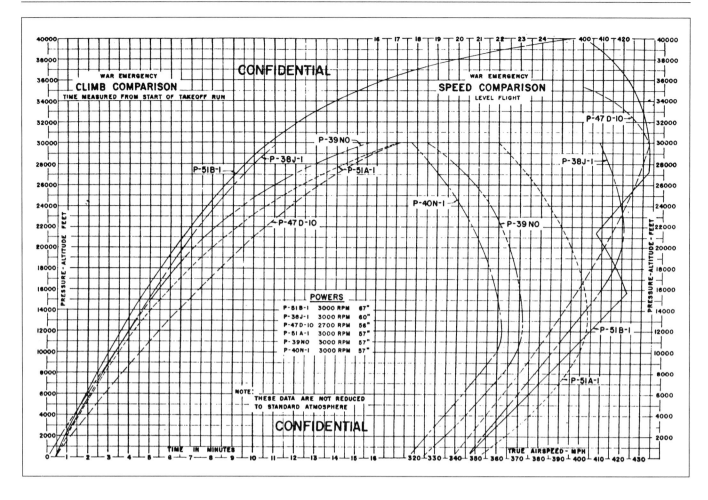

the engine driven pump will maintain flight. The fuel selector valve has one position for the main tanks. Selection of either or both main tanks is by use of the proper booster pumps; the auxiliary tanks are drawn from by use of the selector valve with both booster pumps off. Siphoning of gas from one tank while in the air, may be stopped by switching to the booster pump of the siphoning tank. Direct reading fuel gauges for the main tanks are located on the cockpit floor. A hopper type of oil tank with a maximum capacity of 13 US gallons is installed on the forward side of the fire wall. The entire oil system holds 20 US gallons.

35. Long range version of this airplane, the P-51B-5, has essentially the same excellent general characteristics. It has an additional 85 gallon fuselage tank in back of the pilot. This additional internal fuel installation limits the radio equipment to either a radio or an IFF set.

36. The suggested engine settings are as follows:

	RPM	MP	Mixture
Saunter (max range)	1750	29	AL
Liner (Max cruise)	2320	36	AL (low blower)
			AR (high blower)
Buster (Max cont)	2700	46	AR
Gate (War emergency)	3000	67	AR (5 minutes)

37. A conventional pitot-static head is located under the right wing. The air speed position error ranges from approx 20 mph on the high side, at high speed, to approx 8 mph, on the low side, at stalling speed. The long range version uses a separate flush type airspeed static source, located on the left side of the fuselage near the horizontal stabilizer. This air speed system results in a different type of position error. The instrument reads zero error at about 200 mph IAS, with approx 4 mph, on the high side at the stall to approx 5 mph on the low side at about 375 mph IAS. This error is sufficiently low for the pilot to ignore it in estimating true air speed, and is advantageous from a navigational standpoint.

38. Results of combat range tests run with and without droppable tranks, cruise and combat at 25,000ft:
Total fuel carried – 184 gallons internal
Reserve after landing – 20 gallons
Cruise setting flown in manual low blower.

	Dis-tance	Time	RPM/MP	IAS	Approx TAS
Take-off			3000/54		
Climb		13 min	2700/46	160	
Cruise out	220	53 min	2200/29.5	225	320
Combat		10 min	3000/61		
		10 min	2700/46		
Cruise back	220	32 min	2200/29.5	225	320

Total fuel carried – 334 gallons (184 internal, 150 gallons external)
Reserve after landing – 20 gallons
Cruise setting flown in high blower.

	Dis-tance	Time	RPM/MP	IAS	Approx TAS
Take-off			3000/54		
Climb		19 min	2700/46	160	
Cruise out	600	2 hours	2300/36	210	295
(drop tanks at end of cruise)					
Combat		10 min	3000/61		
		10 min	2700/46		
Cruise back	600	1 hour 34 min	2200/33	225	320

The range can be increased slightly if combat conditions allow cruising back in manual low blower.

LEVEL SPEEDS

39. The P-51B-1 is capable of very high speeds at altitude. It is important in operation to keep the wing skin and the finish in good condition, free from rough spots, dents, and deep scratches. Airflow disturbances in the boundary layer region will materially affect speed performance. With wing bomb racks and normal combat load, the average level flight maximum speed is about 435 mph at 30,000ft, at 3000 RPM and 61" manifold pressure. Two 500lb bombs cause a speed loss of approx 30 mph, and two 1,000lb bombs reduce maximum speed by about 45 mph. The bomb racks alone cost approx 15 mph loss in speed.

[The remainder of the report contains details of performance comparisons with other American types and has been omitted from this history.]

5. AFDU Report dated March 1944

AFDU RAF Station Wittering
Report No 107 on Tactical Trials – Mustang III, comparison with Spitfire IX & XIV, Tempest, Fw 190 & Me 109G

INTRODUCTION

1. According to Air Ministry instructions, and ADGB letter reference 32179/Air Trg. dated 28th December 1943, Tactical Trials have been completed on the Mustang III. Aircraft No FZ107 was delivered on 26.12.43, and was checked weighted as for operational load (total 10,100 lbs). For descriptive purposes, brief comparisons have been made with the Spitfire IX No BS552 (clipped wings and fairly old aircraft), Spitfire IX No JL359, normal wings, fitted with SU pump carburettor. Brief comparative trials were carried out against Tempest V No JN737, Spitfire XIV No RB141, Focke Wulf 190 No PM679 and Me 109G No RN228.

BRIEF DESCRIPTION

The Mustang III is a high altitude long-range single-seat fighter, armed with four .5 Brownings in the wings. It is fitted with a V-1650/3 engine (Packard built Rolls-Royce engine of Merlin 61 type), of appoximately 1550 hp. It can carry two long-range tanks or 2 x 500 lb bombs under the wings. In appearance it differs from the Mustang I in that it has a different type of engine, four-blade airscrew, air intake immediately under the airscrew hub, a deeper fuselage behind the wings housing all the radiators and oil coolers, and a slightly larger fin and rudder. It is a very clean looking aeroplane.

Cockpit
The pilot's cockpit is similar to the Mustang I. It has been 'cleaned up' considerably. Of particular note are:

The only undercarriage warning device is a red light by the gunsight, which lights up when the wheels are unlocked. (There is no light when the wheels are locked 'Up' or 'Down').

The cockpit, and in particular the instruments, are of American design and consequently seem oddly placed to a British pilot.

When the engine is started and the mixture lever placed in 'Normal', the locking unit must be tightened, otherwise the pitch control may creep back on take-off.

The tail-wheel only becomes fully castoring when the stick is pushed right forward.

It should be impossible to retract the undercarriage when the weight of the aircraft is on the wheels.

There are three trimming wheels for all control surfaces.

The flap angle is pre-selected by the control lever in the cockpit. There is a safety stop which need only be used when carrying the 120 gallon long-range tanks (i.e. it does not apply when carrying the normal 62 1/2 gallon long-range tanks). This is to prevent lowering of the flaps more than 30 degrees.

The control column is well placed and of the stick variety. It is pivoted in both directions at its base.

FLYING CHARACTERISTICS

The Mustang III is very similar to fly and land as the Mustang I. It is therefore delightfully easy to handle. It is as easy to fly as a Spitfire IX with the exception that the rudder is needed whenever changing bank (in order to prevent skid, and to prevent the sight from swinging off). This soon becomes automatic. The engine feels very smooth.

Flying Controls
These are well balanced and positive, especially at high speeds. In comparison with the Spitfire IX:

The rudder is heavier. It is far more effective as only a small amount of re-trimming is necessary at high speeds (over 400 mph IAS) to keep the aircraft straight. There is no lateral wander.

The ailerons feel lighter, especially over small movements and in general flying. There appears, however, to be a cushioning effect when full aileron is applied. This is because considerably more stick force is necessary when a quick change of bank is desired.

The elevators are considerably heavier. They are not tiring, partly because the change of trim with speed is less.

Formation Flying
Because the aircraft is clean, one would expect station keeping to be difficult, but engine re-sponse is so steady that formation flying is very easy.

Low Flying
The view forwards and downwards over the leading edge of the wings is the same as a Mustang I, and therefore better than a Spitfire IX. This helps to make the aircraft easy to low fly. It was not, however, built for low flying operations and to improve its air-to-air combat the Unit is advising a certain harmonisation which will make the aircraft difficult for ground attack.

Night Flying
Normal flying is quite straightforward. The exhaust glow does not seriously inconvenience the pilot. A different type of exhaust stub would be necessary for night-fighting.

Apart from certain cockpit lighting troubles listed below, the take-off and landing is quite straightforward. Use of the aircraft floodlight is recommended rather than an airfield floodlight, as considerable cockpit dazzle results when using the latter. To prevent exhaust glare on landing, an engine-assisted approach right on to the ground is recommended. With small modification, blinkers could be fitted to this aircraft where a dusk or night landing is anticipated. It is considered that the disadvantage that would be suffered in day combat would outweigh this luxury.

Undercarriage warning light is lethal. Unless a British type instrument is fitted, this light must be covered over.

The cockpit lighting when suitably manipulated is adequate, but it is a strange colour to British pilots.

Compressibility Speeds
Because the Mustang III increases speed so rapidly in the dive, it is not difficult to enter compressibility range at high altitudes (approaching speed of sound). This can only be done in a dive. The maximum permissible speeds at various heights:

IAS	HEIGHT
298 mph	35,000 ft
336 mph	30,000 ft
376 mph	25,000 ft
422 mph	20,000 ft
468 mph	15,000 ft
520 mph	10,000 ft
574 mph	5,000 ft

The following is a summary of the RAE's instructions (Report No Aero 1906) should the speeds at height be exceeded by any type of aircraft. In the dive, the nose may quite suddenly tend to drop. On no account must the trimming wheel be used to prevent it doing so, but only backward pressure on the stick. When the aircraft has reached a lower altitude where the speed of sound is greater, the aircraft will come out of the compressibility range and behave normally, being pulled out of the dive. Had the trimming wheel been used, there would have been a very sudden nose-up tendency on coming out of the compressibility range. The result of such a sudden change of trim is liable to cause structural failure.

TACTICAL COMPARISON WITH SPITFIRE IX

A very close comparison can be made because the two engines are of very similar design and capacity. The tactical differences are caused chiefly by the fact that the Mustang III is a much cleaner aircraft, is slightly heavier, and has higher wing loading than the Spitfire IX (43.8 lbs per sq ft of the Mustang III, against 31 lbs per sq ft).

Endurance
The Mustang III with maximum fuel load, has between 1 1/2 and 1 3/4 the range of a Spitfire IX with maximum fuel load. The fuel and oil capacities are 154 gallons and 11.2 respectively, as opposed to 85 gallons and 7.5 gallons of the Spitfire IX, both without long-range tanks. With long-range tanks, the Mustang can carry a total of 279 gallons of petrol (2 x 62 1/2 gall long-range tanks) as opposed to the Spitfire's maximum of 177 gallons (1 x 90 gallon 'slipper tank').

The fuel consumption at similar boost and rev settings is approximately the same for the two aircraft, but the Mustang III is approximately 20 mph faster in level flight. Therefore, if the ranges are compared directly according to the fuel capacities of the two aircraft when the long-range tanks are fitted, the Mustang will still have something in hand.

Speeds
The official speed curves are not yet available. This Unit's speed runs have therefore not been confirmed. They show, however, that in general for the same engine settings the Mustang II is always 20–30 mph faster in level flight at all heights. This is also true for the maximum engine setting of 3000 rpm (+18 lbs.) or whatever is available, depending on the height. The best performance heights are similar, being between 10,000 and 15,000 ft, and between 25,000 and 32,000 ft.

Climbs
The Mustang III has a considerably lower rate of climb at full power at all heights. (In a formation take-off, Spitfire IX maintains formation with .. lbs. less boost.) At other engine settings and 175 mph, the two aircraft have a similar climb. The Mustang has, however, a better zoom climb in that it can dive 5,000 feet or more and regain its original altitude at a greater speed. It needs much less increase in power to regain its previous altitude and speed.

Dives
The Mustang III pulls away very rapidly in a slight dive. At the same ... the Spitfire IX requires from 4 to 6 lb. more boost to remain in formation.

Turning Circle
The Mustang is always out-turned by the Spitfire IX. Use of flaps on the Mustang does not appear to improve the turning circle. There is adequate warning of the high speed stall in the form of elevator buffeting, followed by mild buffeting.

Rate of Roll
Although the ailerons feel light, the Mustang III cannot roll as quickly as the Spitfire IX at normal speeds. The ailerons stiffen up only slightly at ... speeds and the rates of roll become the same at about 400 mph.

Search
The all-round view from the pilot's cockpit is the same as the Mustang I, therefore generally inferior to the Spitfire IX, but better forwards and downwards on either side of the fuselage. A sliding hood has been designed and is being fitted to Service Mustangs. This makes its rear view at least equal to, if not better than the Spitfire IX.

Sighting View and Fire-power
The aircraft is fitted with an American 70 mph sight. A bracket for the GM2 sight has been designed and is fitted to most aircraft. If it is not fitted, a Universal Adaptor as shown in Appendix B can be made and fitted by the Squadron. Due to the fact that it is most unlikely that the aircraft will be used against ground targets, the highest possible setting for the guns and sight has been chosen to produce the maximum amount of sighting view over the nose. This gives a vertical view of 180 mph cruising speed, increasing to an unrestricted view at approximately 45 degrees to the vertical, with the guns ∫ degrees cocked up from aircraft datum. This is considerably better than

the Spitfire IX. The guns are cocked up about 2 degrees above the aircraft's cruising line of flight. The fire-power consists of four .5 Brownings in the wings. This is very little compared with the Spitfire.

Armour
Armour plating on the Mustang III is provided for the pilot by means of two plates located behind the pilot's seat. One 5/16" thick extends from just below the bottom of the seat to a point just level with the pilot's shoulders. The other, 7/16" thick, is attached to the top of this plate and affords protection to the pilot's head. Otherwise, protection is provided by the 1/4" armour plate fire-wall, the engine, and the 1 1/2" armour plate glass wind-shield. 1/4" armour plate is also located immediately forward of the coolant tank on the forward end of the engine. There is no armour plate on the fuel tanks, but the tanks themselves are self-sealing.

BRIEF TACTICAL COMPARISON WITH THE SPITFIRE XIV

Maximum Endurance
By comparison the Spitfire has no endurance.

Maximum Speed
There is practically nothing to choose in maximum speed.

Maximum Climb
The Spitfire XIV is very much better.

Dive
As for Spitfire IX. The Mustang pulls away, but less markedly.

Turning Circle
The Spitfire XIV is better.

Rate of Roll
Advantage tends to be with the Spitfire XIV.

Conclusion
With the exception of endurance, no conclusions should be drawn, as the two aircraft should never be enemies. The choice is a matter of taste.

BRIEF TACTICAL COMPARISON WITH TEMPEST V

Maximum Endurance
By comparison, the Tempest V has no endurance.

Maximum Speed
The Tempest V is 15–20 mph faster up to 15,000 ft. There is then no choice until 24,000 ft when the Mustang rapidly pulls away, being about 30 mph faster at 30,000 ft.

Climb
These compare directly with the results of the speed tests. At similar performance height, the Tempest has the better zoom climb.

Dive
The Tempest tends to pull away.

Turning Circle
The Tempest is not quite so good.

Rate of Roll
The Tempest is not so good. This attribute of the Tempest V may be improved upon in later aircraft.

Conclusion
The Mustang has endurance and general performance above 24,000 ft. Conclusions should not be drawn below this height, but the Tempest has a better speed and climb below 10,000 ft.

BRIEF COMPARISON WITH THE FW 190 (BMW 801D)

Maximum Speed
The Fw 190 is nearly 50 mph slower at all heights, increasing to … mph above 28,000 feet. It is anticipated that the new Fw 190 (DB 603) might be slightly faster below 27,000 ft but slower above that height.

Climb
There appears to be little to choose in the maximum rate of climb. It is anticipated that the Mustang III will have a better maximum climb than the new Fw 190 (DB 603). The Mustang is considerably faster at all heights in a zoom climb.

Dive
The Mustang can always out-dive the Fw 190.

Turning Circle
Again there is not much to choose. The Mustang is always slightly better. When evading an enemy aircraft with a steep turn, a pilot will always out-turn the attacking aircraft initially because of the difference in speeds. It is therefore still a worthwhile manoeuvre with the Mustang III when attacked.

Rate of Roll
Not even a Mustang III approaches the Fw 190.

Conclusions
In the attack, a high speed should be maintained or regained in order to regain height initiative. A Fw 190 could not evade by diving alone. In defence a steep turn followed by a full throttle dive should increase range before regaining height and course. Dogfighting is not altogether recommended. Do not attempt to climb away without at least 250 mph showing initially. Unfortunately, there is not enough information on the new Fw 190 (DB 603) for any positive recommendations to be made.

BRIEF COMPARISON WITH THE Me 109G

Maximum Speed
The Mustang III is faster at all heights. Its best heights, by comparison, are below 16,000 ft (30 mph faster approx.) and above 25,000 ft (30 mph increasing to 50 mph at 30,000 ft.)

Maximum Climb
This is rather similar. The Mustang III is very slightly better above 25,000ft but inclined to be worse below 20,000 ft.

Zoom Climb
Unfortunately the Me 109G appears to have a very good high speed climb making the two aircraft similar in a zoom climb.

Dive
On the other hand in defence the Mustang III can still increase the range in a prolonged dive.

Turning Circle
The Mustang III is greatly superior.

Rate of Roll
Not much to choose. In defence (in a tight spot) a rapid change of direction will throw the Me 109G's sight off. This is because the 109G's maximum roll is embarrassing (slots keep opening).

Conclusions
In attack, the Mustang can always catch the Me 109G, except in any sort of climb (unless there is a high overtaking speed). In defence, a steep turn should be the first manoeuvre, followed, if necessary, by a dive (below 20,000 ft). A high speed climb will unfortunately not increase the range. If above 25,000 feet keep above by climbing or all-out level.

COMBAT PERFORMANCE WITH LONG-RANGE TANKS

Speed
There is a serious loss of speed of 40–50 mph at all engine settings and heights. It is, however, still faster than the Fw 190 (BMW 801D) above 25,000 ft, although slower than the Me 109G.

Climb
The rate of climb is greatly reduced. It is outclimbed by the Fw 190 and Me 109G.

The Mustang III is still good in a zoom climb (attack), but it is still outstripped (defence), if being followed all the way by the Fw 190 and definitely outstripped by the Me 109G.

Dive
So long as the tanks are fairly full, the Mustang III still beats the Fw 190 and the Me 109G in a power dive.

Turning Circle
The tanks do not make quite so much difference as one might expect. The Mustang III can at least turn as tightly as the Fw 190 without stalling out and therefore definitely more tightly than the Me 109G.

Rate of Roll
General handling and rate or roll are very little affected.

Conclusions
The performance of the Mustang III is greatly reduced when carrying drop-tanks. Half-hearted attacks could still be evaded by a steep turn, but determined attacks would be difficult to avoid without losing height. It is still a good attacking aircraft especially if it has the advantage of height.

TECHNICAL

Gun Harmonisation
No difficulty was experienced in harmonising the guns in the manner described above. The American Reflector Sight mounting bracket has no adjustment in elevation for harmonisation. The necessary movement was obtained by moving and locking the adjustable reflector glass.

Gun Firing
The guns were fired in the air at varying heights up to 25,000 feet. There was one stoppage, due to a lightly struck cap, otherwise all guns fired

100%. The installation proved satisfactory, and the aircraft is a steady gun platform.

Re-Arming
This was carried out by two armourers only, and time taken was:

First re-arm	– 7 1/2 mins.
Second re-arm	– 7 1/2 mins.

The capacity of the tanks is:

Inboard guns	– 350 rounds each.
Outboard guns	– 280 rounds each.

Cine-gun Installation and Harmonisation
The GASP Cine Camera with 3 inch lens is fitted and was harmonised from the top. No difficulties were encountered.

Air Tests
Films were taken at heights between 5,000 and 30,000 feet, all of which were satisfactory.

Radio
One VHF set is fitted, the control box being fitted on the right-hand side of the cockpit. This position is rather awkward. It was found easiest to use the left hand for operating it.

Oxygen
The American economising system is fitted. It is necessary to adapt the connections at a suitable place if the British type face masks are to be used. If the British 'F', 'G' or 'H' type mask is to be used, it is essential to blank off the compensating valve in the side of the face-piece. The American system draws in an appropriate amount of air at the control box.

Engine Temperatures
These are well controlled if the oil and coolant switches are left on 'automatic'. The temperatures appear to remain constant however the aircraft is flown.

Starting Hints
Starting is quite straightforward if carried out as per starting instructions for Bendix Stromberg Carburettors.

Servicing Hints
The servicing is the same as for Mustang I and IA. Ground equipment is interchangeable, except for propeller kit which has to be exchanged for a Hamilton Propeller Kit, instead of a Curtiss Electric. Flaps have an angular movement of 50 degrees, movement restricted to 30 degrees when carrying ferry tanks (125 gallons) by use of lock bar in flap quadrant. This should be fitted in place by the Rigger fitting the tanks. A restriction is necessary when using combat tanks (62 1/2 gallons).

The rammed and unrammed air control lever in the cockpit of the Mustang III No FZ107 was inclined to creep back half way between settings during flight. This caused the pilot to be unable to produce the required amount of maximum thrust and increased petrol consumption. Much useless flying was carried out before the effects of this were noticed. For use 'at home' it is therefore suggested that for Squadron aircraft the level should be wired in the 'Ram – air' position with copper wire.

CONCLUSIONS

The Mustang III is a delightful and easy aircraft to fly.

Its advantages over the Spitfire IX lie in a considerably greater range and greater all-round speed. It can outstrip the Fw 190 in a dive, followed if desired by a shallow climb. Its only serious drawback is a slightly less rate of climb than the Spitfire IX, particularly at height.

A pilot needs to understand the effect of compressibility speeds. Practices should not be attempted.

RECOMMENDATIONS TO SQUADRONS

1. Pasting – lbs. of boost readings on the face of the boost gauge for ease of reading for British pilots, as below:

BOOST PRESSURE CONVERSION TABLE

Inches of Hg	lbs. per sq/in
22	–4
26	–2
30	0
34	+2
38	+4
44	+7
48	+9
54	+12
60	+15
67	+18

2. Wire-up the air control lever in the cockpit. (Para. 69)

3. For night flying, cover over the Undercarriage Warning Light. (Para. 11a)

AFDU/3/21/36
8th March, 1944

Appendix H - Mustang Survivors

(Inc. those which are airworthy and currently under restoration to fly.
F = flyable; R = under restoration; S = stored)

Military ID	Model	Stat	Civil reg	Owner	Location	Markings/Remarks
	A	R		Bob Collings	Stowe, MA	
	D	F	N513PA	David Arnold	Monte Carlo	*Shangri la*, VF-T
	D	F	SE-BKG	Leif Jaraker	Vasteras, Sweden	Swedish AF#16, K on tail
	D	R		Walter Bagdeserian	San Diego, CA	*Slender Tender & Tall*, HO-T
	D	R		Paul Jurischa	Runcorn, Australia	
	D	R		Robert J. Lamplough	North Weald, UK	
	D	R		Cougar Helicopters	Daytona Beach, FL	
	D	R		Kim Rolfe-Smith	Brisbane, Australia	
	D	R		John MacGuire	Santa Teresa, NM	
	D	R	N4451C	Barone Bros Partners	San Bernadino, CA	Bad accident 10/94
	D	R	NX91KD	L. A. Welcome	Redmond, WA	Ex-*Vendetta* racer
	D	S		Robert J. Lamplough	North Weald, UK	
	D	U	N51KJ	Jerry D. Owens	Scottsdale, AZ	
	D	U	N51RG	Delmer L. Hoagland	Des Plaines, IL	
	RB-51	R		Terry and Bill Rogers	Sherman, TX	Ex-*Red Baron*
	TF-51D	F	N7098V	David Arnold	Monte Carlo	TF-873, 473871-tail
42-103645	C	R	N215CA	CAF, So Minn Wing	St Paul, MN	*Skipper's Darlin*, red tail
42-103831	C	R	N1204	Kermit Weeks	Miami, FL	Red, Paul Mantz racer
42-83731	A-36	F	N251A	Tom Friedkin	Carlsbad, CA	Silver, yellow hub, F-tail
42-83738	B	R	N4607V	John Paul	Boise, ID	
43-12112	B	S			FL	From Lake Hancock, FL, 1992
43-25147	C	F	N51PR	The Fighter Collection	Duxford, UK	*Princess Elizabeth*
43-43335	XP-51G	R		John Morgan	La Canada, CA	*Marjorie Hart*
43-6006	A	F	N51Z	Jerry Gabe	San Jose, CA	Olive drab, 36006 on side
43-6178	A	R	N51KW	Kermit Weeks	Miami, FL	
43-6251	A	F	N4235Y	Planes of Fame Air Museum	Chino, CA	RAF mkgs and camou
43-6274	A	F	N90358	Charles Nichols	Chino, CA	Olive drab/white nose, XA-H
44-10753	D	S	N31FF	Wilson C. Edwards	Big Spring, TX	
44-11807	K	S	N30991	Meryl J. Shawver	Mesa, AZ	
44-12139	K	F	N357FG	James Beasley Jr	Philadelphia, PA	*Frenesi* C5-N, olive
44-12140	K	F	N119VF	Aadu Kareema	San Diego, CA	VF-A
44-12817	F-6K	S	N5151T	Pioneer Aero	Chino, CA	
44-12840	F6-K	R	N151EW	Edward Wachs	Lake Bluff, IL	
44-12852	F-6K	U		Brian O'Farrell	Miami, FL	
44-13016	D	F	NL5551D	Calvin Burgess	Edmund, OK	*Dove of Peace*, LH-X
44-13105	D	F	N71FT	Bill Destefani	Shafter, CA	*Strega* racer
44-13250	D	F	NL151DM	Dan Martin	San Jose, CA	*Ridge Runner III*, WD-A
44-13257	D	F	NL51DL	Ed Lindsay	Sarasota, FL	Camou w/wingtip tanks
44-14826	D	S	N551D	Bruce Morehouse	San Antonio, TX	
44-15651	D	F	NX79111	Jimmy Leeward	Ocala, FL	*Cloud Dancer #9*
44-63350	D	F	N51TK	Charles Greenhill	Mettawa, IL	*Lou IV*, E2-C
44-63542	D	F	N51HR	Ted Contri	Reno, NV	*Sizzlin' Liz*, Nev ANG
44-63576	D	F	N51DH	Evergreen Ventures	McMinnville, OR	Polished, N2, S/tail
44-63577	D	R	N151JT	John R. Turgyan	New Egypt, NJ	
44-63615	D	S		ILOC Corp	USA	
44-63655	D	R	N5500S	Will Martin	Palos Park, IL	
44-63663	D	S	N41749	Wilson C. Edwards	Big Spring, TX	
44-63675	D	F	NL1751D	Roger Christgau	Edina, MN	*Sierra Sue II*, E6-D

44-63701	D	R	N51VT	Vincent Tirado	Miami, FL	
44-63807	D	F	N20MS	Edward Stringfellow	Birmingham, AL	*Tiger Lily,* M-S
44-63810	D	F	N451BC	Joseph K. Newsom	Cheraw, SC	*Angels Playmate,* FT-I
44-63864	D	F	N42805	Kenneth A. Hake	Tipton, KS	FvNr: 26158
44-63865	D	S	N51JK	O. J. Kistler	Long Valley, NJ	
44-63889	D	F	C-FFUZ	Gary McCann	Stratford, Canada	Black w/white horizontal stripe
44-63893	D	S	N3333E	David Tallichet	Chino, CA	YC-D, at March AFB
44-64005	D	F	N51CK	Charlie Kemp	Jackson, MS	*Mary Mine,* E9-Z
44-64122	D	F	N339TH	Wes Stricker	St Louis, MO	339th FG
44-64314	H	F	N551H	Mike Coutches	Hayward, CA	USAF, 464551-tail
44-64375	H	R	N67149	James Parks	Bend, OR	
44-64415	H	F	N49WB	Don Whittington	Fort Lauderdale, FL	RAF camou, KN987
44-72028	D	R	G-LYNE	Ernest Robinson	Darlington, UK	
44-72035	D	F	F-AZMU	Jaques Bouret	St Rambert, France	*Jumpin' Jaques*
44-72051	D	F	NL68JR	Ron Fagen	Granite Falls, MN	*Sweet Revenge,* QP-F 422051
44-72059	D	S	N951HB	Vintage Aero Inc	Wilmington, DE	
44-72086	TF	F	N510JS	Joseph E. Scogna	Yardley, PA	*Baby Duck,* LH-R
44-72145	D	F	NL51PT	Pete McManus	Miami, FL	*Petie 3rd*
44-72192	D	F	N5460V	Mustang Pilots' Club	Hollister, CA	*Straw Boss 2,* PE
44-72202	D	F		SAAF Museum	South Africa	
44-72216	D	F	G-BIXL	Robert Lamplough	North Weald, UK	*Miss L*
44-72339	D	F	NL251JC	Jim Cavanaugh	Addison, TX	WD-C, red spinner
44-72364	D	S		Brian O'Farrell	Miami, FL	
44-72401	D	S	N71L	Elmer Ward	Chino, CA	
44-72438	D	F	N7551T	Selby Burch	Kissimmee, FL	600, polished metal
44-72483	D	F	N51EA	Max Vogelsang	Basle, Switzerland	*Double Trouble Two,* SX-B
44-72739	D	F	NL44727	Elmer Ward	Santa Ana, CA	*Man O'War,* QP-A
44-72767	D	S	N6836C	Pioneer Aero	Chino, CA	
44-72773	TF	F	G-SUSY	Paul Morgan	Sywell, UK	*SUSY* AJ-C
44-72777	D	F	NL151D	John Herlihy	USA	*Sparky,* red nose
44-72811	D	F	N471R	Robert Converse	Bakersfield, CA	*Huntress III,* LH-C
44-72826	D	F	NL51YS	Steve Collins	Atlanta, GA	*Old Boy,* JW-T
44-72840	D	S	N7718C	Pioneer Aero	Chino, CA	
44-72844	D	S	N7406	Elmer Ward	Chino, CA	
44-72902	D	R	N335	Violet Bonzer	Los Angeles, CA	*Bardahl II,* #14blk/wht checks
44-72907	D	S	N41748	Wilson C. Edwards	Big Spring, TX	
44-72922	TF-51	F	NL93TF	Jim Shuttleworth	Huntington, IN	*Scat VII,* L2-W
44-72936	D	R	N7711C	Marvin Crouch	Encino, CA	
44-73029	D	F	NL51JB	Jim Beasley	Philadelphia, PA	*Bald Eagle,* B7-E
44-73053	D	R		Fighter Rebuilders	Chino, CA	
44-73079	D	F	N151BL	Bill Dause	Wellington, UT	*Jolley Roger/Bernie's Bo*
44-73081	D	S	N5074K	Michael Coutches	Hayward, CA	
44-73129	D	F	N51SL	Stuart Eberhardt	Danville, CA	*Merlins Magic,* FF-129
44-73140	D	F	NL314BG	Flying A Services	England	*Petie 2nd*
44-73142	D	S	N51BK	Bruce C. Morehouse	Jefferson, TX	Wreck
44-73149	D	F			Duxford, UK	
44-73163	D	R	N51MR	Randall Kempf	Phoenix, AZ	
44-73206	D	F	NL3751D	Charles Osborn	Louisville, KY	*Hurry Home Honey,* C5-T
44-73210	D	F	CF-IKE	Ike Enns	Winnipeg, Canada	*Miracle Maker,* red nose WD-B
44-73254	D	U		Don Weber	Baton Rouge, LA	*Buster,* B7-R
44-73264	D	F	N5428V	Reg Urschler/CAF	Bellevue, NE	*Gunfighter,* CY-U
44-73273	D	U	N200DD	John Deahl estate	Denver, CO	
44-73275	D	U	N119H	Aviation Sales Inc	Englewood, CO	
44-73287	D	F	N5445V	Michael George	Springfield, IL	*Worry Bird,* D7-J

44-73320	D	S	N5463V	Elmer Ward	Chino, CA	
44-73323	D	R	N151MD	Martin Croutch	Encino, CA	
44-73339	D	F	G-SIRR	David Gilmour	North Weald, UK	474008,VF-R
44-73343	D	S	N5482V	Bruce Morehouse	San Antonio, TX	
44-73350	D	F	N33FF	Lee O. Maples	Vichy, MO	
44-73415	D	F	N6526D	Bob Button	Bakersfield, CA	*VooDoo Chile* #55
44-73420	D	F	ZK-PLl	B. Hore/Alpine Fighter	Wanaka, N Zealand	*Miss Torque* #524
44-73423	D	F	N51DJ	Classic Air Parts	Ontario, CA	*Sunshine*
44-73435	D	R	N6311T	Elmer Ward	Chino, CA	
44-73436	D	F	NL51KD	Olympic Flight Museum	Seattle, WA	E2-S, 413926-tail
44-73454	D	F	NL2051D	Richard Bjelland	Galt, CA	*This is it!*, PZ
44-73458	TF	F	N4151D	William Hane	Mesa, AZ	TF-660
44-73463	D	R		Richard Ransopher	Kernersville, NC	
44-73483	D	S	N351D	Waldon 'Moon' Spillers	Verseilles, OH	Components only
44-73518	D	F	N6WJ	Don Whittington	Fort Lauderdale, FL	*World Jet* #38, green wings
44-73543	D	F	NL51SB	Steve Bolander	Libertyville, IL	*Mary Bear*, SB, blue nose
44-73584	D	S	N51Q	Elmer Ward	Chino, CA	
44-73656	K	F	NL2151D	Vlado Lenoch	La Grange, IL	*Moonbeam McSwine*
44-73683	D	F	NL5551D	San Diego Aerospace Museum	San Diego, CA	*Contrary Mary*, WZ-I, withdrawn from USCR, registration transferred to 44-13016 (see above)
44-73693	D	F	N35FF	Bill Rheinschild	Chino, CA	*Risky Business* #45
44-73704	D	F	N6168C	Lou Shaw	Dallas, TX	*Thunderbird*
44-73751	D	F	N5444V	Ron Von Kregten	San Jose, CA	
44-73843	TF-51D	F	N10601	Confederate Air Force	Midland, TX	*Old Red Nose*, VF-G
44-73856	D	F	N7TF	Tom Friedkin	Carlsbad, CA	*Susie*, F on tail
44-73877	D	F	N167F	Anders Saether	Oslo, Norway	*Old Crow*, B6-S
44-73902	D	S	N38227	Wilson C Edwards	Big Spring, TX	
44-73973	D	F	NL151DP	Museum of Flying	Santa Monica, CA	RAF mkgs, DG-P
44-73990	D	F	N51TH	Tom Henley	Emelle, AL	
44-74009	D	F	N988C	Bob Ferguson	Wellesley, MA	*Ain't Misbehavin*, RL-F
44-74012	D	F	N6519D	James E Smith	Kalispell, MT	G4-C
44-74202	D	R	N5420V	Mike Bogue	Oakland, CA	
44-74230	D	S	N5466V	James Norland	Wasilla, AK	
44-74262	D	R	N515J	J. A. Milender	Fort Mojave, AZ	
44-74311	D	S	C-GPSI	Ritchie Rasmussen	Edmonton, Canada	
44-74391	D	S	N38229	Wilson C. Edwards	Big Spring, TX	
44-74404	D	F	NL151RJ	Robert Odegaard	Kindred, ND	*Dazzling Donna*, BC-H
44-74409	D	F	NL51RT	Robert Tullius	Winchester, VA	VF-B Donald Duck/nose
44-74417	D	F	N6327T	Richard P. James	Fennimore, WI	*Donna-mite*, FF-197
44-74423	D	F	N64CL	Clay Lacy	Canoga Park, CA	#64, purple
44-74425	D	F	NL11T	Tom van der Meulen	Lelystad, Holland	*Damn Yankee*, OC-G
44-74427	D	F	N2251D	Brian Hoffner/Kenair	West Palm Beach, FL	*Nooky Booky IV*, G4-C
44-74435	D	S	N130JT	James Chernich	Lake Zurich, IL	
44-74445	D	F	N4132A	Bill Hubbs	Pecos, TX	White
44-74446	D	F	NL1451D	Bruce Jennings	Carson City, NV	*Saturday Night Special*
44-74452	D	S	N74190	Wilson C. Edwards	Big Spring, TX	
44-74453	D	F	N251HR	Kipnis Inc.	Chicago, IL	*Glamorous Jen*, WD-L
44-74454	D	F	N151HR	Hank Reichert	Bismark, TX	*Dakota Kid*, YF-M, 474524 on tail
44-74458	D	F	N351DM	David Marco	Jacksonville, FL	*Sizzlin' Liz*, QP-H
44-74466	D	F	NL10607	Harry Barr	Lincoln, NE	*Barbara Jean*
44-74469	D	F		Classic Air Parts	Miam, FL	*Tally Ho Two*, RAF mkgs
44-74474	D	F	N6341T	Joe Rousch	Livonia, MI	*Old Crow*, B6-S
44-74483	D	F	N51GP	George Perez	Sonoma, CA	
44-74494	D	F	N72FT	Hugh Bikle	Mountain View, CA	*Iron Ass*, 411661-tail
44-74497	D	F	N6320T	Hess Bomberger	Fayetteville, GA	*Vergeltungswaffe*

44-74502	D	R	NX51VC	John Crocker estate	Oakland, CA	*Sumthin' else* racer
44-74506	D	F	F-AZJJ	Rene Bouverat	France	GA-N 4th FG
44-74536	D	F	N991R	Brent Hisey	Oklahoma City, OK	*Miss America* #11
44-74543	D	S	N4543	Richard Vartanian	Shafter, CA	
44-74582	D	F	NL6329T	Joseph Thibodeau	Denver, CO	*Crusader*, FF-582
44-74602	D	F	N3580	Jack Hovey	Oakland, CA	RAF mkgs, HM-P
44-74739	D	F	N51RH	Bob Hoover	Los Angeles, CA	Yellow w/green letters
44-74797	D	R		Luis Villar	USA	
44-74813	D	F	N6301T	Ken J. Wagnon	Danville, IL	*Cripes A'Mighty IV*
44-74829	D	F	ZK-TAF	Historic Aircraft Trust	Auckland, N Zealand	NZ2415
44-74836	D	S		Brian O'Farrell	Miami, FL	
44-74865	D	F	N8677E	Don Novas	Blackfoot, ID	*Mormon Mustang*
44-74878	D	F	N6306T	Tom Wood	Indianapolis, IN	H1-G
44-74908	D	F	N151BP	Bob Pond	Eden Prairie, MN	E2-S 361st FG
44-74910	D	F	NL74920	Charles Nichols	Chino, CA	*Miss Judy*, JA-J
44-74923	D	F	N6395	Sodenal Group	Berne, Switzerland	*Miss Ashley*, red
44-74942	D	F	NL5427V	Tony Buechler	Elm Grove, WI	*Petie 2nd*
44-74950	D	F	NL51DT	Dick Thurman	Louisville, KY	*Slender, Tender & Tall*, HO-T-tail
44-74962	D	R	N51DK	John Dilley	Fort Wayne, IN	
44-74976	D	F	N98582	Jeff Michael	Lexington, NC	*Obsession*, J-MR
44-74977	D	F	N5448V	Chris Gruys	Santa Fe, NM	
44-74996	D	F	N5410V	Museum of Flying	Santa Monica, CA	*Dago Red* racer
44-75007	D	F	N3451D	EAA Aviation Foundation	Oshkosh, WI	*Paul I*, PH-P
44-75009	D	F	N51TC	Ted Contri	Reno, NV	*Rosalie*, NEV-ANG
44-75024	D	S	N96JM	War Eagles Air Museum	Santa Teresa, NM	
44-84390	D	F	N2869D	Doug Driscoll	Pocatello, ID	*Section Eight*, 3E-B
44-84489	D	S	VH-POB	Peter Anderson	Sydney, Australia	
44-84615	D	F	NL55JL	Jimmy Leeward	Ocala, FL	SKoAF #18, K-tail
44-84634	D	F	NL51ES	Ed Shipley	Paoli, PA	*Big Beautiful Doll*, WZ-I
44-84658	TF	F	N51TF	John MacGuire	Santa Teresa, NM	*Friendly Ghost*, TEX-ANG
44-84745	TF	F	NL851D	Stallion 51 Corp.	Kissimmee, FL	*Crazy Horse*, LL
44-84753	D	F	N251BP	Bob Pond	Eden Prairie, MN	*Mighty Moose*, RJ-P
44-84786	F-6D	F	N51BS	Butch Schroeder	Danville, IL	*Lil Margaret*, 5M-K
44-84850	D	F	N15FS	Stan Musick	Brownwood, TX	*SU SU* FF-850
44-84860	TF	F	NL327DB	Daryl Bond	Chino, CA	*Lady Jo!*
44-84896	D	S	N5416V	Kenneth Scholz	Playa Del Rey, CA	
44-84900	D	R	N51YZ	W. C. Allmon Jr	Las Vegas, NV	
44-84933	D	F	N201F	John J. Mark	Oshkosh, WI	JJ-M
44-84952	D	F	N210D	Charles Mothon	Wilmington, DE	FF-330, silver
44-84961	D	F	NL7715C	Steve Hinton	Chino, CA	*Wee Willy II*, G-4-U, 413334-tail
44-84962	D	S	N9857P	Lee Shaller	New Athens, IL	
45-11381	D	F	NL551CB	Gary Honbarrier	High Point, NC	*Glamorous Glen III*
45-11391	D	F	NL51WT	Wallace Sanders	Warrenton, VA	*Nervous Energy V*, 00
45-11471	TF-51D	F	N332	Liberty Aero Corp.	Santa Monica, CA	*Butter Knife*, ex *Stiletto* racer
45-11507	D	R	NL921	Kermit Weeks	Miami, FL	*Cripes A'Mighty 3rd*
45-11513		S		John Smith	Mapua, N. Zealand	
45-11518	D	R		Alpine Fighter Coll.	Wanaka, N. Zealand	
45-11525	D	F	N91JB	Bill Anders	Eastsound, WA	*Val-Halla*, FF-525, red tail
45-11540	D	F	N151W	James Michaels	Hartland, WI	*Queen B*, blue nose
45-11553	D	F	NL51VF	Mustang Air Inc.	Wilmington, DE	*Shangri La*, WZ-1
45-11558	D	F	NL151BJ	Bill Jones	Sun Valley, CA	Bare metal
45-11559	D	F	N51MX	Warbird Operators Inc.	Indianapolis, IN	*Mad Max*, MX-A
45-11571	D	S	N51T	Tony de Allesandris	Reno, NV	

45-11582	D	F	NL5441V	Planes of Fame Air	Chino, CA	Yellow tail w/diag stripes Museum
45-11628	D	F	NL151X	Bill Hane	Mesa, AZ	*Ho Hun!* CY-H
45-11633	D	F	N5413V	William G. Lacy Jr	Honolulu, HI	
45-11636	D	F	N11636	Mike Bertz	Lakewood, CO	*Stang Evil*, WD-KK
67-14866	TF	F	N20TF	Tom Friedkin	Carlsbad, CA	FAB camou, tiger teeth
67-22579	D	F	N251RM	Russell McDonald	Park City, UT	FF-579
67-22580	D	F	N2580	Chuck Hall	Rialto, CA	*Six Shooter*, RF-K
67-22581	D	F	C-GMUS	Ross Grady	Edmonton, Canada	*What's Up Doc?*
A68-1	CA-17	F	N51WB	Wiley Sanders	Troy, AL	*Jeannie too*
A68-100	CA-18	F	NL51AB	Norm Lewis	Louisville, KY	*Flying Dutchman*, HL-N
A68-104	CA-18	F	VH-BOB	Bob Eastgate	Point Cook, Australia	A68-104, black spinner
A68-105	CA-18	R	VH-JUC	Hourigan/Pay Syndicate	Tyabb, Australia	RAAF A68-105
A68-107	CA-18	F	VH-AUB	Colin Pay	Scone, Australia	RAAF #07, A68-107
A68-110	CA-18	R	VH-MFT	Mustang Fighter Trust	Cabooltur, Australia	
A68-118	CA-18	F	VH-AGJ	Jeff Trappett	Latrobe Valley, Australia	*Eclat*, A68-118
A68-137	CA-18	R	VH-PPV	RAAF Museum	Townsville, Australia	CV-P, RAAF KH791
A68-170	CA-18	R	VH-SVU	RAAF Museum	Point Cook, Australia	*Duffy's Delight*
A68-175	CA-18	F	NL64824	Art & Dan Vance	Santa Rosa, CA	*Million Dollar Baby*
A68-187	CA-18	F	N919WJ	Frank Borman	Fairacres, NM	*Su Su II*, TF-839, 44-74839
A68-192	CA-18	F	G-HAEC	Rob Davies	Duxford, UK	*Big Beautiful Doll*
A68-198	CA-18	F	NL286JB	Bill Bruggeman	Anoka, MN	*Short-Fuse Sallee*, AJ-T
A68-199	CA-18	R	VH-BOZ	RAAF Museum	Williamtown, Australia	
A68-39	CA-17	F	N551D	Jack Erickson	Tillamook, OR	Red nose/tail, 0-7
A68-71	CA-17	R		Derek Macphail	Perth, Australia	

Below: *Flying Dutchman* returning from a photo-sortie out of Oshkosh. (*FlyPast* Collection)

Note: The foregoing has been compiled using information from the 1996 edition of Dennis D. Bergstrom's *Gallant Warriors* publication, copies of which can be obtained from Mr Bergstrom at 4218 E. Montgomery, Spokane, WA 99207. *FlyPast* magazine has been used for updates.

INDEX